PHILANTHROPIC STUDIES

Robert L. Payton and Dwight F. Burlingame,
*General Editors*

*When the Bottom Line Is Faithfulness*

# WHEN THE BOTTOM LINE IS FAITHFULNESS

## Management of Christian Service Organizations

Thomas H. Jeavons

*Indiana University Press*

*Bloomington and Indianapolis*

The paper used in this publication meets the minimum requirements of American
National Standard for Information Sciences—Permanence of Paper for Printed
Library Materials, ANSI Z39.48-1984.
⊚™
Manufactured in the United States of America

**Library of Congress Cataloging-in-Publication Data**

Jeavons, Thomas.
When the bottom line is faithfulness : management of Christian
service organizations / Thomas H. Jeavons.
p.   cm.—(Philanthropic studies)
Includes bibliographical references and index.
ISBN 0-253-33089-0 (cloth : alk. paper)
1. Church charities—United States—Management.
I. Title.  II. Series.
HV530.J43   1994
361.7′5′ 068—dc20     93-30292

1 2 3 4 5 99 98 97 96 95 94

# CONTENTS

# Preface

WHAT MOTIVATES PEOPLE to write books? If the work is not fiction, born of the creative urge to tell a story, and if it is not for money or to serve some other purpose such as improving one's professional status, then I suppose it meets one of two other needs. Book writing is a way to address, perhaps help resolve, some need or question or issue that the author believes truly merits the attention of a community or of society. Or, it offers a means to explore in a disciplined and thoughtful way some questions or issues that command the author's own curiosity or attention. This book is, for me, a response to both of the last two possibilities.

I have spent fifteen years as a staff member, chief staff officer, and board member of several different religious organizations—service agencies, denominational structures, and even a small trust—and out of that experience have developed a keen interest in how such organizations operate. More particularly, I have developed an interest in how they could work better to serve those they are intended to serve, to give witness to the values they are intended to promote, and to meet the broader needs of the society in which they exist. As I have learned more about the traditions and practices of philanthropy in this country, about the place and function of the "independent sector" in our society, and especially about the place of religion and religious organizations in shaping and giving expression to philanthropic or altruistic values and instincts, I have become even more curious about how religious organizations both fit into and facilitate the development of these traditions and practices. Writing this book has provided me the occasion to examine these questions carefully and in some depth.

On the other hand, it is also my hope that this book will be of significant practical value to those trying to manage and govern religious organizations, especially religious service organizations. When I encountered particular problems as the executive of a denominational structure, I often looked at management literature for helpful ideas about ways to address these problems, and I was often disappointed. That literature, written from the point of view of those experienced in organizations whose primary purpose is to make a profit, and directed primarily to others in a similar context, often did not speak to the situations I faced. And if it did, the ways it suggested approaching such situations often conflicted with the values I held as a Christian trying to run an organization that should give testimony to Christian values.

This is not to say that there were never any helpful insights to be gained from general management literature, but it often required substantial and sophisticated efforts at translation to apply ideas suggested there in a very different environment. The fact is, management in a religious context or environment is different than in a secular environment. There are values—moral values, "ultimate" values if you will—that need to be honored and expressed in the decisions and actions of a religious organization that are frequently of little concern in a secular organization. Certainly, the nurture and promotion of such values is not a part of the stated mission of most secular business or government organizations. What I wanted and could not find in most management literature was counsel about how to think through the management problems I encountered, in the context of needing to have the organization affirm its values in its policies and actions.

This book, then, is an attempt to help others with that problem, with the need to consider management issues *in an organizational context in which the affirmation of moral values is as important as the completion of a task.* Much of this book is given to analyzing and describing the organizational context and environment of religious organizations for just this reason. The public's expectations about the place and function of religious organizations in our society—as voluntary associations, as philanthropic organizations, as service agencies—are crucial factors in determining which approaches to management will be successful, useful, and appropriate, and which will not. Also crucial, obviously, are the theological tenets of the faith community a particular organization represents and the expectations of the members of that community.

Finally, I have come to see how religious organizations have been the "archetype" of nonprofits. The origins of the "independent" or "voluntary" sector in the realm of religion suggest why so many nonprofit organizations—not just those that are explicitly religious—have been, still are, and are still expected to be "values-expressive"; and that is the characteristic that most essentially distinguishes them from business and government organizations. Insofar as that is true, then secular nonprofits may have something to learn from well-run religious organizations that have long recognized that their mission is twofold; not simply to provide services, but also to give testimony to specific social, moral, and spiritual ideals by the way they provide those services.

The pages that follow offer research, analysis, and personal reflections on this range of issues. Pursuing this study has been an interesting and satisfying exercise for me—spiritually as well as intellectually—because it has given me an opportunity to wrestle with questions that are personally fascinating and, I believe, vitally important for the voluntary sector and a set of organizations that are profoundly significant to American society as a whole. Finally, though, my hope is that reading this volume will be helpful and useful for others, especially those concerned with or responsible for understanding, supporting, governing, or managing religious organizations.

I know from my own experience that it is not possible to provide any formulaic answers to the problems of management in religious organizations. Still, I have tried to point to better ways to think about these organizations and their management, and to suggest approaches to management issues and problems that may be more readily adapted in specific situations in religious organizations.

# Acknowledgments

THE WORK THAT follows could never have been completed without the help and support of numerous people. The many who offered ideas, words of encouragement, and a myriad of small acts of support are too numerous to mention. Some, however, contributed to my efforts in ways that require specific recognition.

My thanks go to the Indiana University Center on Philanthropy and the Lilly Endowment for the grant that supported my research and my completion of my doctoral studies. In addition, I am especially grateful to the officers and members of the Association of Evangelical Relief and Development Organizations (AERDO) who permitted, facilitated, and participated in the survey process that set up my field studies. And I am even more indebted to the participating agencies that gave generously of their time and insights.

This work would not have been possible without the guidance, discipline, and encouragement of Robert Herman, Steve Levicoff, Robert Payton, William Pickett, and Charles Rodriguez, who constituted the best doctoral committee a Ph.D. candidate could imagine. They were generous with their time and wisdom, and exceedingly helpful as critics of and respondents to my work. They cannot be responsible for any of the flaws in this work, but certainly deserve some credit for much of what is valuable.

Finally, I need to express my gratitude to my family and the members of my own religious community for their personal support and to the group of spiritual "fellow travelers" with whom I have been joined over the past decade in difficult but rewarding efforts to try to keep religious institutions faithful and vital organizations for the benefit of all people.

# Introduction

*Religion, Philanthropy, and American Culture*

A MERICAN SOCIETY HAS a number of characteristics that distinguish it from the societies of other industrialized Western nations. Observers and scholars of American culture—historians, anthropologists, sociologists, political scientists, and others—suggest these unique features are the result of many different influences. These include the social and cultural attributes of the different kinds of people who settled the United States; the economic and political trends and dynamics that were influential in shaping Western culture more generally during the past three centuries; and even the physical and aesthetic qualities of the American landscape. Clearly, however, one of the most important influences in shaping American society and culture has been religion.

The people of the United States have long been, and continue to be, among the most religious—in terms of belief in God and active participation in religious life—of any industrialized nation (Gallup and Castelli, 1990). The effects of religion and religious life on this society, on public life in the United States, are many. Religion's influence can be clearly seen in the development and prominence of one of the distinctive attributes of the American political economy, that is, in its "voluntary" or "independent" sector. While a few other nations have significant numbers of private nonprofit organizations and noteworthy traditions of philanthropic giving, in no other country have these organizations and traditions played the same kind of central role in shaping cultural, civic, and political life they have in the United States (Hall, 1984, 1989; Bremner, 1988; O'Neill, 1989).

This independent sector and the organizations within it have become the subject of increasing attention and study in recent years. There are a number of reasons for this. Partly it is a function of the increasing sophistication of the field of organizational theory and behavior, which has led to scholars' being interested in looking at different kinds of organizations, beyond large industrial and governmental concerns. Partly it reflects the interest of social scientists—especially economists and political scientists—in examining how those facets of our lives not fully encompassed by commerce and government are represented in organizational structures and dynamics that might otherwise fall into their fields of study (see, for example, Boulding, 1973; Douglas, 1983).

And certainly it reflects the increasing importance of nonprofit and voluntary organizations for our society as a whole in recent decades; first as a result of their proliferation under the Great Society programs of the Johnson administration, and then as a result of the Reagan and Bush administrations' efforts to limit the government's role in delivering social services and caring for those in need.

Over the last ten or fifteen years we have seen the publication of numerous books about the economics of nonprofit organizations (for example, James and Rose-Ackermen, 1986; Weisbrod, 1988); the place and function of nonprofits in our civic life (for example, Johnson, 1988; Van Til, 1988); and about the management of these organizations (for example, Borst and Montana, 1977; Hay, 1990). We have also seen the development of journals devoted to articles about nonprofit and voluntary organizations (*The Nonprofit and Voluntary Sector Quarterly*) and their management (*Nonprofit Management and Leadership*). It is important to note, however, that as interest in the independent sector and nonprofit organizations has been increasing, attention on the part of scholars to the religious roots of the sector and to religious organizations has been almost nonexistent.

This has certainly been apparent to those of us with backgrounds in religion and the church as well as the secular nonprofit realm. The absence of references to or considerations of religion and religious elements in studies, articles, and books about nonprofit organizations and their functions is often conspicuous. In fact, this phenomenon has been documented recently by one researcher who found that

> of 916 projects listed in the 1986–87 compendium of research in progress [on nonprofits and voluntarism] compiled by Independent Sector (Hodgkinson, 1988), only 4.7 percent deal specifically with religion . . . [and in] Daphne Layton's (1987) listing of 2,195 books and articles on philanthropy and voluntarism, only 2.1 percent deal specifically with religion. (Hall, 1990a, p. 38)

Clearly this failure to include religion and religious organizations in the study of the nonprofit world makes no sense. The centrality of religion and religious organizations to the tradition and activities of philanthropy and nonprofit organizations is indisputable.

According to the most recent figures on philanthropic giving, in 1989 more than 47 percent of total contributions went to religion (AAFRC, 1990). Independent Sector's study, *Giving and Volunteering in the United States*, found that two-thirds of individuals' contributions go to religion (Hodgkinson and Weitzman, 1990, p. 21). Moreover, churches and religious organizations are not just the recipient of funds; they are also an important source of funds for charitable service work and other nonprofit organizations. In 1986, religious congregations provided $19.1 billion for charitable service work, of which $8.4 billion was in the form of outright grants to other organizations. This means 46 percent of the $41.4 billion donated by individuals to congregations in 1986 went to service activities on behalf of other people (Hodgkinson, Weitzman, and Kirsch, 1988).

What is more, these are only figures on amounts of money given to religion and its uses. Recent studies highlight the major role religious commitment and participation in religious life play in motivating people to give both money and time to nonreligious organizations and causes (Hodgkinson, Weitzman, and Kirsh, 1988; Hodgkinson and Weitzman, 1990). Studies of the history and development of the independent sector and nonprofit enterprise document the importance of religion as a key motivating and guiding factor in much of this activity (Hall, 1984, 1989; O'Neill, 1989; Stackhouse, 1990).

## The Purposes of This Volume

The point of all this is that too little attention has been, and is being, paid to the vital role of religion and religious organizations in the tradition and practice of philanthropy, and in the place and functions of nonprofit organizations and the independent sector. Organizational studies pay too little attention to the nature and behavior of religious organizations. This book begins to redress that situation, particularly with respect to concerns and questions about management. This volume has three objectives in this regard:

1. to indicate how religious organizations—especially religious service organizations—are an integral part of the American cultural traditions of philanthropy, voluntary association, and nonprofit enterprise, as well as part of "the church";

2. to consider the distinctive place these organizations occupy in our political economy and culture, representative of the cultural traditions just mentioned as well as their own theological traditions; and how then, as a result, certain societal expectations both support and place limits upon them; and

3. given this special context for their existence and operation, to consider how it shapes the ways in which religious organizations can and should be managed.

I will undertake to meet these objectives for the additional purpose of outlining the shape and principles of a philosophy of management for religious organizations.

First, I will examine and reflect on a wide range of literature about the traditions of philanthropy and voluntary association in America. As noted, these traditions occupy a unique place in our national culture in terms of their centrality in and power to affect the civic, social, and even economic life of our nation. That being so, we cannot hope to understand fully the context for management of a group of organizations—religious organizations—that have been shaped by these traditions if we do not understand the traditions themselves.

It will be important in this effort to look very closely at the relationship between religion and philanthropy. There are, we know, many nonprofit organizations that have no religious roots or concerns but are still nonprofit by charter or statute and philanthropic in nature. On the other hand, there are hardly any religious organizations that are not nonprofit by charter or statute; most all are dependent upon voluntary giving for support; and most are "philanthropic" in some sense in their mission. Accordingly, to comprehend what the purposes, functions and character of management should be in religious organizations requires careful consideration of ways in which this society's expectations about philanthropy and philanthropic organizations relate to its understanding of and expectations about religious organizations, and to religious organizations' expectations—usually theologically derived—of themselves.

This last point raises another question about the distinctive character of religious service organizations, a question we must consider if we are to understand them. That is, How does theology shape their mission? Different organizations have different theologies and different missions. However, focusing on Christian service organizations generically, we can examine how central theological tenets of the Christian tradition move toward imposing a twofold mission, involving both service and witness, on the church and all its agencies by emphasizing the need to integrate the discovery, proclamation and practice of faith.

Finally, I will draw on the insights of organizational theory to explore the nature and functions of religious organizations. While comprehension of an organization's context or environment is crucial to considerations about its management (Lawrence and Lorsch, 1967; Senge, 1990), the intrinsic structure and character of an organization also need to be carefully examined in thinking about how it ought to be managed. This may be more true for religious organizations than for others, because the structure and character of religious organizations may—later I will argue, should—derive from and reflect commitments to central theological principles.

The purpose of the first part of this volume is thus to draw a picture, as complete and detailed as possible, of the background and context within which questions about the management of Christian service organizations should be considered. The basic assumption is that the context for management of Christian service organizations is significantly different from that of other types of organizations, so different approaches to management are required.

The second part of the book turns to an exploration of specific and practical questions about the management of Christian service organizations. Here we look at management literature and at the findings of a set of field studies of specific religious organizations that raise, illustrate, and begin to answer what seem to me to be key questions.

All the organizations in these studies are Christian service organizations; almost all are United States–based and work in the fields of international relief and development. The opportunity to observe these organizations closely as they carried on their day-to-day business, as they tried simultaneously to serve people in need and to make a witness to those people and others about the Christian faith these organizations uphold, was immensely educational. This section of the book articulates some of the insights about organizational behavior and management practice that emerged from those observations.

The opening chapter of this section outlines the scope and methodology of the study from which the empirical data informing my reflections were drawn and describes the seven organizations that were the subjects of this study. The following chapter considers a number of vital questions about general organizational and management concerns, especially as these relate first to philanthropic organizations and then to religious organizations. A crucial issue, for example, is how to define the mission and the meaning of "effectiveness" for a religious service organization.

Succeeding chapters explore the general issues outlined in more specific areas of operation and management of special importance to nonprofit organizations. The major areas or functions of operation and management addressed include: (1) issues of creating and sustaining a Christian organizational culture and, in this context, basic principles for human resource management relating to both volunteers and paid staff; (2) practices and principles of resource development and fund-raising; and (3) roles and activities of boards and executives in the leadership and management of these organizations, including approaches to and uses of formal planning that take into account the distinctive aspects of a religious organization.

The final aim of all this is to suggest what some essential principles undergirding good practice in the management of religious service organizations—a philosophy of religious management—might look like. If this sounds somewhat tentative as a goal, that is for good reason. I recognize in beginning this effort how different the operative values of different religious traditions are. All the organizations I have studied in preparing to write this volume are Christian, Protestant, and mostly evangelical in their orientation. Thus, all the data I have been working with, as well as my own ecclesiological experience and perspective, are likely to lead me to give more weight to one set of religious and moral values—specifically, those rooted directly in New Testament writings. A Catholic undertaking this study and focusing on Catholic organizations might well see some things differently. Even more so a Jew, and certainly more so someone coming from outside the Judeo-Christian tradition.

That caution noted, I still contend that there are, at least within the Judeo-Christian tradition—which remains the religious tradition that dominates American culture—a core of common moral and social values that religious organizations in our society are expected to affirm and promote. These core values would surely include: faith and trust in God; a commitment to dignity, equality, and justice for all people; a commitment to caring for and empowering people who cannot (presently) care for themselves; and a belief that some ideal of stewardship should define our relationship to material goods and the natural world. It is around such values, and their nurture, expression, and promotion, that the missions of religious organizations center; and it is these values (at a minimum) that a set of principles for management for religious organizations must honor.

So, tentative though they may be, this volume suggests a set of principles for the management of Christian service organizations. These will be, I believe, generally useful in application to the management of other religious organizations, and I will examine briefly how that may be so. Just as important, though, readers who have followed through the data, analysis, and arguments in this volume that lead to the articulation of these principles will have been introduced to ways of thinking about management in, and significant questions about, religious organizations that they can apply in a similar analysis of their own experience and faith traditions. Perhaps they can then better develop their own set of principles, which may be different from what they find here.

Finally this volume concludes with a few observations about how what I have suggested are important principles for the management of religious organizations may be pertinent to other kinds of nonprofits. Insofar as some of those organizations are subject to many of the same kinds of public expectations about promoting and maintaining certain values, and are intended to be "values-expressive" in much the same way as religious organizations, many of the principles for the management of religious organizations will apply equally well to them.

# PART I

# The Context of Religious Philanthropic Organizations

## Historical, Societal, Theological, and Organizational Elements

THE FIRST PART of this volume analyzes the cultural and sociopolitical environments by which Christian service organizations have been shaped and in which they operate in the United States. It includes a theological examination of and reflection on the most distinctive feature of many of these organizations, that is, the dual-faceted character of their missions, which combine a desire to offer practical services to those in need with a specific intention to share and promote the faith that inspires that service. Part I concludes with an examination of these organizations as organizations, focusing on the ways in which they are like or unlike other organizations, and examining them in the frameworks provided by a range of organizational theories.

This may all be seen as preface by pragmatic souls who want simply to look at practical, instrumental questions about how best to manage Christian service organizations. These people may want to move right into a discussion of nuts-and-bolts issues about how to operate these organizations so they are "most effective." But I contend that this preface is crucial and essential. The fact is we cannot meaningfully define "effectiveness" for these organizations if we do not understand the historical circumstances and social and spiritual dynamics that gave rise to them, as well as the societal expectations that surround them. We cannot think clearly and usefully about how these organizations should be managed if we do not understand their place and function in our society's political economy, and their most salient characteristics as organizations. The point of the next four chapters is to describe and explore the context and distinctive characteristics of these organizations, matters of which we need to be aware in addressing questions about how they can best be managed.

# 1

## Dimensions and Tensions of Philanthropy and American Culture

IN HIS ESSAY ON "American Philanthropy and the National Character," the noted historian Merle Curti says:

> While American patterns of giving for religion, welfare, education, health, science and the arts owe much to British and continental examples, they have, apart from the question of magnitude, reflected a distinctly American character. They have also helped shape that character. In other words, philanthropy has been both index and agent. (1958, p. 424)

This chapter explores the development of the tradition and practice of philanthropy in the United States, focusing especially on how it has, in Curti's words, both "reflected" and "helped shape" our political economy and culture. Before beginning such an exploration, however, it is probably important to define terms, particularly the term "philanthropy."

### What Is Philanthropy?

The word *philanthropy* comes from two Greek words: the verb *phileo*, meaning "love," the sort of love evidenced between friends; and the noun *anthropos*, meaning "man," as the generic Greek term for humankind. In its origins, then, "philanthropy" refers to the love of a person for the rest of humankind. In its English uses, it has acquired and lost a variety of connotations over time, but has usually referred to the actions of giving to and caring for others—particularly those less fortunate than the giver—which express and reflect that kind of love.

At times in American usage the term philanthropy has been understood, by the general public at least, to refer primarily to the giving of the wealthy, either to cultural activities that were of special interest to them, or to charitable causes that cared for those less fortunate. More recently, however, there has been an effort on the part of practitioners and scholars to recapture the broader sense of the word, which includes all giving by any private person or party

*3*

(poor as well as rich) for any public purpose. Thus Robert Payton, one of the leaders in this movement, suggests all "voluntary action for the public good" is philanthropy (Payton, 1988). The philosopher Mike W. Martin, another scholar in this area, believes that, given the public's difficulty in agreeing on what is "good," we would do better to talk about philanthropy as "private giving, of time, labor or money, for public *purposes*" (Martin, 1991).

For the purpose of the discussions that follow, I accept and use as an operative definition of philanthropy a description elaborated by both Payton (1987 and 1988) and Martin (1991), which suggests philanthropy encompasses all "voluntary private giving [including donations of time and labor as well as money] for public purposes."

## Philanthropic Ideals and the Origins of American Culture

It can be easily demonstrated that philanthropic ideals and philanthropic practices have played a central role in this nation's efforts to define itself from its earliest days. One of the most prominent statements of the purpose for founding one of the earliest English-speaking communities in North America emphasizes that community's obligations to become "A Model of Christian Charity" (Winthrop, 1983 [1630]). While the descriptions of the intended character and purposes of this community in John Winthrop's sermon (by this title) to the settlers of the Massachusetts Bay Colony are explicitly religious, many of the ideals he spelled out for their life together can be readily translated into secular terms. In other words, many of the ideals for the shape of society and public life for a new nation, which were planted in this first foundation, can be understood in civic and moral terms as well as religious terms.

This is in no way to diminish the significance of their religious character. I want to insist, in fact, on the importance of understanding the connections between the religious—particularly Judeo-Christian—ideals of this nation's founders and forebears and their social ideals. Chapter 2 is devoted to exploring those connections, especially as they pertain to the traditions of philanthropy, voluntarism, and nonprofit enterprise. The point to be made here is that, at their origins, many of the communities that would evolve to become the United States embraced and affirmed what we can fairly call philanthropic values and practices as defining ideals and practices for their civic life and culture. This was true not only in Massachusetts and New England, but in all the colonies.

We can trace the evolution of philanthropic ideals and practices along with the evolution of attributes of America's national culture over time, and see some fascinating and striking correspondences between them. To make such a claim is to assume we can speak in some meaningful way of an "American culture." That claim has been made and soundly defended by a number of scholars, including Curti (1958) and Hall (1984).

For instance, pursuing the same line of inquiry as I am pursuing here, Curti asks,

> What has been the relation of philanthropy to the national character? Many social scientists . . . reject the validity . . . of the concept of national character. Yet the belief that there is a cluster of more or less distinguishing American traits and values has persisted through our history, varying in expression from time to time, from place to place, from subculture to subculture. (1958, p. 421)

It is interesting to note how the definition of a "national character" (or "culture") implied here—as the distinguishing characteristics or traits of a community corresponding to that group's basic values—corresponds to the definitions of culture favored now by the most insightful organizational theorists (Schein, 1985).

The historian Peter Dobkin Hall also contends there is an "American culture," although he takes a different tack in defining it. He speaks of "culture, not as a set of aesthetic and intellectual formulations, but as a set of social institutions used by a people in organizing the entire range of their fundamental activities." Hall goes on to observe that

> American culture as it had come to exist by the beginning of the twentieth century . . . was a mass culture involving the coordination of activities of nearly one hundred million people across a geographical area of over three and a half million square miles; and the greater part of this task of coordination was conducted by private for-profit and nonprofit corporations. (1984, p. 2)

Curti's and Hall's views of culture are not incompatible. In fact, they serve in an interesting way to illuminate and confirm Curti's earlier claim about the role of philanthropy as "both index [of] and agent [in]" the shape of America's national character. The "traits and values" Curti cites are surely reflected in the structure and functions of many of the "social institutions" of which Hall speaks; and many of those social institutions—especially the nonprofit ones— were created expressly to maintain and reinforce some of those traits and values, as Hall's history of the development of private institutional forms in the United States convincingly demonstrates (1984). So, accepting the notion that there is an American character or national culture, we can go on to ask how the traditions and practices of philanthropy have reflected and helped shape that character over the last three hundred years.

## Philanthropy at the Nation's Beginnings

In his sermon to the new settlers of Massachusetts, John Winthrop said they needed to "be knit together in this work [of building a new community] as one man . . . [to] entertain each other in brotherly affections . . . [and] to abridge themselves of their superfluities for the supply of each other's necessities" (cited in O'Connell, 1983, p. 32). At a functional level, this plainly describes the need for "voluntary action for the public good." What John Winthrop said this new community required was for its people to be always ready to sacrifice personal gain or comfort to provide for the needs of the community and persons less fortunate than themselves.

Of course, this group found the motivation and rewards for such behavior in their religious beliefs. Altruistic behavior was a demonstration of their faith commitment, to be rewarded in the next life. Nevertheless, the note sounded here, the need for people to take care of one another and share of their bounty (when they had such) with those less fortunate, defined one characteristic of life in the colonies and in the new nation of the United States. This was especially true in rural and small-town settings and, indeed, continues to be evident today in such settings.

The structures and processes of philanthropic practice in the earliest days of this society were, by our standards, fairly informal. Care for the poor was handled primarily through the church (congregation or parish) or town. In many areas, as in New England, those civic and ecclesiastical structures were intertwined. In the countryside or wilderness, people simply cared for each other in whatever ways were needed in times of crisis, as best they were able, knowing full well that they could expect—and might need—similar care themselves someday.

Still, as some towns became cities and the economy became less wholly agrarian, the needs some communities faced grew more complex, and new and different kinds of voluntary associations and nonprofit organizations began to develop to address various needs. It is this tendency to organize to meet the needs of individuals and the community as a whole that Alexis de Tocqueville describes in his well-known observations.

After traveling in the United States for only nine months in 1831–32, de Tocqueville returned to his native France to write about his observations of the young nation, producing one of the best-known commentaries on the American national character, *Democracy in America*. In a chapter on one of the features of public life in the United States that he found most interesting, "The Use Which Americans Make of Public Associations in Civic Life," he observes:

> Americans of all ages, all conditions, and all dispositions constantly form associations. They have not only commercial and manufacturing companies . . . but associations of a thousand other kinds—religious, moral, serious, futile, general or restricted, enormous or diminutive. . . . As soon as several of the inhabitants of the United States have taken up an opinion or a feeling which they wish to promote in the world, they look out for mutual assistance; and as soon as they have found each other out, they combine. From that moment on they are no longer isolated men, but a power seen from afar, whose actions serve as an example. . . . Nothing, in my opinion, is more deserving of our attention than the intellectual and moral associations of America. (1984 [1835], pp. 198–201)

Through the course of the nineteenth century, the creation of associations for civic, moral, and religious purposes became, as de Tocqueville's observations indicate, widespread. The practice of philanthropy, as giving and acting to care for those in need, thus often became a matter of common action pursued through such organizations. In addition, as the work of associations to address community needs, promote culture, or champion some cause was meant to serve the public good, then giving time and labor to these associations can be seen as a form of philanthropy. Obvious examples of the kinds of voluntary work for public purposes just cited would be volunteer fire departments, community lyceums, and temperance groups, respectively.

At that point in time, assumptions about the importance of community, as well as the experience of community, were still formative for philanthropic practice. Even with the growth of cities, recognition of one's interdependency with and obligation to "neighbors" remained a vital underpinning of philanthropic efforts, and this is reflected in the formation of many voluntary associations. As the obligation of citizens of Puritan communities in New England to "bear one another's burdens" was preached by people like John Winthrop and Cotton Mather, so the possibilities for organizing to care for citizens' common interests were demonstrated by the leadership in forming community organizations shown by people like Benjamin Franklin, who lived in one of the largest of those early cities, Philadelphia.

Still modeling the essence of philanthropy—that is "private voluntary giving for public purposes"—people like Franklin and Stephen Girard went beyond being individual philanthropists to become the creators of some of the earlier philanthropic institutions (Bremner, 1988). Before there could be widespread development of such institutions, however, there were structural and legal problems that had to be addressed.

Prior to independence, and even for some time afterward, many of the colonies and states lacked the authority or legal mechanisms to create private corporations, and also lacked the legal jurisdiction of "equity" under which trusts can be enforced. This meant it was impossible for voluntary associations to become nonprofit corporations as we know them today, legally autonomous and able to act as corporate entities. Furthermore, as trusts were not enforceable, it was impossible to establish a secure endowment as a funding base for such a group (Hall, 1984, 1987). As Hall notes, only after a number of crucial cases were decided—like *Dartmouth College v. Woodward* (1819); and the *Girard Will* case (1844)—"were private nonprofit corporations placed on a firm legal footing under federal law" (1987, p. 6). Even then, many states did not allow such developments for many years.

Nevertheless, despite occasional obstacles, the growth of philanthropic giving, voluntary association, and the formation of nonprofit corporations continued throughout the eighteenth and early nineteenth centuries. During this time and in the decades following, America began to industrialize, cities grew quickly, and immigrants came in large numbers to work in new industries and live in those cities. With the immigration of many people who were not Protestant Christians and not from England, new forms of voluntary associations, nonprofit organizations, trusts, and philanthropic giving appeared to address new problems.

As difficulties relating to housing, public health, education, welfare, and crime multiplied in new urban environments, there was recognition that they needed to be quickly and effectively addressed before they destroyed the existing social order. This does not mean that charitable activities were undertaken primarily as a palliative for social unrest, although some were probably so motivated. The degree to which this was the case, and how we should interpret the motivations of nineteenth-century philanthropists—including religious philanthropists—is the subject of an interesting historical debate (see Griffin, 1957; Banner, 1973; Heale, 1976). Finally, the evidence supports the claim that these philanthropists' intentions were largely to do good, although, as in almost all philanthropic activity, there certainly were cases where motives were mixed.

Still, perhaps what was most strikingly different in that situation from the way Americans would view these problems today was the lack of any sense that the emerging social ills were primarily government's problems. From our perspective, in the United States of the twentieth century, this may be hard to understand, because it is now the dominant assumption that the government is finally responsible for the social welfare of the people; but the social philanthropic ideals expressed in John Winthrop's sermon held sway, virtually un-challenged, through the middle of the 1800s. This meant that it was still the expectation of most citizens that they should care for one another's needs through those means they could create and control, whether that was the church or some charitable organization created specifically for these purposes.

In this respect, religion and religious organizations, particularly local con-gregations, continued to play a powerful role. Many local "charitable societies" were, in essence, auxiliaries of churches through which congregations' mem-bers, usually the women, undertook charitable and social-welfare activities for those in need in their own communities. This kind of organization could play an important role in providing assistance to families and individuals in need in smaller towns, and even in some neighborhoods in larger cities. Such orga-nizations often evolved over time to provide the foundation for the more "pro-fessional" social-service organizations that started to appear in the latter half of the nineteenth century (Joines, 1990). Even in those cities that had already grown too large for this kind of congregational agency to be effective, and es-pecially in neighborhoods and among groups that were outside the Protestant church fellowship, religious affiliation still often provided the basis for orga-nizing assistance. This took two forms.

First, some Protestants created service agencies, "charitable societies" and the like, to reach out to the new populations. These groups were not always explicitly church-related, but they were usually begun by religious people out of religious motivations. Their efforts were most often aimed—following the Biblical priority (Isa. 1:17)—at the "widows and the orphans," at trying to pro-vide assistance, education, and sometimes health care especially to children in poverty. Religious groups ran orphanages, homes for unwed mothers, and hospitals. These groups usually made sure that with the provision of services came a concerted effort at "moral reformation," for it was assumed—especially in the cases of families in poverty, and women and children in trouble—that the root causes of such difficulties were moral and spiritual.

A second form of religiously rooted philanthropic practice emerged among the growing populations of Catholics and Jews, who stood outside the Protes-tant mainstream. These people were often separated from the Protestants, and sometimes internally divided as well, by ethnic differences. For example, not only were the Jews separated from the Protestant mainstream of American cul-ture by religious differences; but the first groups of Jews in this country—who arrived primarily in the 1700s—were for the most part German in background, creating another line of separation from the dominant English culture, and a line of separation from many Jews arriving in the 1800s who were primarily from Eastern Europe (Smith, 1984). Such circumstances led to the development of philanthropic agencies, sometimes in the form of mutual-benefit organizations, in the Jewish community to help Jews, and in the Catholic community to help Catholics. Among the different ethnic populations, particularly among the Catholics, these organizations were often set up along ethnic lines.

Yet, in these cases, many efforts were still undergirded by and reflective of religious and philanthropic ideals and traditions of long standing. For instance, the Jewish community in the United States structured their efforts for relief and mutual assistance around the ideals of *tsedakah*, a time-honored ideal in Judaism embodying principles and practices for the maintenance of a "righteous" community that upholds and respects the dignity of all its members (Neusner, 1988).

Yet another religious manifestation of this growth of philanthropic and organizational activity was the development of what came to be called the Benevolent Empire. This encompassed a whole host of Protestant organizations, often connected by common trustees and members as well as common religious interests and beliefs, that undertook a wide range of both evangelistic and social-service activities. Interdenominational in nature, these organizations pursued the causes of missionary work, temperance, the Sunday-school movement (which, we should remember, was the adult literacy movement of its time), and the founding of colleges. Interestingly, as the cause of abolition grew more prominent, the controversy surrounding it undermined the unity of these Protestant philanthropic endeavors (Bremner, 1988).

Just prior to the Civil War, American society was struggling to continue to live out its founders' dreams for the creation of a nation marked by people's willingness to care for one another and for the common good as a matter of religious, moral, and civic principle. In America's earliest days, prior to independence and the beginnings of industrialization and urbanization, it was often possible to achieve this through informal acts of caring of neighbor for neighbor, and through the activities of churches that represented a faith tradition with which almost everyone in the community identified. Following independence, and especially in the nineteenth century, the growth of cities and industry, combined with religious and ethnic diversification in the populace, began to necessitate the development of more formal and more sophisticated mechanisms for carrying on philanthropic activity.

In addition, while the natural inclinations of all Americans to organize themselves for these and other purposes, on which de Tocqueville comments, continued to be manifest, various "elites" began to look for ways to establish and support organizations—nonprofit enterprises—that could more effectively meet specific social needs and promote those religious, moral, and social values these elites believed were essential to the nation's greatness. This was made possible by the improving quality of the juridical structures and practices that allowed for the creation of private corporations, testamentary trusts, and endowments (Hall, 1984).

Again, what may be most noteworthy in all this from a twentieth-century perspective is that, for the most part, up until this point, it continued to be the public's assumption that "the common good," including the welfare of individuals in need, should be cared for through *private means rather than government*. Generally speaking, most early settlers came to America with a negative experience of government as oppressive; indeed, many were fleeing the persecution of such governments. They tended to be, not surprisingly, highly distrustful of government. It is important to note, however, they also tended to be distrustful of people of great wealth—which was often associated in their experience with the aristocracies and the capricious exercise of quasi-public authority.

The clear preference of the early inhabitants of the United States was for individuals in communities to care for public needs through community-based institutions, like the local church. The people's concern about excessive concentrations of private wealth was a contributing factor to the slow development of a statutory basis for private corporations, and other legal forms, that would allow for the accumulation and transmission of large concentrations of wealth. As the circumstances of society, commerce, and industry changed, however, such legal and corporate forms came into existence, providing possibilities not only for the development of private, for-profit corporations but also for the establishment of institutions committed to philanthropic work.

By the middle of the 1800s, critical changes were taking place in the United States that challenged the validity, or at least the viability, of the founders' ideals. Society was diversifying. Significant differences in religious beliefs and traditions were now appearing among its members. There were also greater disparities in individuals' economic status as the accumulation of private wealth on the part of a few individuals and families grew, and the appearance of these disparities was heightened by the abject poverty of many people in rapidly growing cities. As a result of these conditions, we begin to see the emergence of some new issues—or, at least, issues that take on a new significance—around questions of (1) whether large-scale philanthropic giving and philanthropic organizations are truly serving the public good, and (2) what the government's role should be in addressing large-scale social problems.

## The Evolution of Philanthropy in the 1800s

Robert Bremner notes that, by the middle of the 1800s, in the face of increasing differences among classes, "early Americans began to voice the suspicion that philanthropy was a device used by the rich to atone for their way of acquiring wealth" (1988, p. 42). Leading writers and social critics like Emerson and Thoreau voiced such sentiments. Yet the diaries and letters of philanthropists speak more of motivations of religious values like "stewardship" or of personal satisfaction in giving than they do of guilt. Bremner observes that the philanthropists of this age were likely to cite "a feeling of religious duty, because they enjoyed giving, because some appeal touched their heart" (p. 43) as the motivation for their generosity.

Regardless, whether the reasons for giving were religious or not, or even genuinely "altruistic" or not, it is in this period that we begin to see very large gifts for secular purposes like schools, libraries, and hospitals. This is indubitably a function, at least in part, of economic factors, as with the growth of industry and commerce there were more persons with sizable fortunes. It is probably also a function of the recognition on the part of some industrialists and merchants of the importance of these kinds of institutions for the further development of the nation's civic and commercial infrastructure.

The increasing awareness of the interdependency of the interests of commerce and many of the societal needs addressed by philanthropic or nonprofit institutions also led businesspeople and others to begin asking questions about the efficacy of philanthropic giving and charitable or nonprofit institutions in meeting those societal needs. In his analysis of our culture, Curti notes that the "American national character has emphasized practicality and efficiency" (1958, p. 422). Certainly many observers share this view, suggesting "pragmatism" is a central facet of the American character. While philanthropic practices and institutions were intended to give expression to specific social and religious ideals from the time of the first English settlements in America, they were also always intended to meet specific practical human needs. In the 1800s, particularly in the last half of the century, we see increasing emphasis on questions of the practicality and efficiency of philanthropic methods and institutions in solving social problems.

Simultaneously, we see for the first time people beginning to ask if some of the needs addressed by private philanthropy should not be the responsibility of government. In the 1840s and 1850s, Dorothea Dix was campaigning for the state—first Massachusetts and then the federal government—to provide support for building and operating asylums for the "indigent insane." Her crusade raised for the first time at the national level the question of governmental versus private responsibility for the care of the poor. And it is not without significance that she attempted to make her case on practical economic as well as moral grounds, arguing that it would be less expensive for the state to provide care for the insane in institutions where they might be cured than to have to pay for their maintenance for life in other institutions—in those days, usually prisons.

It is also interesting to note that in 1854, when President Franklin Pierce vetoed the bill Dix had proposed providing public lands for asylums and schools for the deaf, he did so on the basis of a "slippery-slope" argument. He said that, while the cause was worthy, he could not approve the appropriation because, "If Congress has the power to make provision for the indigent insane . . . it has the same power to provide for the indigent who are not insane" (Bremner, 1988, p. 66). President Pierce was, in other words, worried about establishing a precedent that could be used later to argue for greater federal support for social-welfare programs. In his argument we find—in addition to prophecy—the first example of many debates to be had about public versus private responsibilities for social welfare.

In any case, the latter half of the nineteenth century saw the government still, by and large, staying out of the work of social welfare; but interest on the part of business and community leaders in putting that work on a more businesslike or "scientific" footing was on the rise. During this period, there was a phenomenal increase in the size, range, and value of philanthropic activities. This relates to the continuing increase in the range and depth of social problems, but it also relates to newfound capacities for and interests in organizing such work.

One of the more curious elements in this history has to be the role of one particular institution in laying the foundation for the greater organization of charitable work. This is the United States Sanitary Commission (USSC), an organization of private citizens created to provide logistical support and advice to improve the conditions in military camps and hospitals during the Civil War. With the corps of Civil War nurses that Dorothea Dix organized, the USSC became a precursor of the American Red Cross.

The corps of Civil War nurses involved thousands of women beyond those actually doing the nursing. They organized to provide support and material for the nurses, an effort that engaged many American women for the first time in voluntary activities that reached far beyond their own communities. The organizational skills developed in this context would later be put to use in a number of philanthropic movements and institutions—as well as political movements, such as the suffrage campaign—of national scale.

One major part of the work of the USSC was coordinating the activities and contributions of women's groups. It arranged for and coordinated the delivery of donated supplies for the troops. It also inspected and helped design and improve camps and hospitals to ensure more sanitary conditions. The men who gave their time to managing and overseeing this service were largely college graduates with substantial expertise in relevant fields. The development of the USSC created a first model of a "professional organization" in philanthropic service. Moreover, many of the men involved in this work took their experience and ideas and went on to play key roles in directing local and national charitable organizations after the war, bringing with them that model and the underlying concern for efficiency.

In the aftermath of the Civil War there was, in fact, a burgeoning of activity and organization around charitable causes. Indeed, some felt there were too many people and too many organizations trying to relieve the poor, and quite possibly too much charity being proffered. Two concerns were prominent: first, that in all this activity there was significant duplication of services—which apparently was true—and hence great waste and inefficiency; and second, that the relief work was being undertaken in the wrong way, tending to create dependency on charity among the recipients rather than encouraging and equipping them to attain self-sufficiency.

We should recognize that this second concern was not a new one. All the way back in the 1600s and 1700s, we find people like Cotton Mather and Benjamin Franklin articulating concerns about charity encouraging sloth. In his famous "Essays to Do Good" (1710), Mather exhorts his readers to be cautious: "If there be any idle persons among [your neighbors], I beseech you, cure them of their idleness. Don't nourish 'em and harden 'em in that, but find employment for them" (cited in O'Connell, 1983, p. 46). And Franklin writes, "I am for doing good for the poor, but I differ in opinion about that means. I think the best way of doing good to the poor is, not making them easy in poverty, but leading or driving them out of it" (cited in Bremner, 1988, p. 17). In truth, this sense of caution and uneasiness about charity has been evident in the American philanthropic tradition all along. Bremner observes, "The constant effort of American humanitarians since the days of Cotton Mather had been to restrain and discipline, not to expand, the charitable impulse" (p. 143).

So, in the latter part of the 1800s—amidst great wealth and great poverty, with philanthropic activities increasing in both size and number—the concern about charity being counterproductive and creating "pauperization" among recipients was again prominent. Hand-in-hand with this concern was the question of the efficiency of charity more generally. These concerns, along with the emergence of the social sciences and the growth of knowledge about organizations and administration, led to the development of the "scientific philanthropy" movement. This approach to giving and charitable work came to dominate American philanthropic practice by the end of the century. It may have been given its most succinct and powerful statement in Andrew Carnegie's essay, "Wealth" (1889). About the values undergirding this perspective, Hall comments, "Though employing a rhetoric of benevolence, 'scientific' philanthropy's desire to put charity on a businesslike basis was anything but humanitarian. [It was] far more concerned with efficiency and 'race progress' than with alleviating suffering" (1990, pp. 46–47).

This movement and way of thinking about the work of charity and philanthropy was so pervasive and persuasive that even many of those working in religiously based organizations soon came to adopt its views. Other religious people saw the clash between the values of this perspective and the values of the Judeo-Christian tradition more clearly, and rejected "scientific" philanthropy "believing that Christian charity involves far more than the economical provision of services. As, if not more, important was the creation of a community of feeling, a set of human bonds, which are in themselves perhaps far more valuable than the service." (Hall, 1990a, p. 52).

The most important institutional manifestation of scientific philanthropy was the development of the "charitable organization society" (COS). The first COS actually appeared in London in 1869, but the model was soon imitated in the United States. Bremner describes the movement as follows:

> The basic idea of the charitable organization movement was to promote cooperation and higher standards of efficiency among older relief-dispensing agencies. . . . With varying degrees of success . . . the charity organization societies acted as clearinghouses and bureaus of information. They maintained registries of all applicants for relief, with detailed records of the assistance given or refused by cooperating societies, and they undertoook searching investigations of the need and worthiness of the cases referred to them. (1988, p. 94)

The clearinghouse function a COS offered was important to many of those who needed help as well as to the agencies, because many charitable organizations and aid-granting agencies had very narrow focuses and could provide only one of a number of services an indigent person or family might need. The investigations of the "worthiness" of the applicants could be more or less useful depending on the criteria for worthiness. The evidence indicates these criteria unfortunately often had more to do with applicants' backgrounds and racial, ethnic, or religious factors than with need.

A key element in the relief process the COS movement promoted was "visitation." The poor were visited in their homes by volunteers under the supervision of paid agents or secretaries of the charitable societies or agencies. These visits were to serve two purposes: first, to investigate the conditions and claims of an applicant for relief; and second—on the assumption that many of the poor people's problems were caused by a lack of character or virtue—to create a relationship with the volunteer wherein the poor could be "instructed and uplifted." While we might now find the rationale for and character of the visitation paternalistic and condescending, it led (ironically) to two important transformations.

In the long run, it laid the groundwork for the transformation of the COS movement and scientific philanthropy into what we now call "social work." The fact is that, in many cases, actually getting the well-intentioned if misinformed volunteers and staff into the homes and communities of the poor made some of them understand that these people were in need not (for the most part) because they lacked virtue, but rather because of the economic and social environment in which they existed. This led to some of these volunteers and staff beginning to understand the real, systemic causes of poverty and wanting to do something about them. And that contributed greatly to the development of more modern and enlightened approaches to social welfare (see Bremner, 1956).

In the shorter run, this whole movement led to a lively and vitally important public debate about the purposes of philanthropy and voluntarism. While the champions of a more humane, idealistic, moral, or religious perspective did not necessarily win that debate, it provided the occasion for them to re-think and restate the traditional ideals for philanthropy in a new era. In a society that was beginning to grow notably more secular and individualistic, that was important. The maintenance of civic virtues, of which philanthropy is surely one, requires they be regularly articulated and discussed in public discourse.

Another development that should be seen as a fruit of the scientific philanthropy movement was the creation of large, general-purpose foundations, a development that Andrew Carnegie and John D. Rockefeller gave great momentum. Where previously wealthy individuals had usually created trusts or endowed institutions to support one particular kind of service—whether medical, educational, or for the care of those in need in some way—these newer foundations were directed toward research and policy formulation, toward finding or designing the solutions to problems rather than just alleviating suffering.

These kinds of institutions could be innovative and potentially useful as philanthropic instruments. On the other hand, they could also serve as vehicles through which the wealthy could protect their estates from taxes and exercise ever more power in the public sphere. General-purpose foundations became the focus of considerable controversy when they were created, with much debate about whether they represented genuine "philanthropy" at all or simply another way for the wealthy to extend and preserve their own interests and privileges.

Scientific philanthropy can be seen to embody the values we might expect someone like Andrew Carnegie to bring from a business background. What is more, Carnegie is in many ways representative of the civic leaders of that time in holding those values and promulgating them in public life. As this approach to philanthropy became dominant, it transformed the criteria by which people judged the effectiveness of charity and service, and the nonprofit organizations that provided them. Concerns for fidelity to biblical ideals of compassion and alleviation of suffering (or even long-range improvement) in individual's lives, became secondary to considerations of efficiency in the use of resources for the purposes of promoting the "progress" of "the race" or "the nation"—as defined by an intellectual and industrial elite.

Thus, as America entered the twentieth century, the role and purposes of philanthropic giving and voluntary association were contested. For some, philanthropy continued to express profoundly important religious and moral ideals for the shape and character of American society, providing an avenue through which to try to build a compassionate society wherein neighbors cared for neighbors and those with plenty shared with those in need. For others, philanthropic practice was seen more as an obligation of the rich to give something back to society for the purposes of improving social conditions and the chances of continuing the material and scientific progress of society as a whole.

## Philanthropy in the Twentieth Century

There are a number of characteristics that distinguish philanthropy and voluntary action in twentieth-century America from philanthropy and voluntary action in earlier periods. Some of these relate to issues of scale. Others are a function of the changing relationship between private philanthropy and government.

We have already noted the beginnings of the creation of large, general-purpose foundations. If this trend was launched by Carnegie and Rockefeller, it was reinforced by others like Julius Rosenwald, W. K. Kellogg, Eli Lilly, and the Mellon family. The result is the presence in American society of a number of philanthropic institutions with enormous economic and political influence, capable of highlighting specific problems or issues, assuring they will get the attention of business and government leaders, and forcing consideration of specific policies or approaches to solutions through research and experimentation in these areas generated by the foundations' own resources.

Another dramatic change in philanthropic practice has been the refinement of the art and science of fund-raising. Here, too, the most obvious change involves scale. While institutions dedicated to helping others and serving the common good have been asking people for money for a long time, it is safe to say—as we come to the close of the twentieth century—that never have so many been asked so often for so much. The techniques of and approaches to fund-raising that have made this possible started to take shape in the late 1800s with the first federated fund drive in Denver (1888); but they began to develop in earnest with Charles Ward's work in implementing the first modern "fund-raising drives" for the YMCA in the early 1900s, and the establishment of the first full-scale "community chest" in Cleveland (1913).

Ironically, it was war that furthered improvements in this key element of the business of doing good works. Fund-raising efforts for the Red Cross during the First World War, and then for relief efforts on behalf of the war's victims, generated the first coordinated, nationwide, fund-raising efforts and greater refinements in fund-raisers' techniques. These circumstances also drew Americans into giving on a large scale for the first time for international causes and concerns. Contributions for overseas missionary efforts had been a key component of giving in many religious congregations for many years, but in the generosity of contributors to relief efforts in the aftermath of the First World War we see for the first time a broad spectrum of Americans viewing persons in other nations as part of a community to whom they should extend care and assistance.

In the last seventy years, the number and size of general-purpose foundations has grown. The scale and sophistication of fund-raising efforts for all kinds of causes have grown, especially with the introduction of television and computer technology. The involvement of Americans and United States–based nonprofit organizations in philanthropic endeavors abroad has continued and grown. What has changed most dramatically since the beginning of this century has been Americans' understandings and expectations of the relationship between private philanthropy and government efforts and responsibilities for the welfare of individuals in need.

If philanthropic giving and activity were raised to new heights during the First World War, they continued at remarkable levels through the prosperous 1920s. In 1918 the American Red Cross collected $175 million, an astonishing sum in those times. After the war, the European Relief Council, led by Herbert Hoover, raised over $30 million in 1921–22 for aid and assistance in those countries that had been devastated by the recent conflict (Bremner, 1988).

Such generosity on the part of individuals was also evident in the success of Community Chest and United Appeal drives at home and in support for cultural and educational institutions as well. Moreover, the beneficence of a number of major foundations that had been established in the first two decades of the century was felt as huge grants in the millions of dollars went to support the improvement of education, research on medical problems, and efforts to improve the conditions of blacks. There were even large gifts from private philanthropists to government institutions, such as John D. Rockefeller's gift of $500,000 to the Library of Congress.

It is in this time frame that philanthropy really becomes an industry (of sorts) in its own right. In the 1920s, we see the establishment of the first fund-raising-counsel firms. The models of federated funding—the precursors of the modern-day United Ways—became firmly established in most major cities.

But, of course, it is easy to be generous when you are prosperous, and these were prosperous times. The many large gifts received by major institutions came from persons who had become very wealthy (mostly) in the late 1800s and early 1900s, and from the large foundations such people had established. The patterns of giving by smaller donors had been established first during the war—a time of great need that united people and encouraged sacrifice—and had then continued in a growing economy.

With the onset of the depression, the challenges to philanthropy, and even more significantly to the societal assumptions that undergirded much of American philanthropic practice, were suddenly much larger and different in kind. Most important, the relationship between private philanthropic activity and the government's efforts to care for society's need was dramatically altered.

After the crash of the stock market in 1929, the prosperity Americans had enjoyed since the end of World War I crumbled rapidly. Companies shut down, banks failed, and unemployment rose swiftly. As these effects were first felt in 1930–31, local communities rallied around to help their own in the best traditions of American philanthropy. They raised funds through their community chests (and other vehicles) to provide relief for those in need. The American Red Cross undertook to organize relief efforts on a national scale.

For the most part, earlier concerns about pauperization and being too liberal in providing assistance were set aside, and so were questions about the character of those in need, as the severity of the economic problems became clear. What remained, however, was the expectation that the efforts to provide assistance should be organized and financed privately. The Red Cross even turned down a goverment grant for assistance in 1930.

Herbert Hoover's leadership reinforced this commitment to handling the crisis through private means. This was not simply an effort on his part to protect the federal treasury from having to pay the costs of assistance. It was also an affirmation of American ideals about the place and functions of philanthropy and government, respectively. We should recall that Hoover led the organization of relief efforts in Europe after the First World War, and from his experience had no reason to doubt that charitable giving and private nonprofit organizations could successfully address the most severe economic and social problems. He had grown up in a rural Quaker community; everything in his upbringing would have reinforced the ideals of neighbor helping neighbor and discouraged dependency on government aid.

In addition, in articulating such ideals and encouraging nongovernmental solutions, Hoover was reflecting the bias of most of his audience. When Hoover said, "A voluntary deed by a man impressed with a sense of responsibility and brotherhood of man is infinitely more precious to our National ideals and National spirit than a thousandfold poured from the Treasury of the Government under the compulsion of law" (cited in Bremner, 1988, p. 138), he was voicing a widely shared sentiment. Distrust of government still ran deep in those days—among both the rich and the poor. There was a tendency to see government money as tainted, at least for charitable purposes, and to be concerned about the growth of government programs.

Finally, however, the Great Depression overwhelmed all private initiatives to resolve it and provide relief for its victims. After Hoover's defeat and Roosevelt's election in 1932, the country moved fairly quickly into large-scale government efforts in social welfare, both in areas of relief work and in areas of economic reconstruction. As a result of these circumstances, there was a growing acceptance that the government should play a central role in assuring the provision of certain kinds of social-welfare programs, and a significant diminution of private philanthropy's reputation. In fact, the ways in which Hoover and others championed the cause of voluntary giving and action contributed to a serious disillusionment about private philanthropy on the part of the general public, for many claims were made about what it could do that simply did not hold true.

This is not to say that the role of philanthropy in our nation's political economy has diminished since the Great Depression; quite the contrary. Its role, however, has changed. First of all, after these events, virtually no American expected private philanthropy to provide the most basic forms of welfare, relief, or general assistance in most communities. Second, these events ended up largely resolving—at least for that time—the question of whether private philanthropy's primary role should be to alleviate the suffering caused by social and economic problems or to generate innovative solutions to those problems.

The first issue has been part of the ambiguity of philanthropy in the United

States for most of its history. In the earliest days of the nation, the vast majority of giving was directed to either providing immediate assistance for the poor or developing educational and cultural institutions, although in the efforts of people like Franklin and Stephen Girard we also see endeavors to find new ways to address the causes of poverty and disease. As time went on, philanthropists increasingly directed their attention and resources to efforts aimed at discovering and removing the causes of social problems, rather than just providing relief. This trend toward investing in research and experiments for social progress rather than charitable aid obviously accelerated under the influence of scientific philanthropy and people like Carnegie and Rockefeller. Giving through churches, community chests, and the like continued to go largely for relief and assistance.

One of the ironies of what happened in the Great Depression was that it caused, first, a redirection of philanthropic giving toward relief and assistance—what some would call "almsgiving" instead of "philanthropy." However, the fact that these efforts failed and the government stepped in essentially released philanthropy from that set of expectations after the depression. No longer did most Americans think philanthropy could or should provide basic social welfare. This change gave philanthropists and philanthropic institutions more freedom to support research, innovative experiments in social service delivery, and community efforts to resolve community problems.

After the Second World War, this is precisely the direction philanthropy took. Large foundations tended more and more to support entirely new efforts to solve basic social problems, sometimes even on an international scale—for example, the Ford Foundation's endeavors with respect to world hunger, agriculture, and the Green Revolution. Local United Ways channeled support to community agencies trying new approaches to working with young people in trouble, the handicapped, and other groups needing help, as well as scout troops and traditional charities.

In the 1960s and 1970s, the Johnson administration's Great Society programs and the Nixon and Carter administrations' "revenue sharing" facilitated the proliferation of nonprofit enterprises in community-service activities by channeling large amounts of federal funds to service agencies. Some of these agencies, being truly community-based and representing constituencies often previously unrepresented, became not only providers of service but also advocates for social justice on behalf of those constituencies (Fink, 1990). Thus, in an interesting reversal of the traditional model, we had government funding (albeit, often indirectly) the kinds of values-expressive advocacy activities of voluntary associations that had been associated with their status as private organizations.

Certainly, one of the most striking features of the public discourse about social welfare issues in the last ten years has been the revival of the whole set of questions about public versus private responsibilities that were so prominent around the time of the Great Depression and the New Deal—and seemed to have been resolved. In their eagerness to get government out of the business of providing for basic social welfare, the Reagan and Bush administrations revived Hoover's arguments about voluntarism being an essential aspect of the American social order, crucial to our national moral fiber, which will be undermined by too much government funding for social services. They challenged basic assumptions about these services being government responsibilities, on moral as well as economic grounds.

Recalling the way philanthropy and voluntary organizations have reflected two aspects of the American character—moral concern and practicality—they claimed both: (1) that care for those in need should be provided voluntarily by persons in their community as an exercise that would reflect and build up that which is finest in our national character; and (2) that this kind of care would be provided more effectively by local and private agencies than by government. Reagan administration officials even went so far as to revive nineteenth-century language about the "worthiness" of those receiving public aid, clearly attempting to impugn the character of many public-welfare recipients in hopes of justifying or excusing the withdrawal of assistance on moral grounds.

Some saw this as a crassly political effort on the part of these administrations to excuse government from its proper responsibilities for caring for those who cannot care for themselves. Others saw it as a legitimate effort to renew attention to values that are essential in our culture and political economy. Either way it is obvious that, for example, the famous speech George Bush gave in accepting the Republican nomination for president in 1988—in which he first used the image of "a thousand points of light"—was meant to evoke and appeal to these basic values and images in American culture. There can also be no question that the success the Reagan and Bush administrations experienced in their campaign to pass responsibilities for social welfare back to the private sector can be attributed to the fact that the civic and philanthropic ideals for our society articulated by John Winthrop more than 350 years ago, and Herbert Hoover 60 years ago, still have remarkable currency.

Whether or not the public believes the government must be ultimately responsible for providing basic social-welfare services, clearly many Americans still believe this nation's social structures and public life should be marked by the qualities and shaped by the activities that philanthropic giving and voluntary associations ideally embody. We should conclude this examination of philanthropy's role as "index and agent" in shaping American culture by reviewing the essential facets of those qualities and activities, and by noting the apparent tensions between some of them.

## Key Dimensions and Tensions of American Philanthropy

This brief review of how philanthropic practice evolved in the United States reveals that a number of values or ideals in what Curti calls the American "national character" are both embodied in and have been shaped by that philanthropic tradition. One fascinating aspect of this tradition is the way in which values or characteristics that are often seen as opposites are juxtaposed and held in tension—a tension that is, ideally, creative. Key elements of our national culture that are so reflected in the tradition of philanthropy are:

1. the tendency to individualism as well as the desire for genuine community;
2. the tendency to idealism as well as the tendency to pragmatism; and
3. the desire to preserve traditional values as well as the desire for innovation.

The rest of this chapter summarizes and analyzes the history we have just reviewed in relation to these ideals and values.

The curious integration of both individualistic and communitarian values is a facet of American culture on which a number of observers have commented (Slater, 1976; Bellah et al., 1985, 1991). These two seemingly opposing sets of cultural dynamics and ideals have been evident in Anglo-American culture from its origins. The American notion of what constitutes a good society originally embraced them both, albeit sometimes uneasily.

This is evident, for instance, in the beliefs and communities of the New England settlers to whom we have pointed. John Winthrop's "model of Christian charity" emerges from a Calvinist theological system, which contends that individuals are "saved" individually—so at one level their faith is strictly a matter of their personal relationship with God—but in that salvation they are called to live out their faith in a "covenanted community"—so at another level the expression of their faith requires a commitment to sharing their life with others.

The lives that Alexis de Tocqueville observed years later reflected these same ideals in tension in small towns and in rural and wilderness settings, even if the basis for the values was more practical and less theological. On the one hand, many of those settling the American frontier were seeking individual freedom, pursuing their fortune, and striking out "on their own" in the process. On the other hand, in these settings, perhaps even more than in the cities, people came together to help each other out, and created the kinds of voluntary associations that de Tocqueville so lauded, in order to ensure there would be a sense of community for mutual support in times of trouble. Our forebears in these settings lived lives that were much more isolated than those of modern urban Americans in one sense, and yet they were much more fully and meaningfully interconnected in another.

The truth is the pursuit of the "American dream" of individual fame, fortune, and personal fulfillment has always required affirmation of and participation in community. It is when the creative tension and balance between the pursuit of individual achievement and the affirmation of our interdependency begins to break down that our society seems to be in real trouble, as it may be now. In the book *Habits of the Heart* (1985), it is recognition of the reality of this interdependence and the restoration of that balance that Robert Bellah and his colleagues urge upon us.

Philanthropic practice in this nation has reflected, and sometimes helped sustain, this creative tension. There has been a great deal of individual initiative in giving and service, and there has been a willingness to unite in associations and to create nonprofit corporations whenever a task or cause required more unified and sustained efforts. Many people have associated philanthropy with the spectacular giving of very wealthy individuals to great institutions and endeavors, yet it can be argued that what has sustained the philanthropic tradition in this country has been the consistent participation of small givers and volunteers in countless ways to sustain a great host of small organizations and service providers—from local congregations, to storefront nonprofits, to the more than 2000 local United Ways.

Indeed, many argue it is this latter form of participation that has been crucial to creating and sustaining a communitarian spirit (Etzioni, 1968; Boyte and Evans, 1986; Ellis and Noyes, 1990). In this view, it is through participation in the granges, PTAs, local civic associations, and environmental groups, for example, that individuals come to identify the "common good" and their stake in it, and learn how to pursue it with others. Voluntary associations and nonprofit organizations are, accordingly, generally expected to demonstrate strong commitments to democratic processes in their own operations and governance—as a function of their role as nurturers and sustainers of a participatory, democratic spirit for a larger society. They are expected to recognize and honor individual rights and individual initiative, but also to provide the institutional structures through which individuals may define and pursue *common goals* for their lives *together* in the public sphere.

As these organizations frequently have demonstrated such values, or at least strived to do so, they have reflected the idealistic streak in American culture. Yet if operating in such ways—or other factors—leads to organizational paralysis, or just obvious inefficiency, these organizations will find themselves criticized for failing to honor another American value, pragmatism.

Part of the vision that has shaped the American character stems from the earliest aspirations of English settlers who, leaving behind what they viewed as a corrupt culture and society in England, saw America as the place where they could build a society free from the imperfections of the society they left behind. Certainly the high idealism evident in such a vision has been upheld and renewed by social reformers throughout our history.

Some of the first white settlers also came for economic reasons, however. And all came to a strange and harsh environment wherein their first concern was to figure out how to survive, and then prosper. Absent even the primitive advantages of seventeenth-century European civilization, these first colonists had to find new ways to do things. From these origins the spirit—and myth— of "American ingenuity" was born and came to occupy a central place in our national self-image. This too grew and was sustained over the years. Necessity was sometimes the mother of invention, as was the desire for wealth, and the United States led the way in the development of many industries and technologies.

American philanthropy has echoed both the idealism and the pragmatism of the national character. In a manifestation of a "can-do" mentality, voluntary associations and nonprofit organizations have been the vehicles for one social reform movement after another and have led the way in meeting many social needs, as we have seen. In these efforts, they have often tried both to address practical problems and to give expression to values and ideals.

There may be no better example of this synthesis of idealism and pragmatism than John D. Rockefeller. While the ways in which Rockefeller ran his corporations and made his fortune certainly raise questions about his ethics and values, his life evidenced a sincere desire to "do good" and improve society through his philanthropy. Biographies show that his religious ideals deeply influenced his giving; but at the same time he brought an industrialist's concerns for efficiency to this process (see, for example, Nevins, 1959). Manifesting his sense of how these values needed to go hand-in-hand he said, "We must always remember that there is not enough money for the work of human uplift and there never can be. How vitally important it is, therefore, that the expenditure should go as far as possible and be used with the greatest intelligence" (cited in Bremner, 1988, p. 114). Thus, in its endeavors to meet and solve social problems while—at least sometimes—making visible high moral ideals for human relationships and public life, and in its effectiveness in doing so, philanthropic practice has both reinforced and made manifest the distinctive combination of idealism and pragmatism that marks the American character.

In keeping with this tradition, Americans today still generally hold high expectations of nonprofit, philanthropic organizations in both aspects. They often expect such organizations to show higher ethical standards for openness, integrity, and accountability than business or governmental organizations; but they also expect their philanthropic enterprises to perform. Questions about their efficiency, about administrative costs, and about the efficacy of the services they provide are very important to many donors; but the appeals of these organizations to donors are often based on the values they try to embody in their work. So both kinds of ideals need to be honored—and, again, sometimes held in a creative tension—in the organizations' operations and governance.

Finally, it is in this necessity to balance moral idealism and efficiency that a third set of cultural values comes into play, and those are the values of cultural preservation and innovation. Philanthropy and nonprofit organizations have been alternately condemned and praised for coming down too much on one side or the other of this balance.

For instance, some who have studied the tradition of philanthropy and voluntarism in this country suggest that one of its greatest contributions to society, indeed one of the reasons for its existence, is its capacity for innovation. These people argue that because nonprofit organizations are not constrained by the need to produce a profit or by the need to represent a political consensus, they can try new approaches to addressing social needs, support new kinds of art, and champion new and controversial causes. They also argue that the history of philanthropic practice demonstrates such organizations have often done so, much to society's benefit (see, for example, Douglas, 1983, O'Neill, 1989, Drucker, 1990b). Yet others who have studied this same tradition criticize philanthropic practice because it has functioned as a conservator of social values, often reinforcing the positions and ideals of powerful elites, and not infrequently inhibiting change in public perspectives on social needs, true innovation in cultural matters, and progress toward a more just social order (see, for example, Ostrander, 1984; Neilsen, 1985; Odenhal, 1990).

It has been fairly pointed out, for instance, that large foundations are generally reluctant to support radically new approaches to meeting social problems, and have consistently underfunded programs directly addressing the concerns of certain constituencies—especially women and minorities. They have also been reluctant to support the work of agencies with controversial advocacy agendas. On the other hand, one can draw up a long list of the beneficial innovations in medical care, social services, and education that resulted from foundation-supported programs. In addition, groups with different social agendas are creating new foundations, and some controversial causes have become the focus of philanthropic activity that exemplifies the national tradition. A current example would be the philanthropic and nonprofit activity concerned with AIDS.

Odenhal (1990) has argued that the giving of the wealthy in this country has gone largely to support the arts and education of the sort they prefer, rather than meeting the needs of the poor or supporting new or different forms of arts and education. While this may be true more often than not, it is also true that innovations in art, education, and other spheres have always been championed by a few risk takers and had to gain some acceptance before they drew more general support. And others—not just the wealthy—who appreciate ballet and opera, or who have profited from higher education in elite institutions, will argue the broad public benefits of the charitable giving that has supported these activities and institutions.

In fact, philanthropic activities and institutions have always been able and likely to fill both roles—as conservators of societal and cultural values; and as innovators in creating new forms of service and art and fomenting change in the public realms of policy and politics. Curti insightfully explores this dual role in his essay, "Tradition and Innovation in American Philanthropy" (1961). And Hall's book on *The Organization of American Culture* (1984) shows how the "cultural elite" of New England created new organizational forms—many of them nonprofit—and generated many interesting innovations in education and other realms of public life, *all while intending to preserve and promote more traditional values*. That philanthropic organizations can serve as both conservators and innovators is but one more reason to appreciate their role in American culture. It is also another way in which philanthropic practice has mirrored as well as shaped the national character.

While many of those who came to this country from Europe came to get away from the social order they knew and to create a "new order of the ages"— *novus ordo saeclorum,* as it says on our money—they also recreated many of the patterns of the societies they left behind. Many characteristics of American society are distinctive, and many manifest the fact that settlers of this new world held on to many of their traditional values.

So, even today philanthropic and nonprofit organizations may be either conservators or innovators or both. With regard to this set of societal expectations, perhaps, the issues of which philanthropic organizations need to be most conscious have less to do with questions of progressive versus conservative than with questions of whom they serve. They may be aligned with either conservative or progressive constituencies and still expect to be accorded the special status and privileges of "philanthropic" organizations. This situation obtains so long as they are not primarily serving "themselves," that is, those who create and run them. If we give credence, however, to what Robert Michels (1949 [1915]) tells us about voluntary organizations, we should expect to see that kind of organizational behavior—that is, self-serving behavior—frequently.

For example, foundations survived the criticism in the 1950s that they were too radical, and criticism in the 1980s that they were too conservative; it was the apparently well-founded criticisms in the 1960s that they were serving the private interests of those who formed them that led to significant government intervention and reforms. Another example is that many church organizations raise large amounts of money for (relatively) narrow purposes—some socially conservative, some liberal—and have not suffered from inordinate public criticism; but when some were discovered to be raising money primarily to support the opulent lifestyles or personal empire-building instincts of their boards or founders, they found themselves in deep trouble. Finally, it seems that whether conservative or innovative, if supposedly philanthropic activities and organizations are directed to contributing to "the public good"—in a manner that accords with a reasonable definition of that term—they will be acceptable in society's view and our public life.

## Summary and Conclusions

Reviewing, then, I have argued that the tradition of philanthropic practice in the United States has reflected, and has helped shape, key elements of the American national character. We have seen how this is manifest in the parallels between what many observers have cited as prominent attributes of our national culture and what we have shown to be central values and ideals for philanthropic practice. Especially significant among the attributes and values of both American culture and American philanthropy are the three sets just discussed—individualism and the desire for community, idealism and pragmatism, and the desire for cultural preservation and the drive toward innovation.

Tracing philanthropic practice and the national character over time, we have seen how these different attributes and values have evolved, and how the relative weight given to them has changed. I have shown how, taken as a whole, this history and these ideals have created an identifiable set of public expectations about the place, functions, and behavior of philanthropic nonprofit organizations in American society that may both support them and place constraints upon them. In sum, they are expected to meet both individual and community needs and aspirations; and they are expected to embody and give expression to many of the nobler values of our society by the manner in which they operate to meet those needs.

I said at the beginning of this chapter that the ideals shaping both our national character and our tradition of philanthropy could be described as moral or civic values, but they were expressed first in explicitly religious terms. We now need to explore those religious elements and their place in this culture and tradition of philanthropic practice.

# 2

# Philanthropy and Religion in America

The fields of activity we most readily associate with nonprofit
organizations include health care, education, religion, the arts and a vast
array of social welfare services. In medieval times these would have come
primarily within the jurisdiction of the church rather than the state.

—James Douglas

IN CHAPTER 1 we saw how the tradition of philanthropy—the practices of
voluntary giving, service, and association for public purposes—has always
been a central feature of the American national character. Examining the origins of this tradition, we noted how John Winthrop described what could be
called "philanthropic" values and practices in a sermon to the first settlers of
the Massachusetts Bay colony and said that these values needed to define the
life of the community they would form. We also noted, however, that the values and practices Winthrop described were, for these early Americans, explicitly religious in source and substance. This was, after all, a sermon. The observation of James Douglas that opens chapter 2 also reminds us that, in fact, much
of what we in the United States now see as the business of philanthropic and
nonprofit organizations was once almost entirely the business of the church.
In this chapter I want to look more closely at the relationship between religion
and philanthropy, particularly as that has played out in American culture.

## Religious Ideals and the United States' Self-Identity

If it is true that the American national character has been distinguished by
philanthropic values and practices, it has also certainly been distinguished by
the uniquely religious emphasis of public as well as private life in this country.
The interest in religious matters, affirmation of religious values, and participation in religious life of citizens in the United States is the highest of any developed nation in the world. What is more, this is not just a recent occurrence.
While there has been a decline in membership in religious congregations since
the 1950s, that appears to have been reversed in the last few years; and belief

in God and participation in religious life in America have been, relative to other countries, consistently high over the last fifty years, and probably over the course of our history as a nation (Gallup and Castelli, 1990; Hodgkinson and Weitzman, 1990).

This is in keeping with our national origins. The sermon of John Winthrop, "A Model of Christian Charity," which we cited as a description of philanthropic values, was even more a pronouncement of religious mission. The settlers coming to New England in the 1600s saw themselves as being on a religious "errand into the wilderness" (Miller, 1956). There were, as we noted, economic reasons for the migration too, but the dominant images in public discourse about the society being formed in America were religious images. This land was "a new Eden," or a wilderness to be tamed by "a new Israel." The new society being formed was to be the biblical "city on a hill." Moreover, the enduring power of these religious images is shown by the fact that they have had currency in public discourse throughout our history, even in the present, frequently being employed by political leaders hoping to evoke deeper responses from the American public (Adams, 1989).

The use and influence of such religious imagery in public life, permeating our national political culture and persisting over the centuries, is sometimes described as the phenomenon of "civil religion." In his insightful analysis of American civil religion, Robert Bellah observes, "In the beginning, and to some extent ever since, Americans have interpreted their history as having religious meaning. They saw themselves as being a 'people' in the classical and biblical sense of the word. They hoped they were the people of God" (Bellah, 1975, p. 2). Historian James Moseley claims, "Americans often think of their nation—especially of its origins—in religious terms. We remember Pilgrims and Puritans 'risking their all' for 'religious freedom' in the New World. Historians use religious metaphors [such] as righteous empire and redeemer nation to describe the developing national consciousness" (Moseley, 1981, p. 30).

In fact, the testimony of many historians and social scientists is that the United States has been from its origins, and continues to be, a nation where religion and religious ideals play a key role in shaping national values and public life. That being so, the questions I want to focus on more closely have to do with the relationship of those religious ideals to the tradition and practices of philanthropy. Have religious ideals and values created and supported philanthropic ideals and values? If so, how? Moreover, if religious ideals and values have played a major role in shaping the philanthropic tradition, what then are the place and function of religious institutions in philanthropic practice? Is the relationship such that religious institutions would be subject to the same kinds of societal expectations we have argued apply to philanthropic institutions more generally? Are churches and religious organizations seen and treated, for the most part, as voluntary associations in our society; or do they have a radically different place and function in the social order?

## Religious Ideals and Philanthropic Practice

Clearly religious ideals—specifically Judeo-Christian, biblical ideals—have provided one of the essential moral and practical foundations for the development of the tradition of philanthropic practice in Western culture. The Old Testament tells us that God wanted the people of Israel to create and sustain a community of "justice and righteousness," *mishpat* and *tsedakah* (Gen. 18:19, Ps. 33:5, Isa. 33:5, Amos 5:24). It was only this kind of community that could be the "city on a hill" and "light to the nations" (Isa. 49:6) that God desired Israel to be.

Reading carefully, we see that one of the distinguishing features of such a community was supposed to be the way it cared for its weakest and most vulnerable members. So the law and the prophets' messages resound with admonitions and exhortations to care for "the poor, the widows, the orphans, and the sojourners" in the community (Lev. 19:10, Deut. 14:29, Ps. 10:18, Isa. 10:1–2). Thus, prior to New Testament times, we find in Jewish practice specific traditions for providing for those in need. These include leaving portions of the harvest in the field to be gleaned by the poor (Lev. 19:10, Ruth), and developing ways for the more prosperous in the community to provide aid to those in need without demeaning them (Neusner, 1988).

Jesus' teachings renew and personalize these emphases. Jesus told his disciples that "loving your neighbor as yourself" is one of the two "great commandments" on which "hang all the law and the prophets" (Matt. 22:34–40). In a hundred different ways, Jesus tried to make his disciples understand that serving others is the essence of a faithful life, and that "it is more blessed to give than to receive" (Acts 20:35). Furthermore, these ideals were often actualized in the lives of Christians in the early church, where we find that care of those in need and methods for collecting and distributing donations for these purposes were among the first concerns attended to as a religious community (Acts 6, 2 Cor. 8).

These religious traditions and values provided the background, the archetype, and the images, for John Winthrop when he wanted to draw a picture for the earliest Anglo-Americans settlers of what their life together should look like. He told them that the only way they could prosper as individuals and as a community in their new settlement—which was largely conceived of as a religious mission—was "[to] entertain each other in brotherly affection; [to] be

willing to adbridge ourselves of superfluities, for the supply of others' necessities. . . . We must delight in each other, make each other's conditions our
own, rejoice together, mourn together, labor and suffer together: always having before our eyes our commission and community" (cited in O'Connell, 1983,
p. 32). In short, the ideals and images that were so powerful at the outset in
shaping the nation's image of itself as an especially moral, caring, and genuine
community—and hence in undergirding the prominence of philanthropic practice—were explicitly religious.

What is more, this was true not only at the outset. It has remained true
throughout American history. This religious imagery has been evoked again
and again in the United States in times of crisis, particularly when political
leaders wanted to move the people to increased giving and acts of sacrifice and
voluntary service for the public good. So, three hundred years after Winthrop,
when Herbert Hoover tried to engage the American public's energy and resources for private (rather than governmental) relief efforts as the Great Depression set in, the heart of Hoover's appeals was framed in religious terms.
He told the nation, "It is indeed *the spiritual* in the individual and the nation
which looks out with keen interest on the well-being of others . . . and gives
us a sense of belonging to the great company of mankind, sharing in *the great
plan of the universe and the definite order which pervades it*" (cited in Adams, 1989;
emphasis added). And certainly the efforts of the recent administrations to call
forth the American public's interest in voluntary service, efforts that have centered on the imagery of "points of light" and "neighbor helping neighbor," are
calculated to appeal to 'quasi-religious'—if not explicitly Judeo-Christian—ideals and values.

Indeed, secular charities freely employ religious imagery with a sense they
are appealing to those deeper cultural motifs and personal instincts that undergird philanthropic giving in this society. A representative example is the poster
that recently appeared in Washington, D.C.'s subway system as part of the
"Combined Federal Campaign"—a kind of "United Appeal" for federal employees. This poster, which asks these employees to designate part of their
contributions for support of an AIDS clinic in Washington, shows two hands
poised over a plate on which are piled bread and fish. The poster says, "Perform a miracle." The text on the poster asks for support for the clinic's "compassionate efforts" to care for those with AIDS.

Mind you, this clinic has no formal connections to any religious body
whatsoever. Indeed, we can be sure that at least some of the religious congregations in the city would take strong exception to some aspects of the clinic's
program. Yet the clinic shows no inhibition about invoking images from the
New Testament—the Sermon on the Mount and the feeding of the five thou-

sand—in trying to elicit a compassionate response and contributions from the public, much of which they know does not explicitly identify with a Christian fellowship. The clinic draws on these images because it knows how strongly values of compassion and charity are linked with religious values even in an increasingly secular society.

We could catalog many more examples of political leaders and secular charities using metaphors and images that intentionally evoke religious themes and ideals in efforts to secure the public's support for particular voluntary efforts or causes, but that is not the point of this discussion. Rather, the point is to demonstrate that religion and religious values have long undergirded the tradition and practice of philanthropy in this country. Religious images and metaphors have long been used to make appeals for contributions to the common good because they are, in fact, highly effective in evoking deeply rooted— sometimes buried—elements of our sense of identity and purpose as a society whose cultural origins are largely in the Judeo-Christian tradition.

In fairness, we should note that another heritage, the classical, Roman-republican heritage, has also played an important role in shaping America's national culture and the philanthropic tradition. Scholars sometimes point to the ways in which the classical Roman tradition provides additional values, symbols, and ideals that may contrast with, but mostly complement, our Judeo-Christian heritage in both the formation of our national culture (Bellah, 1975) and the tradition of philanthropy (Payton, 1987). Indeed, Robert Payton argues that "the prototype of the great American philanthropist is to be found in ancient Rome" (1987, p. 27), not in the Scriptures.

This classical heritage, Payton suggests, emphasizes giving and service for civic purposes out of reasoned commitment, whereas the Judeo-Christian tradition emphasizes giving and service for purposes of alleviating personal suffering on the basis of spiritual and emotional motivations (Payton, 1987). Curti, in his essay on "Tradition and Innovation in American Philanthropy" (1961), also highlights this distinction between the classical, civic-oriented and the Christian, charity-oriented strains of philanthropy. This analysis is helpful in that it points out another source—beside the influences of the social sciences, and condescending and self-protective biases of the upper-class—for the more civic-centered, analytical, and cautionary aspects of American philanthropy.

On the other hand, there can be no question that many of those working and giving to remove the causes of social problems rather than, or as well as, to alleviate personal suffering have also been responding to the emphases on justice and right order in social structures that stand out in the prophetic elements of the Judeo-Christian tradition. Look, for example, at the lives and works of people like Jane Addams and Dorothy Day. What is more, studies of current patterns of giving and volunteering demonstrate how crucial the role of religion continues to be in the nonprofit world, to civic and cultural as well as charitable and social-service organizations—in fact, to both secular and religious organizations. Two nationwide surveys of the organization Independent Sector (IS) highlight this (Hodgkinson and Weitzman, 1990; Hodgkinson, Weitzman, and Kirsch, 1988).

Begin with the issue of who receives most charitable giving. As noted earlier, Independent Sector's study of *Giving and Volunteering in the United States* shows that almost two-thirds (64.5 percent) of household (personal) charitable contributions went to religion, specifically to churches, synagogues, and other religious congregations (Hodgkinson and Weitzman, 1990, p. 26). The survey of the American Association of Fund Raising Counsel (AAFRC) Trust for Philanthropy, *Giving USA*, shows that almost 47 percent of total charitable giving (not just that of individuals) went to religion, for a total of 54.32 billion dollars in 1989 (1990, p. 7). In short, by far the largest beneficiaries of Americans' charitable instincts are religious congregations and organizations.

This may not be surprising to some. However, to understand fully the importance of religion and religious institutions to the tradition and practice of philanthropy, it is even more important to look at how religion may be a source of philanthropy. Here the picture is also impressive, and probably more surprising to most people.

First of all, while religious congregations may be the largest recipients of charitable givers' largesse, they do not direct all those funds to buying robes or decorating their sanctuaries. Indeed, a large percentage of these funds is either spent on service programs run by these congregations, or given away to other nonprofit service agencies. Independent Sector's 1988 study, *From Belief to Commitment: The Activities and Finances of Religious Congregations in the United States*, shows that religious congregations are, in fact, an important source of social services and funds for other nonprofits (Hodgkinson, Weitzman, and Kirsch, 1988). In 1986, out of 41.4 billion dollars donated to religious congregations, $19.1 billion was used for programs other than worship and religious education or for donations to other groups (p. 5). In other words, almost half of the contributions received were used to provide services other than religious programs, most of which benefited the larger community. Moreover, the significance of religious groups as a source as well as a recipient of charitable contributions is highlighted by the fact that they provided more money in 1986, $8.4 billion, to other nonprofit organizations than did foundations (p. 4).

These studies tell us there can be no denying the economic significance of religious organizations as part of the realm of philanthropy and nonprofit enterprise. Yet equally striking and significant is the role of religion as a motivation in individual giving to, and volunteering for, secular nonprofit activities. Again, the results of the IS studies are noteworthy.

For example, the most recent IS study (Hodgkinson and Weitzman, 1990) tells us that "respondents who reported attending religious services in the past year (78 percent) on average contributed 2.4 percent of their household income [to charities including their congregations], compared with .8 percent of average household income contributed by the 22 percent who did not attend" (p. 6). This disparity increases with increases in the level of participation, so the level of contributions is 3.8 percent of income among those who attend religious services weekly (p. 215). While one might attribute this disparity solely to people with religious commitments giving large sums to their congregations, these studies also show that those who participate in the life of a religious congregation are significantly more likely to give to secular groups. Two-thirds of those who are members of congregations give to nonreligious groups, whereas only 58 percent of those who are not members do so (p. 39).

Similar results appear with respect to volunteering. People active in religious life are more likely to give of their time—and to give more of it—than those who are not; and this includes giving their time to causes and activities outside of their congregations as well as within them. And, as with cash contributions, no small portion of the time and energy volunteered to congregations goes into programs designed to serve the larger community. All in all, almost half (48 percent) of the over one billion volunteer hours per month given to local congregations are devoted to social-service activities (Hodgkinson, Weitzman, and Kirsch, 1988, p. 5).

Simply put, in addition to being the largest beneficiaries of Americans' charitable instincts, religion and religious congregations are clearly among the most significant nurturers of those instincts. In the final analysis, there can be no doubt that religious faith and religious images have played a powerful role in shaping our national self-identity and characteristics, and therefore in forming the culture in which philanthropy has flourished. Clearly, religious ideals have also shaped the goals to which individual giving and service have been directed. Finally, religious faith and commitment have been and continue to be among the most crucial elements in motivating such giving and service—including giving and service to secular causes and organizations (Hodgkinson, Weitzman, and Kirsh, 1988; Hodgkinson and Weitzman, 1990).

Thus, the relationship of religion to philanthropy is intimate and vital. It is also, however, complex, and we would be missing something very important if we limited our examination of this relationship only to questions of how religion has shaped individual—albeit sometimes collective—decisions and behavior concerning giving and volunteering. Equally important are questions about how religion and religious institutions have influenced the social and political structure of Western nations—especially the United States—to allow for the development of the "voluntary," "third," or "independent" sector, in which philanthropic and nonprofit organizations have come to operate with considerable freedom from government interference.

## Religion's Role in Creating the "Third Sector"

There is substantial foundation for the argument that the voluntary or third sector as a whole owes its existence to religion and religious groups. James Douglas (1987, p. 43) points out that a great many of the activities of present-day secular nonprofit organizations were once within the purview of the church in Western societies. This does not mean that endeavors such as education, health care, or social-welfare services would not be undertaken if religious groups had not started activities and organizations for these purposes. But it does suggest that the fact that these endeavors can be pursued by private organizations in our culture derives from the work of religious groups establishing precedents for the idea that such endeavors, even though they take place in the public sphere, should be allowed to go on largely free of government control.

In other words, in addition to the fact that many specific institutions— schools, hospitals, service agencies, and others—were begun by religious groups, there is good reason to believe that religious activity created the "social space" in which our political economy allows these "independent" voluntary organizations to exist. Indeed, this social space was carved out first within the religious sphere, and then between the religious and political spheres (Adams, 1986; Stackhouse, 1990). It can be argued that it was precisely because religious groups claimed to be giving expression to values of ultimate importance in undertaking service and advocacy activities of various kinds that they succeeded in establishing this social space for their independent existence.

The essence of this argument is that religious groups—often "sects and advocates of marginalized faiths" rebelling against established and state religions—established the right of voluntary association for themselves, and that right came to be transferred to other charitable and values-expressive organizations. As Max Stackhouse explains it,

> In the name of God, they claimed the right to be, to organize, to care for the neighbor, and to set forth their views publicly. . . . What religious communities fought for was eventually institutionalized: *The right of people to form intentional religious associations outside established religion* was

more and more tolerated, acknowledged, celebrated, and subsequently expanded to include non-religious charitable and ethical organizations.

Stackhouse further claims, "These chapters in church history . . . are what has made modern, Western societies more or less safe not only for religious pluralism," but for the host of organizations and causes represented in the independent sector today (1990, pp. 25–26; emphasis added).

This historical phenomenon was essential to allowing the establishment, early on in the formation of the American political economy, of an independent sector. The sector was originally populated, as we saw in the last chapter, primarily by religious and quasi-religious organizations who justified their existence in terms of their claims to the right to undertake certain kinds of work, often service work, as an expression of fundamental religious and moral convictions and commitments. It is no accident that the first network of nonprofit organizations of national scope was something we now call the Benevolent Empire, a host of Protestant organizations, formed by church people and churches but standing outside the formal church structures, for purposes of advocacy for Christian causes and delivery of Christian service. Indeed, for much of the first century-and-a-half of this nation's existence, churches and other religious groups provided and delivered most of the social services as an expression of commitment to the biblical admonition to "love thy neighbor" (Lev. 19:18; Luke 10:27).

This view accords perfectly with the distinctive character of churches in American culture. In this society, they have been and remain, for the most part, fairly prominent voluntary associations in local communities—perhaps with ties to national private organizations (denominations)—whereas, in other Western societies, they are far more likely to be local branches of a national, official, government-approved, if not government-controlled, organization—that is a "state-church."

The prominent theologian and ethicist James Luther Adams, in his essay on "The Voluntary Principle in the Forming of American Religion" (1986), makes a convincing case that churches are the quintessential voluntary associations in American society. Going back to the beginning of Christianity, he points out, "The Christian viewed the church in its origin and development as the work of Divine grace. . . . Yet the church [has always] appealed to the individual for a voluntary decision to join" (p. 175). Confirming Stackhouse's point about churches setting precedents for other forms of independent private organizations working in the public realm, Adams reminds us that Thomas Hobbes, the conservative British social philosopher, was worried (in 1650) about the dangers to government of allowing freedom of religious association—in other words, the development of "free churches"—contending that this would lead to demands for other "freedoms of association," challenging the state's authority in the public realm. As it turned out, Hobbes was right. Finally, Adams contends, the American experience of voluntary association exemplified in the Protestant free-church tradition was extended into society at large as it began to be seen as a model that could serve purposes other than just those of the church as a worshiping body—in other words, purposes of specialized outreach and service. That model began to be applied in the formation of missionary societies, charitable societies, temperance unions and the like. The Benevolent Empire was the first flowering of those possibilities.

Thus we can see that religious organizations—especially religious service organizations, but in many cases even congregations—can and should be viewed as integral parts of the American tradition of philanthropy and voluntary association. Religious faith and the primacy of religious claims to freedom of expression in proclaiming and enacting ultimate moral values played a key role in creating the possibility for organized philanthropy and nonprofit enterprise to develop and flourish. And insofar as religious congregations in the United States represent a kind of archetype for other types of voluntary associations and philanthropic organizations, they should surely be seen as part of that realm. It seems appropriate to inquire then about what expectations society holds for religion and religious organizations if they are viewed as part of the philanthropic world.

## Religion and Philanthropy in the Public View

Given the degree to which philanthropic values and religious values are interwoven—indeed, in some instances, they are identical—and given the degree to which religious organizations are involved in philanthropic activities, and secular philanthropic organizations appeal to religious values and motives, it seems perfectly reasonable to assume that the public will view religious and other philanthropic organizations in much the same light. That being so, we could also assume that religious organizations will be subject to very similar societal expectations regarding their behavior, governance, and management. The evidence for the premises of this argument is compelling in the historical as well as the sociological and economic data we have just reviewed. What is more, this conclusion is confirmed by consideration of some contemporaneous cases of religious organizational behavior—or misbehavior—and the public's responses.

To look at just one prominent example, consider the case of the "Televangelist Scandals." Recall the furor over the transgressions of Jim and Tammy Faye Bakker. While much of the press coverage focused initially on the sexual transgressions of various parties—the "juicy gossip" angle of this sordid tale—

finally the most scandalous elements of the story centered around the Bakkers' misuse of funds. Indeed, in interviews with the public and remarks of media commentators, the harshest judgments were usually reserved for the way the Bakkers betrayed the PTL Club's contributors with their extraordinary diversions of the organization's funds to personal ends.

I would argue that in this reaction we can see how similar, at least in some ways, are the public's expectations of religious and secular philanthropic organizations. Jim Bakker's sexual morality may have been an overriding concern for some Christians, and something that those who wished to mock Christianity reveled in ridiculing, but for the larger society the bigger issue seemed to be the way in which the Bakkers took advantage of the nonprofit tax-exempt status and the self-proclaimed philanthropic purposes of the PTL Club to defraud contributors to their organization. In this respect, the public's reaction was most similar to the responses we see to stories of abuses in fund-raising in cancer research or education or other areas of secular philanthropic activity.

By way of contrast, we should note that it is rarely "big news" when some business cheats its customers in the regular course of commerce. Moreover, contemporaneous with the Televangelist Scandals were a number of cases of defense contractors defrauding the government (and the taxpayers) out of billions of dollars, amounts exceeding the Bakkers' wildest dreams. Yet, at that time, the press and general public's indignation over these corporate crimes seemed nowhere near as intense as that generated by the Bakkers' transgressions. Why?

Because the American public has higher expectations of religious (and secular) nonprofit organizations, especially when they claim to be engaged in philanthropic endeavors. The fact is that as consumers we almost expect to be disillusioned at the behavior of for-profit firms trying to increase their profit margins at our expense. As taxpayers, many of us assume that large corporations will cheat the government when they think they can get away with it. But we fully expect—indeed demand—greater integrity of religious or philanthropic organizations. We tend to believe they will and should operate out of a different "values base"—of course, most religious organizations *explicitly claim* to be operating out of a different values base—and so the public expects greater integrity in their operation. The Bakker case makes clear how similar societal expectations of religious and nonreligious philanthropic organizations are, at least in matters of fiduciary responsibility and operational integrity.

## The Changing View of the Church

Finally, though, if we are trying to ascertain whether society at large looks at religion and religious organizations and philanthropy and philanthropic organizations in similar ways, we should consider another body of data, one that centers more specifically on Americans' views of "the church." One of the questions that is provoked by examining literature about the nonprofit sector is whether religious congregations (and denominations) should be categorized—in the language of the tax code—as "mutual benefit organizations" or "public benefit organizations." This is to ask, "Do these organizations and the activities they undertake primarily serve their own members or a larger public?" The question is important because—among other things—one traditional, historically justified reason for the tax-exempt status of religious organizations (including congregations) was the assumption they provided public welfare services that government would have to provide in their absence (Karl, 1989).

The data from the studies of Independent Sector and others (cited above) demonstrate clearly that churches, synagogues, and other religious bodies continue to contribute to the public good in significant, tangible ways. Moreover, the history we have reviewed supports the view that religious organizations have been central to philanthropic practice, and have often been seen as such. It is undoubtedly true, however, that the role of religion and religious organizations in American society has changed significantly over the last fifty years (especially), as have the public's assumptions about the role of religion and "the church." That should lead us to ask if those changes have altered the public's expectations of religion and religious institutions.

In a careful and comprehensive study, Robert Wuthnow (1988), a sociologist from Princeton University, documents the changes in the role of religion, and Americans' perspectives on religion and religious institutions, in the last forty-five years. His analysis confirms the argument that religious organizations are likely to be subject to the same kinds of societal expectations as secular philanthropic groups.

Wuthnow's work shows that a major cause of the changes in American religion between 1945 and 1985 was the entrance of government into many areas of activity—especially social services—that had been primarily in the domain of religious institutions. In other words, just as the relationship of government to private philanthropy more generally had changed in this realm, so too did the relationship of government to religion, because so much religious activity was philanthropic activity. This change, Wuthnow claims, altered the way people saw religion's role in society and, so, the reasons for and manner of individuals' identification with specific religious groups.

It is important to recognize that while it is true that congregations have always been, in essence, voluntary associations in the United States, it is also true that the reasons many persons make commitments to particular congregations have often been historical and familial. The most frequent reasons for people affiliating with specific traditions and congregations have centered on how these groups embodied the theological perspectives those people have been taught are true, or the fact that these were the groups to which their family had always belonged, or some combination of these circumstances.

Until fairly recently, adults were very likely to join the congregation—or at least the denomination—in which they were raised as children. So, as Wuthnow points out, a 1955 survey "showed that only four percent of the adult population—one person in twenty-five—no longer adhered to the faith of their childhood" (1988, p. 88). Though it is hard to get comparative data for earlier eras, it is safe to assume switching denominations (or even congregations) was, if anything, even less likely in previous decades when it was even more common for people to live all their lives in one community.

This contrasts sharply with the findings of a 1988 survey, which showed that now one out of three Americans (33 percent) have switched their religious affiliation from the one in which they were raised (Gallup and Castelli, 1990, p. 28). In this kind of environment, where denominational loyalty is less and less significant, congregations obviously become even more essentially voluntary associations. The question which then presents itself is, Why do people choose to belong to one particular congregation (or denomination) and not another?

The answers to this query, at least as far as denominational affiliation is concerned, cannot have much to do with doctrine. One of the more pronounced trends in American religion in the last half-century has been the movement toward ecumenism and the decreasing significance of doctrinal differences, at least between denominations. Ironically, this has been accompanied by the increasing significance of what might be called 'quasi-doctrinal' differences—cast in terms of liberal versus conservative views of theological and social issues; but the various parties representing these views are as often encompassed by denominational labels as they are divided by them.

Wuthnow (1988) argues that this situation began to develop in the aftermath of World War II. Then, he shows, religious institutions, and especially congregations and denominations, began to take on a different role and became less important as structures for influencing public life and public policy. In that time, Wuthnow notes, "Religious individuals and organizations would be enjoined to work actively in the world for goodness and righteousness" (p. 49). However, the focus of that activity shifted from affecting institutions and entire communities of individuals to addressing more specifically individuals as individuals. This transition may mirror the beginnings of the decline of assumptions about the viability of many communal structures in America as people became more mobile, both geographically and economically. In any case, despite the long-standing historical ideal of religion and religious life being a largely communal phenomenon, an ideal supported by millennia of theological reflection and centuries of American cultural practice, at that point the individualistic streak in American culture (always present) came strongly to the fore in religious life.

At that juncture in our national history, as Wuthnow describes it, "Descriptions of the religious body often paid little or no attention to such vital aspects of its functioning as fellowship, mutual caring and sharing, the collective enactment of religious rituals, or the cultivation of moral obligations through actual experiences of bonding and reconciliation. In place of these, emphasis was placed primarily on the spiritual growth of individuals. *The corporate body became subtly transposed into a service agency for the fulfillment of its individual members*" (1988, p. 55).

If this accurately describes the way many Americans now view their congregations—and my own experience as a denominational executive working with many congregations suggests it is—then these organizations are being viewed as being as much "mutual benefit organizations" as "public benefit organizations." This suggests one of the primary reasons individuals commit to membership in particular congregations centers on their sense that these groups can fulfill particular personal, practical, spiritual, and associational needs. Again, my own experiences and those of others I have talked to largely confirm this conclusion. However, that is not the whole story. While the above description is accurate, it is not complete.

It may be true that individual Americans now tend, more and more, to shop around for a congregation with the key question being, How does this group meet my needs? rather than, How am I called to be part of, or even render service to and through, this body? Yet, it is also the case that the needs many individuals feel they must have met are needs to be part of a religious body that will transmit what they see as essential moral values from one generation to the next. They seek religious bodies that will give expression to those values in service and witness to the community.

If this is true, and there is good data to confirm that it is (see Gallup and Castelli, 1990, especially pp. 253–56), then we have another reason to believe that churches will be expected to function in many ways like voluntary associations, especially philanthropic ones. The experience of many clergy, and other persons deeply involved in the activities of religious congregations, confirms this. Many I have talked with say that two of the most important factors in individuals' choices about religious affiliation these days are the character of a congregation's religious education (and child-care) program and the character of its outreach into the surrounding community.

This correlates with Wuthnow's observation that coincidental with the changes in the role of religion and the focus of religious congregations in the 1950s came a strong renewal of emphasis on religious education. In that context, he notes, "religious education was motivated by the desire to inculcate moral values" as much as a desire to deepen doctrinal understanding or loyalty (1988, p. 69). This description of the purposes of religious education still fairly characterizes many religious education programs, particularly in "mainline" Protestant churches.

This once more highlights the curious way in which the efforts of churches to meet the personal needs of members and potential members may mesh with society's needs and expectations for them to contribute to the public good. This kind of religious education now not only attracts young parents who may have abandoned organized religion after their own adolescence, it may also undergird the development of a new generation of citizens who will assimilate values traditionally seen as necessary to sustaining the kind of compassionate society Americans have always wanted to believe they have. That churches have been choosing this role strengthens the claims of observers of religion in American life, like James Reichley, who says that, "From the standpoint of the public good, the most important service churches offer to secular life in a free society is to nurture moral values that help humanize capitalism and give moral direction to democracy" (1983, p. 359). Reichley's view on this matter is virtually identical to Benjamin Franklin's position on the value of religion (see Franklin's *Autobiography*, 1964 [1791]).

So, to this point, the evidence suggests that Americans now expect—and may always have expected—religious congregations to fulfill two roles and behave like *both* mutual benefit *and* public benefit organizations. Yet, there is one more piece of Wuthnow's analysis that is particularly pertinent to our interests. This has to do with the increased prominence and importance of what he calls religious "special purpose groups." This is even more significant for our considerations, because most religious service organizations would fit into this category.

Wuthnow reminds us that "American religion has been characterized by a long history of special purpose groups. Alongside its numerous sects, churches and denominations has functioned an impressive array of organizations devoted to the attainment of more focused purposes" (1988, p. 106). This "array" would obviously include many of the groups we cited in the last chapter. In his review of changes in American religion, however, Wuthnow goes on to say, "The most striking feature of these special purpose groups is the tremendous number that have been founded in the last two decades" (p. 112). Interestingly, affiliations with such special-purpose groups (rather than denominational ties) are now often one of the better indicators of individuals' theological commitments. Finally, what may be most significant for the argument being presented here, "As far as the society as a whole is concerned, these organizations may be the ones that increasingly define the public role of American religion" (p. 121).

Note these organizations include many "Christian professional associations" and "support groups" as well as agencies devoted to particular kinds of advocacy, ministry, and service. Nevertheless, if Wuthnow's analysis is sound, it strengthens the claim that religion and religious groups are now increasingly likely to be seen as being much like other organizations in the nonprofit sector that are committed to public service or the promotion of particular moral and social values. As that is true, they will also be subject to the same kinds of societal expectations and constraints as those other organizations.

Thus, the picture Wuthnow paints is one of a society in which people are drawn to religious organizations primarily because of the ways those organizations can meet their personal needs; but many of those needs center on the desire to strengthen and transmit—to family and others—moral values, both in word and deed. So, it also makes clear that the majority of people continue to expect religion, and especially religious organizations, to contribute to the public good: first, by providing a moral underpinning for individuals in both public and private life, by upholding moral ideals in the public realm; and second, by providing specific practical, charitable, and philanthropic service.

## Summary and Conclusions

In summary, there is a large body of evidence to indicate that religion and religious organizations have served, and still serve, as primary inspirations for, formative influences in, and important expressions of philanthropic ideals and practices in our society. Looking at how they do this, we can see that religious organizations have often functioned and are often viewed as philanthropic organizations. This is true for congregations and especially true for "para-church" and service organizations. So these groups also must reflect and accommodate some key attributes of the American national character in ways that conform (as we saw in the last chapter) to our society's expectations of philanthropic organizations—especially competing values of individualism and community, and idealism and pragmatism. That is, these groups are subject to many of the same societal expectations regarding their (organizational) behavior as secular philanthropic organizations.

Altogether then, the evidence from the preceding historical, sociological and economic analyses suggests what is most distinctive about philanthropic organizations generally, and religious service organizations particularly, is their values-expressive character. Reflecting especially the desires and expectations that they should be both idealistic and pragmatic, Christian service organizations especially tend to have a sense of mission that has two distinct but inseparable aspects—both to provide a service and to give witness to and try to promote the religious beliefs that inspire that service. Other philanthropic organizations may be like this, but—as a rule—not so explicitly or to the same degree. This a critical factor that sets many Christian service organizations apart from other task-oriented organizations in our political economy.

In addition, however, to the *external* factors we have examined that lead to and support the twofold missions of these organizations, there are *internal* reasons they are likely to have such missions. We cannot understand these organizations well, we cannot fully comprehend either what they are or what they should be—at least from the point of view of the traditions that gave them birth, and that they claim to represent—if we do not see how the religious belief system that undergirds them also encourages the integration of service and witness, faith and works, preaching and practicing.

In short, in order to have a complete and useful picture of the context for management of Christian service organizations, we must examine what God (and the church, in an ideal sense) expects of them—at least as far as we can see indications of this in the Scriptures and the history of the church—as well as what society expects of them. The next chapter is devoted to exploring (from a Christian perspective) the theological mandates for combining witness and service that help shape and reinforce this distinctive characteristic of these organizations.

# 3

## "I Will Show You My Faith by What I Do"

### *The Mandate for Combining Witness and Service*

W E HAVE SEEN how there are external societal forces that serve to increase the likelihood that Christian service organizations will have a distinctive twofold mission—to embody moral and spiritual values as well as to provide practical services. Equally important forces that push in this direction, however, are the internal mandates and dynamics of Christian beliefs and practices, which command an integration of faith and works. All through the record of the teachings of Jesus in the New Testament, we hear him telling his disciples that they must *both preach and practice* their faith.

Jesus' disciples are told (in Matt. 25:31–46) that the most important evidence of their faith, that which will be viewed as incontrovertible, will be the record of their care for and service to those most vulnerable or most in need. Nor are they encouraged to serve silently. Quite the contrary, Jesus instructs them to "let your light shine before men and women, that these men and women may see your good deeds and praise your Father in heaven" (Matt. 5:16). In many places in the Scriptures, Christians are exhorted to serve their neighbors and one another; to care for the poor, the widows, and the orphans; and to be helpful to and treat with dignity "the least of their brethren." They are encouraged to see this as another way of making God's love visible to those who have not experienced it (see Matt. 20:26–27, Luke 10:25–37, Gal. 5:13 and Phil. 2:5–18).

It is with this understanding in mind, with the expectation that one's faith should become visible and meaningful to others in actions of caring for and service to them, that the writer of the Epistle of James challenges his brothers and sisters in faith by asking:

> What good is it my brethren if a man or woman claims to have faith but has no deeds? Can such a faith save him or her? Suppose a brother or sister is without clothes and daily food. If one of you says to him or

her, "Go, I wish you well; keep warm and well fed," but does nothing about his or her physical needs, what good is it? In the same way, faith by itself, if it is not accompanied by action, is dead.

But someone will say, "You have faith; I have deeds." Show me your faith without deeds, and I will show you my faith by what I do. (James 2:14–18)

This passage has been used to make many points in a long history of scriptural interpretation, but whatever else it does it urges the reader to view belief and behavior as inseparable. It says that the best way of proving one's beliefs is by demonstration in action and suggests that proclamations of belief not accompanied by matching behavior are of marginal credibility.

The writer of the Epistle of James certainly is echoing a central theme in Jesus' teaching in arguing that faith and works are inseparable. Furthermore, this passage lifts up the possibility that doing good works creates powerful opportunities for witnessing to others about one's own faith. In this light, we can fairly assert that those engaged in Christian service should, at the least, be mindful of those opportunities that providing service might create for them to share the faith that inspires that service. They need to think about the possibilities for integrating service and witness.

Of course, establishing that Christians should be mindful of these opportunities is not the same as establishing that they are obligated to take advantage of them; but in fact the passages we examined in Scripture suggest that we can take this argument that extra step. The disciples are not merely encouraged, they are commanded to let their light shine (the Greek verb is in the imperative), so that their good deeds will become a testimony to God's love (Matt. 5:16). Passages like this that encourage service should be seen as part of a unified voice in the New Testament, the same voice that commands evangelization when the disciples are sent forth to "preach the good news to all the creation" (see Luke 9:2, 10:1–12; Mark 6:7–13, 16:15). So, what I am arguing here is that when people create agencies or organizations for doing "good deeds" using the term "Christian" in their name or the explanation for what they do, they have a special obligation to make sure the way they perform that service (and operate more generally) reflects Christian ideals and beliefs, because it will be seen as—and ought to make—a statement about their faith.

Some might contend that we cannot or should not put the same kinds of expectations on organizations that we put on individuals. It is true that, in the Gospels, Jesus' teachings are largely addressed to individuals, offering testimony about God's love for them, and instructions and guidance to them about how to live a life of faith in response to their realization and acceptance of that love. Some theologians urge us to be wary about applying Christ's teachings in organizational contexts, in the church, or in larger society (see, for example, Niebuhr, 1932, and 1943), and that is a caution well considered. But we also need to recall that, from the earliest days of the church, its members and leaders have often seen it as a single corporate entity (see Rom. 12, 1 Cor. 10:17, Acts 4:32), as an organic whole, with the implicit understanding that the teachings of Christ and tenets of faith do apply to the whole—and certainly to various bodies, congregations, and such within the whole—in much the same way as they do to its individuals members.

This being the case, it is reasonable to ask that any organization that calls itself Christian, or identifies itself with some branch or part of the Christian tradition, consider how it represents that tradition to the larger world and honors Christian tenets in its corporate life—in its organizational behavior, if you will. In the context of an inquiry about the character and management of Christian service organizations, it is not only reasonable but important to ask about the ways in which these organizations uphold the ideal of wholeness and integration in the life of faith highlighted in the New Testament and other sources of the Christian tradition. It is important to ask if (or how) they try to make the most of the opportunities for witness that service creates.

Now, in addition to the fact that the New Testament plainly articulates an imperative for such integration, there are three other issues that relate to and reinforce the need to combine faith and works, to unite witness and service. These can be seen in terms of the benefits that accrue when this is done, or the problems that arise when it is not done.

The first of these themes centers on the incompleteness or inadequacy of good works performed without faith. In this perspective, it can be said that a Christian service organization that does not operate daily with a vital understanding of the inspiration (in the literal sense) for the service it offers, is likely to find that service is not all that it can and should be. The second of these themes highlights the need for an integration of faith and works, and of witness and service, to facilitate spiritual growth in those serving as well as those served. The third point is raised by a reading of Christian literature combined with a consideration of the state of contemporary society, which together suggest that today in many instances service will often be the most, sometimes the only, effective way to make a witness about God's love to nonbelievers in an increasingly secular society.

## The Faith at the Heart of Good Works

Clearly, the performance of good works does not necessarily derive from, nor have to demonstrate, Christian faith. Many people who are not Christians are involved in works of charity, compassion, and altruistic service. Indeed, history provides for us no shortage of cases in which the non-Christian neighbors of Christians have shamed them by displaying considerably more compassion for those in need than did those who claimed to be followers of Jesus. Nevertheless, over the centuries, many Christians have been involved in, and some have dedicated their lives to, the performance of goods works, and the New Testament makes some claims about the special character of those good works.

In his letter to the Romans, Paul writes, "All things work together for good for those who love God and are called according to God's purposes" (Rom. 8:28). This claim is made in that context as a word of encouragement to Christians for times when they experience hardship or trouble. It is intended to give them a foundation for hope in times of distress, but it has broader implications. If it is a true claim, it also tells us something about what one can expect if one is engaged in doing good deeds inspired by one's faith—that is, because one "loves God" and is acting on the basis of a "calling according to God's purposes."

We all know, as the old poem says, that the best-laid plans often go awry. Most people who attempt to do good works experience at some point the fact that their efforts may have unintended consequences—some good, but some bad. And certainly we all know that the best-conceived and best-executed endeavors to help those in need or solve some human problems are often inadequate. Are they then wasted?

The answer that Christians may offer to that question, if their efforts have been made in the most sincere and well-conceived way they can manage as an expression of their faith, is certainly not. One of the promises we find in the New Testament is that, even though such efforts to do good may frequently have unintended consequences—sometimes not helpful—and not achieve all that had been hoped, they will "work for good." In fact, a theme that we find woven through the whole of the Scriptures is that God will take whatever efforts people make in a sincere effort to do good, and find some way to allow them to bear "good fruit." One of the messages that permeates the stories and history found in the Bible is that no loving act is lost ever from the sight of God; and even if it does not evoke the responses or changes that one hopes for, this does not mean that it has no value or cannot be the ground in which God plants some new possibility for the fulfillment of noble aspirations.

So we find another reason for Christians to try to root their efforts to do good works in a vital and thoughtful faith, and be mindful of the connection between service and witness. When these efforts are a part of their intention to demonstrate their love of God, and to act "according to God's purposes," then they may trust in the promise that these things will "work together [with other circumstances] for good."

In addition, when the good works Christians undertake are not fully informed and shaped by the tenets and experiences of their faith, they will often be lacking some special qualities and characteristics that would—perhaps should—distinguish their service as Christian. This becomes particularly significant when one considers some of the nonmaterial aspects of caring for others which are generally ignored—for better or for worse, because they are generally considered unimportant—in secular approaches to charity and social service. Thomas Aquinas provides a useful schema for considering these matters.

Thomas makes a useful distinction in his *Summa Theologica* (1964 [1273]) between "corporal" and "spiritual works of mercy." In fact, the attention paid by different types of organizations to these different types of work may offer an interesting measure for determining whether the organizations are *functionally* religious or secular. (For a more extensive inquiry into the characteristics that define an organization as religious see PONPO Working Paper #197 [Jeavons, 1993].) On the list of "corporal works," Aquinas places visiting, giving drink, feeding, rescuing, clothing, bringing people together, and burying people; on the list of "spiritual works," he puts giving advice, instructing, consoling, reproving, forgiving, bearing with, and praying for people. The obvious distinction here, simply framed, is that the first list is a list of practical services that can be provided without having any particular religious beliefs and without (with the possible exception of visiting) the establishment of any meaningful relationships between the service providers and those served, whereas the second list is a list of personal and spiritual services that require religious convictions and the creation of a genuine relationship between the parties involved.

Genuinely Christian service agencies whose work is truly an expression of faith will, I believe, attend to the spiritual as well as the corporal works of mercy in what they do—at least in some, if not every, aspect. That means they will undertake the work they do because of their religious convictions and in a way that creates real relationships among the "servers and the served." It also means opportunities for witnessing about their faith will arise out of the works of service performed, and be welcomed. So, as efforts to integrate faith and works are realized in the way these agencies go about providing service, in order to provide these essential distinctive qualities to service often lacking in work of secular agencies, the possibilities for integrating service and witness will emerge naturally and be realized, and will reinforce the distinctive characteristics of these organizations.

## In the Service of Spiritual Growth

One of the goals for a Christian life, or more specifically for spiritual growth in that life, is "perfection," defined in theological terms as becoming like Christ, who is seen in the Christian faith as the perfect embodiment of humanity as well as divinity. While some Christian theological systems appear to put more emphasis on the initial experience of "being saved" than on continuing growth in faith, as a whole the Christian tradition has stressed that after one has been become a member of the church it is expected one should continue to grow to become more like Christ.

We see the origins of this expectation in Jesus' own teachings, when he tells his disciples that the goal for their lives is that they should "be perfect . . . as [their] heavenly Father is perfect" (Matt. 5:48), and in the Epistle to the Ephesians where Paul writes that the purpose of God's gifts of grace is to bring individuals into unity and knowledge of Christ so that they might become "perfect, attaining to the whole measure of the fullness of Christ" (Eph. 4:13).

More simply put, one of the ideals for the life of faith in the origins of the Christian tradition was that Christians would grow toward "perfection," and "perfection" was understood to mean becoming Christ-like. Moreover, this ideal for and expectation of spiritual growth was evident not only in New Testament times, but throughout the long history of the church. This aim for spiritual formation was discussed at length in the works of early theologians. Its continued significance is manifest by the fact that one of the most important pieces of devotional literature of the late Middle Ages—a guide for living a spiritual life—was entitled *The Imitation of Christ* (Thomas à Kempis, 1989 [1441]), and that book continues to be read by devout Christians even today.

To acknowledge this as the goal of spiritual growth raises another question, however, of what it means to be Christ-like. While different Christians have answered that in different ways, and being Christ-like may in fact involve the development of different qualities for different people, the tradition suggests there are some common denominators. The most important of these may be the qualities of servanthood. Paul tells the Philippians that to imitate Christ is to be like one who "did not consider equality with God something to be grasped, but made himself nothing, taking the very nature of a servant, being made in human likeness" (Phil. 2:6–7).

The individuals who picked up on the quest for spiritual growth and perfection most obviously and dramatically in the early centuries of the church were the first monks. Indeed, the earliest monks took this quest so seriously they felt they had to escape from any contact with the distracting and corrupting influences of the world by withdrawing into solitude. But this form of Christian contemplative life as a pursuit of perfection was soon challenged by people like Basil of Caesarea (A.D. 330–379) and Benedict of Nursia (A.D. 480–547), who pointed out that it would never be possible to attain perfection in solitude because it denied the individual the opportunity to serve others, and the practice of such service was essential for spiritual growth.

Thus, in his *Longer Rules* (1952 [370]), Basil reminded monks that if they sought perfection they must remember that "the Lord by reason of his excessive love was not content with merely teaching the word, but so as to transmit to us clearly and exactly the example of humility in the perfection of charity, [He] girded himself and washed the feet of his disciples." Basil then asked those who would live in solitude, "Whom, therefore will you wash? To whom will you minister? In comparison with whom will you be the lowest, if you live alone?" (1952, p. 252)

Basil's point is that the fullness of a Christian life of faith and real spiritual growth cannot be attained apart from the experience of community and the practice of service. Certainly many congregations (as we discussed earlier) have programs to serve their communities, and provide numerous opportunities for members to serve one another; but Christian service organizations also provide an important venue for individual Christians to engage in service and experience the kind of spiritual growth that Basil and others describe as essential to a life in faith.

Thus, we encounter another reason to be concerned about the integration of faith and works, one relating more to the way these organizations serve the church. Christian service organizations that operate out of a strong and active faith commitment provide avenues through which Christians who desire to serve others because of their own faith commitments may experience profound spiritual growth, reinforcing the integration of service and witness. In this, these organizations may serve the church as a community in important ways as well as the individuals to whom they direct their services, because the continuing spiritual growth of its members should always be a central concern of the church.

Furthermore, when the integration of faith and works, of service and witness, does not occur, those who are drawn to work in these organizations because the organizations have espoused Christian values grow frustrated and cynical. (We will discuss some examples of this in later chapters.) But when this integration does occur, individuals who are growing in this way are more likely to be able to offer service to others in ways that testify to their Christian values and beliefs, facilitating that integration of service and witness we have suggested is ideal. In this too the church is served, for if Robert Wuthnow's observations are correct, these organizations have become the most prominent elements of the church for the public—those the church would like its witness to reach.

## Service as the Most Powerful Witness

The third very important reason that Christian service organizations should be intent upon making a witness as well as providing a service also relates to how they can—perhaps should—serve the church. We just observed that, by providing avenues for the kind of service experiences that facilitate the spiritual growth of Christians, these organizations serve the needs of members of the church as well as others. And we noted that when they function in this way, and spiritually committed and vital Christians are working in them, the depth and clarity of the witness these organizations can make in their work grows—both to their benefit and that of the church.

Finally, a key consideration is that the depth and clarity of the Christian witness these organizations can offer to an increasingly skeptical and increasingly secular public may, in fact, never have been so important to the future of the church as it is now. While it is true, as we pointed out before, that the United States is the "most religious" of any of the industrialized nations, by almost any measure; it is also true that the United States is becoming an increasingly secular society. The fact is that, over the past several decades, church attendance has been dropping (with the possible exception of the last few years), and certainly many other indicators suggest the influence of religious values on life in our society is weakening. All of this says that the church's (and churches') endeavors to spread the faith—to convince people that the Gospel message is true, and that the ideals and values Christianity promises can bring wholeness and meaning to their lives and society—are meeting an increasingly indifferent, if not hostile, reception.

The question of whether it is the message or the ways in which it is delivered looms large in this regard. Our society is one in which talk is cheap, institutions and their leaders in the public realm make and break promises all the time, and solutions proposed for human problems that are not framed in the common currency of our public discourse—which is to say in technological, political, or economic terms—are generally dismissed as unrealistic if not simply irrelevant. In such an environment, how can the church offer a message of hope and have it heard? How can the church make the claims that God's love is real and changes lives, that Jesus' teachings offer helpful guidance in building more fulfilling and useful lives for individuals and communities, that spiritual elements of life, which can neither be seen nor measured, can have a significant effect, perhaps be the key, in giving our lives the quality and stability that most of us long for? More precisely, how can the church make these claims and have them taken seriously in larger society?

Preaching on the street corners will not do it. For the most part, people will see that as either corny or crazy. Preaching in the churches mostly reaches those who already at least espouse religious commitments, though good preaching, among other things, is crucial to helping them grow in those commitments. Even preaching on the airwaves, it is now recognized, reaches a relatively small, mostly already convinced segment of the general populace. So, how?

In a culture that is still as pragmatic as—if not more pragmatic than—idealistic, the best and perhaps only way to get these ideas taken seriously is to *demonstrate* their validity. For those who believe the Christian faith has answers to our society's problems, that means proving it. This is the last reason it is so important that Christian service organizations integrate service and witness in their work. Because of the work they do, Christian service organizations may be able to reach the public with the Christian message in a way many churches cannot.

For churches, the circumstances just cited mean that they have to put time and energy and resources into making the "good news" tangible in their communities—into providing "good news for the poor, freedom for the prisoners, recovery of sight for the blind, release for those who are oppressed" (Luke 4:18)—if they want the Christian faith to be taken seriously. Some churches do a fair job of explaining their convictions, but others need to do more in the way of demonstrating them.

Yet there are many kinds of service, many ways of establishing the solidity and relevance of Christian beliefs and ideals, into which churches cannot enter because they are too small or lack resources. Indeed, these are often the most visible and dramatic realms of service and the kinds of service that many Christian service organizations do undertake, with considerable visibility. Such organizations have the opportunity, on behalf of the church, to make their service a form of witness, and find ways within that framework to point people to the faith that inspires that service, with a potential to reach a skeptical public in ways an average congregation never can. For the sake of the church in this day and age it is crucial to have Christian service organizations achieve this integration of service and witness.

## Summary and Conclusions

In this chapter, I have argued that the most powerful reasons for Christian service organizations to integrate service with witness, to hold to and honor this distinctive twofold mission, come from within the tradition they represent.

Simply stated, one message of the New Testament is that faith and works must be united, and for any Christian service organization that takes its scriptural heritage seriously that means there must be attention to the ways the organization's work conveys the values and ideals of the faith tradition it represents. To honor the teachings of Jesus, the organization must try to operate in such a way that its "light shines" so that others will "see their good deeds and praise God."

In addition, I have showed how three other factors promote the concern for the integration of faith and works in Christian service organizations' operations. First was the admonition in Scripture that the role of faith in actually shaping the work may be a key to ensuring its efficacy in "working for good." Second was the value of this integration in creating the opportunities for spiritual growth for the Christians who work in these organizations, which benefits both the organizations and the church as a whole. Third was the fact that, if these organizations do not achieve this kind of integration, disabling them from making an effective witness for Christian beliefs and ideals through the work they do, one of the most important—and potentially most effective—channels for the church's witness in an increasingly secular society would be sorely diminished.

Combine this internal mandate and theological reasons for Christian service organizations to carry forward a distinctive values-expressive mission with the historical and societal influences that also mold them in this way, and it becomes easy to see how these organizations come to have, and should be expected to maintain, such unusual dual-faceted purposes. This only begins to tell us what we need to know, however, if we are concerned about the management of these organizations.

Even if we have a relatively complete picture of environmental and internal influences that serve to shape Christian service organizations in unique ways, we still need to know more about how they are like or unlike other organizations in structural and functional terms. We turn next to looking at these organizations through the lenses of organizational theory.

# 4

# Religious Organizations as Organizations

## A Theoretical Inquiry

THIS CHAPTER TURNS our attention to what scholars of organizations—organizational theorists—might see if they focused on Christian service organizations. The literature about organizations has given little attention to religious bodies, and what attention it has given them it has directed almost entirely toward congregations and denominations (see O'Dea, 1961; Benson and Dorsett, 1971; Hinings and Foster, 1973; Scherer, 1980, 1988), with a few exceptions (Lofland and Richardson, 1984). Indeed, it is ironic that what is probably the best-known analysis of an organization with religious roots, Patricia Denton and Mayer Zald's study of the YMCA (1963), documents the organization's transformation into a secular service agency.

Some organizational theorists offer typologies for organizations that explicitly provide a place for religious organizations (see Parsons, 1960; Etzioni, 1961). They do this, however, by downplaying the possibilities of religious organizations' being task-oriented, or at least casting doubt upon the potential concreteness or specificity of such organizations' tasks. These theories might lead us to believe that the only functions of religious organizations in our society are to maintain cultural patterns; to nurture or promote cultural, moral or religious values; or to provide structures for association and fellowship among those whose values are similar. Such descriptions and conclusions fit many congregations fairly well, but they are largely incongruous with the missions and self-understandings of most religious service organizations.

My interests here are primarily in these religious *service* organizations—which, as we have seen, often intend to combine a commitment to specific and stable concrete goals in service with harder-to-measure goals in nurturing and sharing faith. These groups have rarely been the subject of organizational studies. So, what follows is in large measure a first effort to consider how the insights of organizational theory apply to such bodies.

## How the Difference Makes a Difference

The most important questions in this inquiry relate to issues of what distinguishes Christian service organizations as organizations, structurally and functionally, from other kinds of organizations. If there is no meaningful difference, this effort is unnecessary—we can assume organizational theories now extant apply to these Christian agencies without concern for how such applications might yield different results, or even challenge the premises of those theories. But I believe we need here, at the least, to see if any implications of consequence do follow from applying specific organizational theories to Christian service organizations. The questions I believe should command our attention have to do with how the essential purposes, dynamics, or functions of such organizations may be altered by the fact the organizations are religious in origin and governance.

The historical, sociopolitical, and economic data and analyses we have already reviewed support an argument that religious service organizations are usually distinguished by their values-expressive character. The theological reflections we have undertaken move beyond description to prescription in this regard, telling us the Christian service organizations ought to be values-expressive, witnessing as well as serving, if they are to be true to their Biblical heritage.

I have argued that Christian service groups thus also need to accommodate and uphold elements of both pragmatism and idealism as organizations that fit within, and are viewed as part of, the tradition and practice of philanthropy in the United States. They are expected to provide a service, but they are also expected to honor, nurture, and promote specific moral and spiritual ideals as those ideals provide the particular inspiration for their service. This we saw to be in keeping with an expectation society places upon philanthropic organizations generally, in some measure, but places on religious service organizations even more clearly, in part because these organizations often claim this expression of values is an essential facet of their mission. We have shown that this should be a more prominent facet of the life of many religious organizations because the values or ideals to be honored and promoted arise from profound spiritual and theological experiences and commitments, giving these values and ideals greater salience and authority for those involved in the work of these organizations.

A review of the history of specific religious service organizations will reveal that the reasons for the founding of most of them—and, as we saw, the reason there is a "social space" (Stackhouse, 1990) in our political economy for them—arise from their commitments to giving expression to values they hold to be of *ultimate* significance in their work. In light of these circumstances, we can say that religious service organizations, especially Christian service organizations, should be (almost by definition) as concerned with the message their work sends as with the immediate practical effects of their service. In practice these two things tend to be intertwined, raising a set of issues for these organizations as organizations which, I believe, are distinctive to them, and which can be illuminated by examining them in the light of some extant organizational theories.

## The Range of Perspectives on Organizations: Similarities and Dissimilarities

The first thing students of organizational theory discover is that there are an extraordinary number of perspectives on, ideas about, and theories of organizations; and while there are radically different views represented in the field as a whole, the distinctions between particular theories are sometimes relatively minor or subtle. As one scholar comments, "Conceptually, there are only slight differences in the way in which various theorists define organizations. . . . Yet, while the various definitions do not seem radically different from each other, the directions taken, the concepts used, and the relationships between them are varied" (Tosi, 1975, p. 2).

If this is so, then as we begin to think about Christian service organizations, and about the ways in which they are similar to or different from other organizations, it is helpful first to look at the similarities and dissimilarities various organizational theories suggest we can expect among all types of organizations. For the purposes of a brief analysis, it is helpful to look at these similarities and dissimilarities as they relate to three critical questions about organizations:

1. What are their goals, and how are they chosen?
2. How are organizations structured?
3. Will they, like natural creatures, always seek "self-perpetuation," even if their stated goals have been accomplished?

### Goals

Virtually all organizational theorists will allow that organizations have goals. Even the most unconventional "natural open systems" perspectives (Scott, 1987), which propose that organizational behavior is an almost random result of the interactions of individuals within a system (Cohen, March, and Olsen, 1972; Weick, 1979), will acknowledge that organizations formulate and articulate goals as a way of justifying actions and decisions taken previously and supporting a "myth of rationality" (Meyer and Rowan, 1977) about organizational operations. Indeed, the far more common view of organizations is that they are collectives specifically created to pursue goals or purposes the individual participants share. So, Chester Barnard says, "formal organization is that kind of cooperation among men that is conscious, deliberate, [and] purposeful" (1938, p. 4); and Amitai Etzioni speaks of organizations as "social units (or human groupings) deliberately constructed and reconstructed to seek specific goals" (1964, p. 3).

Yet, if there is some degree of consensus among organizational theories (and theorists) that organizations have goals, there is considerable divergence on several important points about those goals. First, there is a notable difference in the assumptions about the functions and importance of goals. Are those goals—an organization's espoused collective goals—in fact the focus of individual participants' commitment and energy, as, for instance, Barnard (1938) assumes they should be? Or, rather, do those goals merely state the purposes managers of an organization will pursue by coordinating participants' efforts while the managers struggle to accommodate the individuals' various personal goals to ensure those participants will continue to contribute to the organizations' work? Or, as some theorists contend, are "organizational goals" often ex post facto rationalizations devised to explain what has already transpired in an organization (again, see Cohen, March, and Olsen, 1972; Weick, 1979)?

Second, there is considerable disagreement about how organizational goals are established. Who defines these goals, and how do they do so? Can these goals always be satisfactorily defined in economic terms, as some would have us believe (Taylor, 1911; Williamson, 1981)? If that is the case, then individuals' goals—for personal economic gain—can be seen as subgoals fully encompassed by definitions of organizational goals—for example, the maximization of the value of the firm, or increased profits. Furthermore, whether organizational goals are purely economic or not, a question arises as to whether it is solely the prerogative of the owners or managers of an organization to define them; or should all participants have a voice? From a different perspective, we might ask if it is the case, as for example Barnard (1938) would have us believe, that executive leadership is responsible for articulating organizational goals in some way that is sufficiently morally compelling that all participants adopt these goals as their own.

Here some of the perspectives we cited before (Parsons, 1960; Etzioni, 1961, 1964) offer alternative ways of thinking about organizational goals, and about the ramifications of those goals for organizational dynamics. Etzioni's schema, for instance, provides for three types of organizations distinguished by the types of power they employ—coercive, remunerative, or normative—to pursue different kinds of purposes—social/political, economic, or cultural, respectively. This typology suggests how the variant character of organizational goals may allow, or require, variations in the kinds of incentives organizations offer people to participate in and contribute to them. Parsons's typology moves in similar directions. These approaches may be of some utility in thinking about religious organizations, but have real limitations, as we have already seen, when applied to Christian service organizations.

Then again, even if one believes that organizational goals are larger than economics, questions remain as to who has the right to participate in defining them, how people should be induced to pursue them, and how different points of view are to be accommodated. Indeed, the answers to those questions may lead to more-complicated organizational goals. We cannot simply assume that individuals' goals and organizational goals are identical, whatever the type or nature of the organization under examination.

Given that we can expect various individuals within an organization to have different goals, questions of power become prominent. Whose goals will be most influential in defining an organization's goals? How do some individuals come to have more influence in the process than others? Pfeffer (1982) and Perrow (1986) contend that questions of power—its sources and uses—are among the most crucial in understanding organizations, and claim that too many theorists pay too little attention to these questions. If they are right, and issues—and the exercise—of power are critical in the formulation of organizational goals, then how "rational" can we expect organizational goals to be?

Finally, there is little agreement (across the field) about how mutable organizational goals are, or should be. One group of theorists postulates that while organizations may start out with rationally defined goals, the influence of individuals within them and changes in the environment around them lead to changes in goals, "goal displacement," which have little to do with rational choices for the organization as a whole (see, for example, Michels, 1949 [1915]; Selznick, 1957; Clark, 1965). This group tends to see such changes, implicitly at least, as negative, representing a subversion of the organization's purpose and a deterioration in its character. In contrast, other theorists seem either to ignore the possibility of change in basic goals or assume change will represent a rational, appropriate, and acceptable evolution of the organization (Weber,

1947 [1924]; March and Simon, 1958). Still others, cited before, believing all "organizational goals" to be essentially mythic, do not see changes in espoused goals as highly significant.

## Structure

Theorists agree that, in addition to having goals, all organizations have some formal structure. How much formal structure, and how important the formal structure is relative to the informal structure, are matters of debate; but it is the presence of some formal structure that distinguishes organizations from other types of human collective—for instance, families. W. Richard Scott defines a "formal structure" as "one in which the social positions and the relationships among them have been defined independently of the personal characteristics of the participants occupying these positions" (1987, p. 17). Such a definition, we should note, closely mirrors the key elements of Weber's description of a "bureaucracy"—a term he uses in a technical, nonpejorative sense (1947 [1924]).

Organizational charts, job descriptions, and handbooks for procedures are representative of what we mean when we speak of the formal structure of organizations. Documents such as these specify what the people in particular positions are supposed to do, how they should relate to one another, and what they can be held accountable for in the work of the organization, and by whom, regardless of the personal attributes of the individuals filling those positions. Rare are the organizations that do not have some documents of this type—or, in their absence, a fairly clear and solid understanding of such matters in participants' minds—for these are the elements of organizational life that can ensure some continuity of function over time, and are generally intended to foster effectiveness and efficiency in function in the present. One question that has been central to the debates of organizational theorists, however, is whether one can adequately understand the nature and life of an organization by looking primarily at these elements.

Philip Selznick observes that

> The security of all participants [in an organization], and of the system as a whole, generates a persistent pressure for institutionalization of relationships. . . . Moreover, it is necessary for the relations within the structure to be determined in such a way that individuals will be interchangeable and the organization will thus be free of dependence on personal qualities. . . . But, as we inspect these formal structures we begin to see that they will never succeed in conquering the non-rational dimensions of organizational behavior. (1948, p. 25)

Selznick argues that, while an organization will create formal structures to try to channel individual participants' energy and efforts into the pursuit of the organization's goal, it is inevitable that those individuals will bring their own needs, purposes, and agenda to the organization, and will find ways to satisfy those needs and pursue those purposes outside of the formal structures if they cannot do so within them. Selznick and others (for example, Mayo, 1945; March and Simon, 1958; and Whyte, 1959) argue it is thus as crucial to examine the psychological, emotional, and human factors shaping individuals' participation in an organization and the informal relationships—cliques and the like—within it as it is to look at formal structures.

A different body of literature—that is, stories, both nonfiction and fiction—as well as the personal experiences of most of us who have worked in organizations, confirms the truth in this perspective. We all have heard about, and many of us have experienced, the organization where the president's administrative assistant seems to wield more effective power than the president; or some group of midlevel staff people can, for all practical purposes, control the decision making of senior staff—or board of governors—by controlling the information they receive. Such evidence indicates informal structures and relationships are indeed important. How important they are, over against formal structures and relationships, varies from one organization to the next.

Another question about formal structure is how it comes to be shaped as it is in any particular organization. People like Fredrick Taylor (1911, 1947) contend that formal structure should be logically designed around the demands of the task to be performed, beginning from the smallest unit and working upward. Others, like Weber and Henri Fayol (1949 [1919]) argue it should be rationally ordered around the tasks to be performed, but beginning at the top with a recognition of the administrative requirements dictated by the effective division and coordination of labor.

Clearly, the thinking of Weber and the model of "bureaucracy" (in the technical, nonpejorative sense) have dominated managers' thinking about the development and design of organizations in our culture. Yet there are interesting indications that organizations may derive their structure more from adaptation to specific elements of their environment than from unencumbered, logically conceived design efforts. "Contingency models" offer arguments that organizational structure may be either primarily a function of the technology an organization employs in relation to the external challenges and opportunities it faces (Lawrence and Lorsch, 1967), or a function of its needs for information processing and decision making in that same context (Thompson, 1967; Galbraith, 1977), or a function of its needs for legitimacy in a specific social or institutional context (DiMaggio and Powell, 1983).

Some of these theories have a solid experiential base. The work of Paul Lawrence and Jay Lorsch involved studies of a number of different kinds of organizations and demonstrated that they adopted structural elements appropriate to their "task environment." So, when the technology they employed was subject to rapid change and the external environment was too, they tended to employ less formal structures that allowed them to adapt quickly to threats and opportunities. But when both these factors were more stable, they established more formal structures to ensure greater continuity. Such experiential evidence is also present in DiMaggio and Powell's work, which shows how the adoption of similar forms for governmental structures, school systems, and even cultural organizations in different areas and circumstances is the result of the organizations' desires to mirror whatever is becoming the dominant, and hence "most legitimate" form for such organizations in the eyes of their peers and the public.

The questions of how firm and clear an organization's structure can be, and whether it can (or should) be designed independent of pressures from the external environment, raise another question about organizational structure more generally: how solid or how permeable an organization's boundaries can (or should) be. Even theories that stress the power and currency of interactions between organizations and their environments, and the way in which these relationships shape the organizations—generally referred to as "open-systems" perspectives—recognize that it must be possible to differentiate an organization from its environment to be able to speak of or analyze the organization. So, in his summary of open-systems theories, Scott notes that to emphasize the connections and interactions of organizations (so conceived) with their environment "is not to say that open systems do not have boundaries. They do, of course, and must expend energy on boundary maintenance" (1987, p. 82).

This issue becomes particularly noteworthy when one is questioning how important formal structure is relative to informal structure, and how rationally ordered that formal structure can be. The more broadly one draws the boundaries of an organization, the more important informal structure may be and the more difficult rational design and control are likely to be. This may become an especially serious matter for voluntary organizations. For example, the larger and more varied a philanthropic organization's donor base, and the more that donors are seen as full participants in the organization, the more responsive that organization will need to be to a wide range of different people, and that has powerful implications for organizational structure. For a philanthropic organization that is committed to treating its donors as full members of the organization, then, questions of how it expands its donor base, and whom it reaches out to include—which are questions about its boundaries—have consequences that go well beyond finances. (We will look at some organizations that have experienced or dealt with just these issues in chapters 7 and 8.)

## Self-Perpetuation

One assumption that virtually all organizational theories and theorists seem to share is that every organization will devote itself to its own self-perpetuation. Experience suggests this assumption is generally well founded. The problem is that in much of the literature, especially management literature, the assumption begins to take on a normative tone. That is to say, discussions of how organizations behave seem to accept as a given that it is always appropriate for organizations to seek their own perpetuation, whether or not the purposes for which they were formed have been attained, or are still (if they ever were) socially valuable. Some Marxist critiques appear to be an exception to this rule, but the concerns on which they focus have more to do with who controls—in this case, especially industrial and governmental—organizations than with whether those organizations should be self-perpetuating (Bendix, 1956).

"Rational theorists" (Taylor, Weber, and others) see the rational specification of both goals and means for their attainment, and the formalization of structure, as ways to ensure the efficacy of organizations that should allow them to grow and endure—presumably ad infinitum. "Natural theorists" (Barnard, Mayo, and others) assume that self-preservation is an instinct of organizations like that of humans, and treat it as a morally neutral or positive trait. Only theorists from the "institutionalist school" (Michels, Selznick, and others) look critically at the organizational drive toward self-perpetuation, and it seems then only because they see it as likely to subvert an organization's original goals or purposes.

My purpose in raising questions about self-perpetuation is not to deny that all organizations must, as Scott points out, have "those positions or activities whose function is to maintain the organization itself" (1987, pp. 24–25). To sustain themselves long enough to attain their goals, organizations must, obviously, devote some attention to organizational maintenance and development. We should, however, look at organizations' drive for self-preservation with a critical eye, in part because of the problems institutional theorists identify, which may be especially significant for religious and philanthropic organizations, and in part because for some organizations self-perpetuation beyond attainment of their original goals may be a betrayal of the values they were formed to promote. Christian service organizations, I will argue later, can be an example of this phenomenon.

Given this overview of organizational theory, let us now turn our attention more specifically to Christian service organizations.

## A Framework for Analyzing the Character of Christian Service Organizations

For the purposes of our examination of Christian service organizations I want to borrow a framework for analysis from Scott (1987), who describes three categories of organizational theories as "rational, natural or open systems." A rational-systems perspective, Scott says, views organizations primarily as "collectivities oriented to the pursuit of *relatively specific goals* and exhibiting *highly formalized structures*" (p. 22, emphasis in the original). A natural-systems perspective looks at organizations as "collectivities whose participants share *a common interest in the survival of the system,* and who engage in collective activities, *informally structured,* to secure this end" (p. 23, emphasis in the original). This schema sets up the rational and natural perspectives as being somewhat in opposition. Although in the examination of specific theories, Scott demonstrates there is a continuum between these two, where the relative emphasis given to goal orientation versus organizational maintenance or formal versus informal structure shifts but is rarely completely one-sided. In other words, most theories acknowledge there are both rational and natural elements intermingled in organizations, but differ on the relative significance of these elements.

Scott speaks of an open-systems perspective as viewing organizations as "coalitions of shifting interest groups that *develop goals by negotiation;* [and where] the *structure* of the coalition, its activities, and its outcomes are *strongly influenced by environmental factors*" (p. 23, emphasis in the original). Although he initially contrasts open systems with rational and natural systems, the effective counterpoint to an open system in Scott's schema is, in fact, a "closed system." The most important factor in this facet of the analysis—articulated in the second half of his definition of open systems, albeit ignored in the two earlier perspectives—is whether, or to what degree, an organization is shaped by interactions with its environment.

As one might suppose, then, it is possible to look on these two factors as intersecting dimensions for the analysis of organizations as rational and closed, natural and closed, rational and open, or natural and open. This is how Scott finally treats them (pp. 100–101), and I shall follow his lead in the analysis that follows.

## Rational versus Natural Perspectives

This dimension of the framework for examining organizations highlights the tensions that exist in most organizations between devoting resources and energy to accomplishing specific tasks to produce a product or service in fulfillment of the organization's stated goals, and devoting resources and energy to building and maintaining the organization itself. These two activities are sometimes congruent, but sometimes they are at odds.

Among other things, looking at religious institutions through this lens highlights one useful way to differentiate between churches (congregations) and para-church (including Christian service) organizations. Churches, however strong their evangelistic tendencies, tend to focus more on building and maintaining themselves as organizations as an end in itself, which involves attending to a wide variety of tasks with goals that are often difficult to specify or measure, whereas para-church organizations frequently have much more specific goals—for example, providing shelter for the homeless—and are likely to be concerned about building and maintaining themselves more for the purposes of enabling the attainment of those goals. In the language of the non-profit sector we used before, churches, being more like natural systems, may be expected to act more like mutual benefit organizations. Christian service organizations, being more like rational systems (which emphasize more specific goals), may be expected to behave like public benefit organizations.

Many churches, of course, stress their outreach and service, or public benefit efforts. Clearly, the public at large is unlikely to object to that. The pastor (or other leadership) of a congregation is likely to be in trouble with the body of the congregation, however, if the focus on outreach means there is insufficient attention given to internal needs for ministry and worship. Participants in a religious congregation almost inevitably come with a primary expectation that their own needs should be met first, although many also come desiring to contribute to a particular congregation's ministry to the larger community.

The more interesting situation for our study arises when a Christian service organization gives more of its resources and energy to mutual benefit kinds of activities than to public benefit work, and this can easily happen. In its more innocent forms, such behavior arises because the staff of these organizations, bound together by common religious beliefs and mutual affection, see their place of work as more of a church than a service agency, and may become more concerned with caring for one another than with the quality or quantity of their work. That the staff should want the organization to offer such care for its own is not necessarily a bad thing; indeed, it may be crucial to maintaining the kind of organizational capacities required to engage in some of the ministries the group is undertaking. In field studies (which will be described later), however, I frequently heard managers of such organizations talk about the struggle to maintain a balance between the specific tasks of the organizations and the tendency of staff to divert too much time and energy to fellowship and mutual, personal support.

In its less innocent forms, this behavior arises because the staff may be truly self-serving. They may say, for example, that they are devoting a large percentage of resources to expanding an organization's fund-raising capacities because they want to expand its capacity for service; but, in fact, they may simply be interested in "empire building," creating a larger and more prestigious organization primarily so they can enjoy being associated with such an agency. They may be willing to accept donations or grants that either compromise the organization's ability to make a clear witness to its religious tenets or involve it in work that undermines its commitment to its stated mission, because these funds can provide better remuneration or job security for the staff. In the worst cases, of which we have seen far too many examples in the press recently, the leaders of the service organizations have shown a willingness to divert resources for their own personal enrichment.

The point is all these behaviors represent dynamics that a natural-systems perspective on organizations suggests we should expect to find, and which a rational-systems perspective would propose formal structures and procedures to control. These questions are finally ones of mission versus maintenance.

Philip Selznick offers us a useful distinction between "organizations," as tools people create to facilitate collective action to achieve common purposes rationally defined and articulated; and "institutions," as collective entities that take on their own special qualities and become things people want to preserve for themselves (1957). From a rationalist's point of view, we might wish that religious service organizations would always remain organizations in Selznick's sense; but history as well as organizational theory (see, for example, Kimberly, Miles, et al., 1980) tells us most will become institutions. Insofar as this must be the case, this theoretical perspective helpfully defines a problem for managers of Christian service organizations—which is the need to meet individuals' (staff members' and volunteers') desires to create and be part of an institution, but not allow that to subvert the mission of the organization donors are supporting.

This comparison and contrast of rational versus natural systems perspectives also helps illuminate another critical set of issues for trustees, leaders, and managers; that is, how the formal structure of an organization affects the character of its output (products or services), and whether a given structure is compatible with the basic understandings and beliefs the organization holds or claims to hold. As Scott observes, "To focus [only] on what organizations *do* may conceal from us the more basic and far-reaching effects that occur because organizations are the *mechanisms*—the media—by which goals are pursued. . . . Our organizational tools shape in unexpected ways the products and services they produce" (1987, p. 6; emphasis in the original).

A good example of this presents itself from our earlier look at the history of philanthropic practice. As the delivery of charitable services to individuals moved out of the control of informally structured, religiously oriented, often church-based service groups into the control of more formally structured, "scientifically" oriented, professionally controlled charitable agencies, the formal structures and procedures conceived by those agencies altered the essential nature of the service provided. This is, in fact, the focus of some fascinating studies by Peter Dobkin Hall (1989; 1990a). In these studies, Hall notes that many religious people involved in charitable work have had to reject the techniques of "scientific philanthropy" even though the techniques may have been more efficient economically. Although these people may have desired the gains in efficiency, they saw, as Hall observes, that "Christian charity involves far more than the economical provision of services. As, if not more, important was the creation of a community of feeling, a set of human bonds, which are in themselves perhaps far more valuable than the service" (1990a, p. 52).

Organizational theory and this illustration suggest that service organizations marked by organizational structures that involve narrow and rigid specification of job responsibilities, a high degree of formality in relationships, and strong hierarchies in command are likely to produce services that are narrowly focused, uniform, and impersonal in character. This may not be problematic when constituents' needs are narrow, stable, and purely material, but how often is that the case? And certainly "rigid" and "impersonal" are hardly the adjectives people normally want to describe what they do as a "ministry."

So, it is crucial to look at the relationship between the formal structure chosen for an organization and the likely effects that structure will have on the services the organization provides. Choices made in the interest of economic efficiencies may have highly deleterious—although hard to measure—effects on the quality of services provided. Managers and trustees need to ask if these are acceptable trade-offs. Moreover, it is important to think about how those structures and the services that come from them will represent or embody the values the organization wishes to uphold or promote.

This kind of problem became acutely apparent to me in the apparent contradictions between the values embedded in the organizational structures or forms that many Christian service organizations I examined had adopted and the values that the New Testament says are at the heart of any ministry. Let me describe one of the more striking examples.

A key principle in Weber's highly rational conception of organizations, which is a principle accepted in virtually all work organizations today, is the separation of the responsibilities of a position or office from the personal attributes of the officeholder (see Weber 1947 [1924]; Selznick, 1948; Perrow, 1986, Scott, 1987). Thus, while an officeholder must have certain specifiable technical or professional qualifications, the assumption is his or her personal qualities should be irrelevant to the right to hold the position. Moreover, this is not just the view of "classical theorists" who see Weber's idea of bureaucracy as the basic model for all organizations; it is widely shared among other theorists, and among most managers, who see it as important to have different people interchangeable (as Selznick observed) in professional roles so an organization does not become dependent on finding someone with precisely the same personal attributes to fill a particular job every time.

Yet, most Christian service organizations speak of what they do as "ministry"; and at the heart of the Christian conception of ministry is the idea that it is intensely and essentially personal. Central to the New Testament descriptions of ministry is the idea that people are equipped for particular ministries, to which they are *personally called*, by their "gifts" (1 Cor. 12)—*essentially personal attributes* and characteristics. To ask people to be involved in the ministry of a Christian service organization, then, is to ask them to bring their gifts, their personal attributes as individuals and as believers, to that work. This directly contravenes what a rational-systems perspective on organizations would have one do in designing and defining jobs. The incongruity between the basic assumptions about what is needed for efficiency in rational, task-oriented organizations and the theological underpinnings of some Christian organizations defines another key issue for managing these Christian organizations.

Another structural problem area for Christian service organizations is "hierarchy." The disparity between organizational theory and theological tenet is not quite so cut-and-dry in this case, because the witness of the Scriptures about the place and acceptability of hierarchy is not quite so clear. Still, a strong case can be made from the New Testament for the idea that the church is intended to be a community of equals—at least in terms of people's worth and dignity—where functions are assigned because of "giftedness," "calling," and experience (again, see 1 Cor. or Acts). Many organizational theorists and most managers, however, will insist there has to be a "chain of command" and a "status hierarchy" to ensure control and direction in an organization and to allow for motivation and reward of individuals within it.

There are two reasons that, for Christian service organizations, it matters whether one assumes a rational-systems or natural-systems perspective. First, while managers may say (as one did to me), "For our purposes, it does not matter whether the church is supposed to be a group of equals—this is a [nonprofit] business not a church," it is clear many of those who work in these organizations perceive them to be part of the church, and believe they ought to embody the same ideals. Thus we may have a disparity between organizational (or, at least, the managers') goals and individual participants' goals. Furthermore, we have a perfect example of a situation in which it becomes highly significant whether informal structures and values or formal structures and values are more important in shaping and defining an organization.

Second, while rational-systems perspectives assume formal structure is crucial for certain purposes—organizational control, direction, and reward—natural-systems perspectives suggest that people may be controlled and directed—indeed, better directed—by things other than bosses and rules, and better motivated and rewarded by things other than titles or salaries. That is a point managers of religious organizations should take very seriously, for many—if not most—of their employees are more likely to be there because of some identification with the organizations' mission than for the salary or status that come with their positions.

Of course, in addition to the values-based arguments against hierarchy—which, by the way, can be mustered from non-scriptural sources too (see Ferguson, 1984)—there are more practical arguments as well. Perrow catalogs the complaints (in an interesting choice of subtitles) about "the sins of hierarchy," noting that

> hierarchy promotes rigidity and timidity. Subordinates are afraid of passing bad news up the ladder or of suggesting changes. . . . Hierarchy promotes delays and sluggishness; everything must be kicked upstairs for a decision, either because the boss insists or because the subordinate does not want to risk making a poor decision. (1986, p. 29)

There are then many reasons that those responsible for the governance and management of Christian service organizations should be concerned about organizational structure—about the formal and informal aspects of positions and the relationships among positions and the people who fill them. They should also be concerned about the definition of the goals of these organizations, not only about the content and specificity of those goals, but also about how those goals were defined, or (perhaps) redefined. Our claim here is that all these matters are helpfully illuminated, with potentially key questions being highlighted, by considering how Christian service organizations may be seen through the lenses of rational- or natural-systems perspectives on organizations. And before leaving this area, there is one more point that should be made, related to the claim that managers should be concerned about the nature and process of definition of organizational goals.

One area of controversy between rational and natural organizational theorists, to which we alluded earlier, is whether or not an organization can really have goals—in the same sense a person can—and, if so, how the organization's goals can or should be differentiated from the goals of individual participants. Generally, rational theorists claim that an organization can and does have specific goals; and if the goals are properly articulated (presumably by owners or managers), individuals will adopt them as their own either (1) because they come to believe in the inherent value of those goals, or (2) because they see their own goals are served by contributing to the organization's goals. Generally, natural theorists claim that an organization does not have goals independent of the individual participants' goals; thus, what are called "organizational goals" are those preferences for outcomes that result from some process of barter and negotiation among the participants. If so, the goals of individuals—for example, for job security or economic betterment—are easily differentiated from the goals of the organization—for example, to become the dominant producer in a particular industry.

What is interesting is that both positions assume that individuals need to be convinced to join and contribute to the work of an organization, but will have personal goals for joining or participating that are not identical with the goals of the organizations. Hence, they will need to be coerced, compelled, coopted, or bargained with to induce their contribution to the work of the organization for the support of its goals (Barnard, 1938; March and Simon, 1958; Clark and Wilson, 1961). Christian service organizations may represent the most striking and frequent counterpoint to this shared assumption of both rational- and natural-systems theories.

People frequently come to these organizations as staff, volunteers, or contributors primarily, if not solely, to contribute to the work, "the ministry," the goals the organizations have already defined and articulated. My interviews with numerous staff people and volunteers in such organizations over the last year confirm earlier impressions that such organizations may represent a distinctive case in which individual goals and organizational goals may frequently be fully aligned, if not identical.

This is not to say that staff, volunteers, and those who make donations may not be attempting to meet other needs through their participation. We can be sure the staff people appreciate and generally need their salaries, but we know that in many cases they could make more money performing similar functions for other organizations. In the case of volunteers and contributors, a number of studies look at the personal needs these people may satisfy through their participation, and at how organizations can give individuals opportunities to satisfy those needs without compromising organizational integrity (Anderson and Moore, 1978; Clary and Snyder, 1991; Jeavons, 1991).

Finally, though, the most interesting question arising in this context is how these people may participate in redefining the service organizations' goals over time. As opportunities for ministry change, new problems emerge in the spheres in which these organizations work, or new resources become available to support their work, what roles will staff, volunteers, and contributors who come after the establishment of an organization play in shaping its response to those opportunities? If the organizations have difficulty raising resources—money or volunteers—to support their work, will they change their goals or alter their structures to induce more support? Questions of this type draw us into a consideration of the second axis of Scott's basic schema for analysis of organizations, that is, whether they are open or closed systems.

## *Open- versus Closed-Systems Perspectives*

These perspectives again do not stand in strict juxtaposition, but rather, like the rational- and natural-systems theories, mark out a continuum along which different views of organizations may fall. At issue here is the degree to which various organizations are shaped by the environment around them, or can be designed and function independent of—sometimes in spite of—environmental influences. Again, there are descriptive and normative elements in theorists' perspectives. That is to say, the questions are not only about the degree to which organizations *can* function free from external influences, but about the degree to which they *should* function in this way. What is more, some theorists have turned these questions around to ask not only about the ways in which organizations may be molded by their environment, but also about the ways in which they mold—or "enact"—their environments (see Weick, 1979; Perrow, 1986).

The key issues about Christian service organizations which are lifted up for us by examining these organizations in terms of open- and closed-systems perspectives are matters of organizational stability, integrity, and control. All organizations must wrestle with questions about who or what controls or should control the decision-making processes by which their agendas are set. This harks back to our earlier discussion about who gets to have a say in forming organizational goals.

Yet, in religious organizations, these matters may have special importance, because what may be at issue is whether an organization will strive to attain goals and honor values believed to have been formed in response to *divine in-spiration* and to be of *eternal significance*, or whether it will direct itself toward other efforts, which may not serve these ends. It is one thing for a business to decide to change its focus from consumer goods to providing materials for other manufacturers, for example; it is another for a Christian organization to shift its focus from reaching people with the "Word of God" to providing social and recreational services for the middle class (see Denton and Zald, 1963). Fur-thermore, relatively subtle changes may have profound effects, for if the val-ues-expressive facet of a Christian service organization's work is addressed as much by the way it delivers a service as by the practical content of the service it provides, then seemingly minor changes in the manner of or approach to service delivery can seriously undermine the attempt to fulfill an essential el-ement of the organization's mission.

Thus, questions about how and to what degree organizations adapt to their environments (Lawrence and Lorsch, 1967; Thompson, 1967), about the dy-namics of organizational assimilation (Niv, 1980) and organizational drift (Lodahl and Mitchell, 1980), about goal displacement (Michels 1949 [1915]; Selznick, 1957), and about the character and integrity of "organizational cul-ture" (Schein, 1985) all become extremely important questions for Christian service organizations. And they may all be illuminated by applying some of the concepts of open- and closed-systems perspectives.

The dynamics of organizations' adaptation to their surrounding environ-ments deserve the closest scrutiny from those concerned about the integrity of Christian service organizations—and religious organizations more generally—for one of the most obvious results of such adaptation is secularization. Many observers of American culture, as we noted before, have commented on how it has become much more secular over the years; and the truth of this obser-vation means that the environment to which religious organizations must adapt and may assimilate is one very different from—and often at odds with—the culture these organizations are supposed to represent. Not that this is a new problem. In his classic study of the evolution of Christian monasticism, Herbert Workman argued that the earliest Christian contemplatives, those who fled into the deserts of Egypt, "fled not so much from the world as from the world *in* the Church" (1913, p. 10).

However long the history of this problem, adaptation through assimilation is becoming a more significant issue for Christian service organizations for a number of reasons. First, these organizations are often operating in fields of service delivery—health care, education and day care, international relief and development, and the provision of other social services—in which secular ser-vice organizations are also operating. Thus, Christian service organizations are frequently competing for funding, often appealing to other institutions—corporations, foundations, the government—against those secular agencies; and to do so effectively (they believe, at least), they have to operate like their competitors and the institutions from whom they seek help. They may see this as crucial to their "legitimacy." So there is pressure on many of these organizations to import "modern management practices," without regard to the fact that these are products of and most suited to a for-profit environment; or the organizations imitate the management practices of their secular nonprofit competitors, and similar issues arise.

Paul DiMaggio and Walter Powell, in an exceptionally helpful study of "institutional isomorphism" (1983), tell us we should expect this kind of organizational behavior. Nevertheless, the matter of whether the organizational structures and management practices being adopted are compatible with the work of ministry and religious values is too often left unexamined, and it can become a source of major trouble for these religious entities.

A second pressure contributing to the tendency of Christian service agencies to adopt secular, for-profit management practices—and, through this mechanism, to absorb and assimilate secular values—is the presence of large numbers of businesspeople on their boards. These people bring needed skills to the organizations but often fail to see the significant differences between the character and the mission of nonprofit, especially religious, organizations and those of business organizations. This creates the potential—too often realized—for a replay of the struggle between "scientific" and religious approaches to philanthropy we examined earlier. (Remember, Carnegie and Rockefeller, two of the most successful of businessmen, were the two most prominent champions of scientific philanthropy.)

This problem has been well analyzed and helpfully described as a "conflict of managerial cultures" in a recent article by Peter Dobkin Hall (1990b). Commenting on the role of the businessperson directors in creating a crisis of values for one nonprofit—in this case a cultural organization—Hall notes, "In their [the trustees'] enthusiasm for managerial technology, they failed to understand the need *to match their tools to the task*—and that the duties, responsibilities and ethical standards of boards in nonprofit settings differ significantly from those applicable to business" (p. 160, emphasis mine). These observations could certainly be extended to, and may have even more serious implications in, religious organizations.

A third source of adaptation as assimilation is the tendency in our culture for religious concepts and words to become secularized, creating confusion about the nature of Christian service organizations' work and the real meaning of the criteria for evaluation being applied to that work. In some cases, this is just a manifestation of the type of confusion in individuals described above, where—for example—because it is a religious organization engaged in the work, a trustee of that organization may call a program providing child care a "ministry," even though nothing about the way that care is provided gives any evidence of religious motivation or substance in the work. In other cases, however, the meaning of key words and concepts for thinking about and shaping religious work have been actually altered by their usage in secular culture, so when they are used again in religious organizations they convey the wrong ideas.

The most prominent example of this in my view is the term "stewardship." The case has been made that this was once among the most powerful of concepts and symbols for shaping a life of faith in the Judeo-Christian tradition. Yet, as a result of a number of influences in the early years of Christianity, the concept became "spiritualized" and lost much of its potency. It fell into relative disuse for a long time, and then in recent decades has made a comeback (see D. J. Hall, 1990). But the difficulty is that, having been revived largely in the secular world, the work returns to common usage among religious folks with an altered meaning.

My own discussions with many people in churches and other Christian organizations who are responsible for raising and caring for resources—church treasurers, development officers, and other executives for religious organizations—as well as with other church members, lead me to the conclusion that most of them equate "stewardship" with "efficiency in the use of money." But stewardship means much more than that. It means recognizing that all we have, even our lives, is a gift we hold in trust to use as wisely as possible to further God's intentions for the creation.

The shallower, secularized conception leads to religious organizations regularly making choices that are inappropriate and counterproductive to efforts to witness to the fullness of God's love in their work because of simplistic cost-effectiveness calculations. For example, a service agency may face a choice between two approaches to raising money for the care of needy children. One involves specific donors in the lives of specific children, so that a relationship is established wherein real caring, personal support, and prayer may flow back and forth; the other approach is slightly less expensive but creates no relationships except between donors and the organization. The manager who says that "good stewardship" demands that the organization choose the less-expensive approach has misunderstood the real meaning, the scriptural meaning, of stewardship. Yet the case just described occurred, involving a very sincere, thoughtful, evangelical Christian as the manager, and other cases that demonstrate the same kind of confusion occur regularly.

All this is to say that the problems of Christian organizations having the distinctive character of their work undermined by the dynamics of adaptation and assimilation to the environment are very real, and are predicted by some open-systems perspectives on organizations. One theorist, in fact, tells us this may be a problem only for entities like religious organizations when he argues "assimilation is a problem faced only by deviant systems, that is, by systems that attempt to be different from the world" (Niv, 1980). The question that arises is whether there is some way the dynamics can be countered, or at least ameliorated; and the other theorists say they can be.

"Contingency theorists," who straddle the open- and closed-systems fence, contend that there is no one best way to structure an organization, and believe "that organizations strive to be rational even though they are natural and open systems" (Scott, 1987, p. 97). They offer us two helpful ways of thinking about how that "striving" can be most successful, and thus some clues as to how the threat of assimilation can best be met.

Lawrence and Lorsch (1967) contend that different organizations will be more or less open to their external environments, depending on the levels of uncertainty in that environment and in the nature of the work the organization does. So, for instance, "high-tech" firms, whose products are influenced by rapidly changing technology and whose markets may change with similar speed, will generally need to be more open to their environment, because they must be able to stay up with technological advances and stay ahead of customer demands. The downside of this is that the more closely different elements of an organization mirror the particular environments to which they relate—research to the scientific world, marketing to the commercial world, finance to the banking world—the harder it is to keep them focused on the core mission and values of the organization, and the harder it is to keep them communicating effectively with one another.

On the other hand, Lawrence and Lorsch suggest, the more stable the technology that an organization uses to create its product or service, and the more predictable its environment, the more closed the organization can afford to be. That way it can routinize and control procedures for efficiency, and structure itself and operate in ways that lead to the fullest integration of elements focusing everyone on common tasks and values. The assumption is that there is little risk in operating in this mode because, when consumer or constituent needs or demands change little or slowly, less flexibility or alacrity is needed in organizational responses to the external environment.

One of the significant facets of Lawrence and Lorsch's research in this area was its demonstration of how the various parts of an organization could change in different ways because of their connection to different elements of the external environment. James Thompson's (1967) contingency theory works with a similar kind of insight. Thompson's view is that, while different kinds of organizations, or units within organizations, may be more or less open to their surrounding environment, it is helpful to look at the ways in which the various "levels" of an organization are structured to be more or less open.

Thompson identifies three levels within organizations: (1) the technical level, where the core work of the organization is done—for instance, a classroom in a school or a production line in a factory; (2) the managerial level, where decisions are made about how to coordinate the technical work, how to secure the resources needed for that work from the world, and how to deliver the products of that work to the world; and (3) the institutional level, where the concerns are those of relating the particular organization to other organizations and institutional components of its world. Thompson contends that the institutional components of an organization—the legal or government relations department, for instance—will necessarily be open to the surrounding environment. He further believes that, to promote as much efficiency, stability, and psychological security as possible, organizations will often try to close off their technical functions from the external environment as far as possible. Finally, then, it is left to the managerial level to mediate between the needs and cultures of the two other levels.

How do these contingency theories shed light on the character or needs of Christian service organizations? They do so in a couple of ways. Most Christian service organizations need to be, as these perspectives propose, open in some ways and closed in others. Assuming for the moment that the mission of one such organization derives from a particular sense of divine calling to a special kind of work, let us say helping children in need. It is important then that the organization be open enough to what is going on in the environment to see where those children are, what their needs are, and what some of the best possible approaches are that have been discovered to meet their needs. It is also important, however, that those finally deciding how to pursue this mission be insulated from the pressures working to make this organization and its activity like that of every other children's service agency. It is important that in some way those actually doing the work, actually caring for the children, and those deciding who will be cared for and how, be closed off from the influences of the external environment that might divert them from their special mandate and calling as religious people in a religious organization.

Contingency theories give us some concepts for thinking about which facets of Christian service organizations ought to be open to external influences, and which might function better when relatively free from such influences. Recent history and some of the material we looked at earlier suggest that Christian service organizations may need to be more open in the sense of being accountable to their supporter constituencies, and perhaps even to the public at large. Yet, other examples have come to my attention through my studies and experience that emphasize how easily and subtly the special religious character of these organizations can be eroded by external influences. We will need to look more closely later at how this occurs—through the effects of various resource dependencies and the professionalization of staff, and in other ways. The point is that these other examples speak of the need for religious organizations to be closed in some ways.

A crucial element in this complex of issues is leadership—Thompson's institutional and managerial levels—and how responsive it is to various external and internal constituencies. Robert Michels's ground-breaking work in this area (1949 [1915]) generated a theory called the "iron law of oligarchy," which still has remarkable currency seventy-five years after he proposed it. (The theory, in fact, emerged from a study of a voluntary association—in this case a political party.)

Simply put, Michels proposes that, although organizations form around the desire to attain some specific collective goal, after a while a group in leadership will inevitably become more concerned about preserving its own position and interests as the leaders than about that goal. They will begin to guide organizational decision making and action in ways directed toward the maintenance of the organization—and their position within it—in preference to the attainment of that goal. Thus, Michels says, even the most idealistic, egalitarian, purposive of organizations will eventually come to be governed by an oligarchy; and the leaders are likely to divert the organization's behavior, energy, and resources to their own ends, even if that means changing or sacrificing the organization's original goal.

A careful look at the most prominent of the religious organizations caught in outrageously self-serving behavior recently—the televangelist ministries—shows some of the pattern Michels outlines. Overseen (to misuse the term) primarily by the family and friends of the people who ran them, these organizations seem to have been set up to facilitate this kind of abuse. Still, there are many other, nonscandalous instances of organizational goals being displaced or altered by efforts to ensure organizational survival—and the continuance in leadership of those managing the organizations—that follow the pattern Michels laid out more closely. In these cases, changes in the character and operative goals of the organizations may have been subtle or dramatic, but they seem clearly to have been generated by this natural inclination of leaders to preserve an organization and their own position within it regardless of what that means in terms of changing the organization. (I will describe two such cases more fully later.)

If the dynamic that Michels points out is likely to be at work in Christian service organizations, then there is a need to keep their leaders accountable to a broader constituency. Moreover, whether that constituency—for instance, the donors—is seen as being part of the organization or external to it, is an interesting question with some very practical implications. If it is seen as being outside the organization, it means that the organization should be open to its influence to help avoid what some theorists call "organizational drift" (Lodahl and Mitchell, 1980). This is presuming, for the moment, that these people have become donors because they are committed to the original (or current) purposes of the organization. If the donors are seen as members of the organization who are committed to the organization's purposes, then it is still desirable to have the leadership accountable to this group. But it may now become undesirable to have the leadership open to the influence of outsiders. Why? Because now the organization should be concerned about the influence of others (for example, potential donors) who might wish to change its direction.

Such concerns lead us into questions about the sources of power—power within an organization and power that can be influenced over an organization. Again, these are questions on which open- and closed-systems perspectives may shed some light.

In his study of "complex organizations," Charles Perrow defines "power" as "the ability of persons or groups to extract for themselves [or direct to the purposes they choose] valued outputs from a system" (1986, p. 259). Both Perrow and Scott (1987) finally claim that power in—or over—organizations derives from the ability to provide or control resources the organization needs or wants, either because one has such resources or because one can get them. Resources in this context may mean information, expertise, status, or legitimacy as well as wealth. This idea—that power derives from control over resources—has two highly significant implications.

First, the emphasis on capturing resources suggests another way of thinking about what differentiates Christian service (and other philanthropic) organizations from business and governmental organizations. Paralleling our earlier distinction in terms of goals, we make a differentiation in terms of how organizations relate to other elements of society to garner the resources they need. In this framework, outlined by Ostrander and Schervish (1990), we can see that in our society businesses lay claim to the resources they need—primarily economic goods—by virtue of their ability to participate in exchanges of those goods. Government claims the resources it needs—first, political legitimacy in the form of votes, which then allows it to claim economic goods—by virtue of setting public policy or providing public services of which voters approve. But philanthropic organizations' claims on resources—economic goods and institutional legitimacy—are based on moral commitments. If this is so, it suggests another reason why their values-expressive character and behavior are crucial, for the demonstration of those moral commitments is what legitimates and strengthens those claims.

Second, the view that power derives from the control of resources reveals the mechanisms by which particular individuals become exceptionally important in or to an organization, regardless of their official positions. This view squares with the experiences many of us have had in organizations. We know that persons with no official or significant status, but who have the wherewithal—money, connections, expertise, political skill—to make things happen usually have far more influence over an organization's decisions and actions than persons in the reverse situation. Control over resources is the key.

All organizations have to be open systems to the extent that the resources they need are external to them; but all will try to be closed systems to the degree that they do not want people or influences outside of them controlling them. Almost all organizational theorists seem to believe all organizations will want to be free from external control (although some of the Christian service organizations I have studied may challenge the validity of that assumption in a way I will want to consider more closely later). Our examination of the needs of organizations along this open systems–closed systems axis then indicates that we might expect organizations to try to have people inside them who are capable of securing for them the resources they need—controlling environmental "uncertainty" (see Goldner, 1970; Hickson, et al., 1971)—and that those people would have a significant measure of power in and over organizations. If that is so, it leads to the last issue I want to highlight in this section, which has to do with a concern for who these people are.

When one talks to people involved with Christian service organizations as staff, volunteers, donors, or just observers, one of the questions most frequently voiced is, What makes the organization Christian? My own experience in and around such organizations—as a member, staff person, and researcher—tells me the key elements for shaping their character as Christian are two: the personal characteristics and commitments of their staff, especially in relation to their faith commitments; and the manner in which the staff are managed and led to maintain a Christian "organizational culture." These two factors are, in fact, inexorably woven together because it may be that the most important thing the managers and leaders do is choose and support the staff to develop that culture.

Consider the question of resource dependency in relation to these issues. For many modern Christian service organizations, some of the people most important in securing needed resources are fund-raisers. If these people are highly successful in securing needed resources, they are likely to become influential participants in organizational decision making, first, because virtually all aspects of an organization's program have an effect on fund-raising, and second, because virtually all of the organization's programs can become elements of fund appeals.

What then if this fund-raiser is not a deeply committed, active, and thoughtful Christian? What kind of influence might he or she have on decisions about the organization's programs? What if the professional fund-raiser is more responsive to the goals and values of fund-raising than to the goals of the organization and the values of the faith? Might the fund-raiser steer program decisions toward choices that will readily serve the efforts to raise money but poorly serve the goal of representing the best Christian ideals of service and charity? And, of course, such conflict may be at least as serious in the fund-raiser's own work, where some secular approaches to fund-raising may be incongruous with Christian values. (Again, we will explore these issues more later.)

The point is that the greatest care must be taken by the leadership and management of Christian service organizations in the selection and choice of staff, for however much the organizations succeed in being closed systems at certain levels, the most important resource they need from the external environment is people. With respect to people, the organizations must be, at least occasionally, open systems. If we accept Edgar Schein's definition of an organization's "culture" as "the deeper level of basic assumptions and beliefs that are shared by members . . . , that operate unconsciously, and that define in a basic 'taken-for-granted' fashion an organization's view of itself and its environment" (1985, p. 6), then we can see the only way to create and maintain a Christian culture in an organization is to bring in people whose primary commitments are to Christian "basic assumptions and beliefs." Obviously, in addition, management must also pay attention to the way in which the organization is operating, to see to it that those basic assumptions and beliefs are honored in practice as well as rhetoric.

So, looking at Christian service organizations in terms of this second dimension of organizational analysis uncovers a number of important issues for the life of these organizations, and begins to suggest some ways to address those issues constructively. It points out the need to consider how organizations adapt to their environments, and how this kind of organization needs to be concerned about problems of assimilation in that process. It helps us identify the environmental factors that generate pressure for assimilation, and starts to indicate some strategies for coping with those factors, in terms of structuring these organizations so they may be open in some ways and closed in others. It suggests how questions about the dynamics of leadership, power, and resource dependency are interrelated, and how the need to build and maintain integrity in organizational culture relates to all these concerns. Finally, it suggests a number of more specific problems or concerns for these organizations, which we will consider in later chapters.

## Levels of Analysis

One more set of categories is useful to our organizational analysis. These have to do with the level of analysis, that is, the components or ingredients of organizational life with which one is concerned—individual participants, groups within organizations, an organization taken as a whole, or organizations as part of a larger set of societal structures. The focus of analysis that is concerned primarily with the roles and functions of individuals within organizations may be referred to as "social psychological," that which focuses on groups within organizations or on organizations as collective entities as "structural," and that which is interested in organizations as part of a larger social system or political economy as "ecological" (see Scott, 1987).

The aspect of organizational life at which one looks is important to the conclusions one is likely to draw; looking at organizations in terms of these three levels can be useful in uncovering and exploring different elements of their functions and in gaining a more complete picture of them. For instance, if we were to concern our analysis of religious service organizations only with individuals' motivations and behaviors within them, we might conclude that the missions these organizations develop are determined solely by those individuals' inspirations and beliefs. But if we took an ecological perspective, we might find that some of the organizations developed to fill societal needs that no other organizations could or would fill.

These three levels can serve to draw our attention to different but equally important elements of the work of Christian service organizations. Analysis at the social psychological level calls to our attention issues of how such organizations provide vehicles for the expression and nurture of individuals' faith, and raises key questions about how individuals' other needs are met in them. Focusing at the structural level helps keep before us the importance of questions about the ways in which organizational forms and procedures may or may not encompass religious and cultural values and allow for the fulfillment of the less measurable outcomes intended in their mission. And taking an ecological perspective reminds us that questions about the legitimacy and value of these organizations involve considerations of larger social and economic structures. So, this is one more way in which the framework of organizational theory may be useful in helping us understand the nature and behavior of Christian service organizations.

## Summary and Conclusions

This chapter provides a broad overview of organizational theory and explores the insights that field might provide in an examination of Christian service organizations as organizations. We began by observing that the questions of greatest significance for us were likely to revolve around the differences between religious organizations and other types, and suggested that the single, most important difference might be the unusual "values-expressive" character of these organizations. We explored the similarities and dissimilarities that organizational theories suggest would appear among various organizations, regardless of type.

We then looked at how fundamental points of similarity and dissimilarity among organizations, which are exposed by organizational theories, relate to the nature and importance of the organizations' goals and who has a say in determining those goals, the presence and character of their structure and how formal or informal that structure is, and whether they will or should always seek their own self-perpetuation. Using an analytical framework suggested by W. Richard Scott, we next examined Christian service organizations in the light of what we learned from discussing these fundamental points and from a variety of specific organizational theories. The key dimensions of that framework derive from asking about whether organizations are rational or natural systems and open or closed systems. The examination of Christian service organizations through these theoretical lenses highlighted a variety of issues that may have special salience for these organizations. Finally, we noted that the level of analysis is also important, and demonstrated how that is so.

Through this process, a number of aspects of the character and functions of Christian service organizations have emerged as being of special significance for managers. These include the processes by which their goals are defined and evolve over time, questions about the compatibility of their structures with the values they profess and want their work to embody, problems they face in adapting to their environments without assimilating to them, and the need to manage resource dependencies in ways that do not undermine the organizations' integrity. We have also seen how this organizational analysis has suggested approaches to addressing the problems these organizations may face.

Combined with the previous chapters which explore the societal environment that influences these organizations and in which they must operate, and the theological underpinnings for their missions, this provides us with a fairly complete picture of the context for management of Christian service organizations. This chapter in particular has highlighted some of the dynamics and operations most likely to need the attention of those who manage and lead these organizations. Now we turn to the practical issues of management.

# PART II

# The Management of Christian Service Organizations

THE HISTORICAL, SOCIOLOGICAL, cultural, and theological analysis just completed offers us a number of insights about Christian service organizations and demonstrates two especially important points. The first is that many of these organizations are—and on theological grounds I would claim should be—fundamentally different in at least one aspect from those organizations that are more commonly the subjects of management and organizational studies, which is to say, businesses and government agencies. This overview tells us that Christian service organizations differ from most churches (congregations) in having more concrete and specific organizational goals, and differ from the other types of organizations just mentioned in that those goals are dual-faceted rather than singular, encompassing two distinct but thoroughly intertwined aspects. These dual-faceted goals involve not only completing a specific task or providing a practical service, but also promoting the moral values and spiritual understandings that underlie these organizations' commitment to this work.

Second, the contextual analysis tells us that these organizations belong, and are seen by most people, in the category of voluntary philanthropic organizations. In this regard, they are subject to a specific set of expectations, which we have seen apply generally to philanthropic organizations in American society, and which reinforce the need to embrace a twofold mission as described.

These distinctive characteristics of Christian service organizations create an environment for their operations that is unlike that of business or government, or even many secular philanthropic organizations. The cultural and societal expectations of these organizations are key elements in that environment, as is the organizations' obligation to honor and embody a specific set of spiritual and theological ideals. The ways in which the context is *operatively* distinct, in which it requires different approaches to the *practice* of management, are the subject of the second part of this volume.

The chapters that follow reflect on how the insights of management literature may apply to Christian service organizations, extrapolate ideas and findings from the analysis offered in Part I, and draw on the observations and questions that emerged from my studies of seven specific, Christian-based service organizations. A few words about the nature and methodology of those studies are required for background.

Part II begins with an explanation of the approach to the field studies and an overview of the set of organizations that were studied. Chapter 6 considers generally the management needs of Christian service organizations, with special attention to identifying key issues for and functions in the management of these organizations. Chapters 7, 8, and 9 explore in more detail the needs for and possible approaches to management in three specific aspects of the life of these organizations: (1) the establishment and maintenance of organizational culture and the management of human resources, (2) resource development and fund-raising, and (3) executive and board roles in leadership and planning. Chapter 10 summarizes the findings of this study and offers some thoughts about what may be learned from these findings that could be broadly useful for other types of nonprofit organizations.

# 5

# Christian Service in Practice

## *A Study of Seven Organizations*

O N THE BASIS of an examination of organizational theories, one can specu- late about what the primary concerns of managers of Christian service organizations might be, or perhaps should be. Chapter 4 demonstrated the po- tential utility of such an exercise for identifying some of the aspects of organ- izational life to which those managers—and others who care about these orga- nizations—may need to give the most attention. However, to know in fact what issues are most significant, what functions are most problematic, and what questions are the hardest to answer for Christian service organizations— and for those who lead and administer them—we need to study those organi- zations in action. Recently I undertook such field studies.

## Data from the Field—Methodological Notes

### *The Choice of Organizations for Study*

Six of the seven organizations I chose for these field studies were United States–based Christian service agencies working in the field of international relief and development. The seventh was a community-based Christian service agency whose work in its own area has earned it a very fine reputation in its community and more widely.

For the purposes of this study, I wanted to examine some organizations that were seen as highly effective in their work as well as some that were not, but finding the grounds for that selection was not easy. Christian service or- ganizations vary so much in size, field of mission, and type of organization that solidly objective grounds for comparison do not readily present them- selves. I settled on peer evaluation as the most reasonable way to make that determination. To have a meaningful peer evaluation, one needs a group of organizations that know each other well enough to make informed judgments.

The universe of U.S.–based Christian international relief and development agencies offers such a group. The agencies are interrelated through one or both of two organizational networks. In various configurations, they often work in the same geographical fields abroad, sometimes sharing resources with one another there; and often they raise resources from the same individuals and institutions at home. This creates enough contact and common ground among them to provide a basis for their making a reasonable judgment of each other's effectiveness.

Accordingly, with the cooperation of those two organizational networks, I surveyed thirty-five of the Christian international relief agencies based in the United States and asked them to identify which of their peers were "most effective." I sent the survey instrument to the chief executive officers (CEOs) and board chairs of the thirty-five organizations, as these are the people who are generally most likely to be involved in the organizational networks and have the contact with others in the field.

The survey instrument asked respondents to render their judgments of effectiveness in terms of seven primary criteria. These criteria focused on the capacities and performance of organizations in delivering the service they intend to provide to those in need of it, and on the degree to which the organizations seem to make a "clear witness to the faith tradition they represent."

Twenty-two of the thirty-five organizations (63 percent) either returned the survey instrument or answered the same questions in telephone follow-up interviews. In two cases, questionnaires were returned by both a staff person and a board member in the same organization. (In a number of cases, the CEO passed the questionnaires on to another staff member who was the appointed representative to the organizational networks, or who was otherwise seen as having a more informed perspective than the CEO.)

The results of the survey process indicated that a relatively small subset of this sample of organizations is viewed as most effective by the senior staff and board members of their peers. Only four of the thirty-five organizations in this sample were nominated as "most effective" by more than 20 percent of their peers; two of these were named by almost 40 percent. More than half received no nominations—or only one, and organizations were allowed to name themselves. Outside of the four most effective, only three others received nominations from more than 10 percent of their peers; and in terms of relative rankings—respondents were asked to rank their top five choices—they fell far below the top four.

After some inquiries and discussion, the four most effective organizations agreed to be the subjects of in-depth field studies. Two less effective organizations were also chosen for study. These two were nominated by less than 10 percent of the survey respondents; I chose them for the study particularly to provide a useful comparison to one or more of the organizations in the most effective sample. I looked for two that mirrored at least one of the most effective organizations in terms of size, age, type of constituency, and focus of mission.

The community-based organization—the seventh organization studied—was chosen because it seemed important to see if the same factors and dynamics I might find in Christian organizations whose work was focused overseas would also be found in a Christian agency whose service focus was local. If nothing else, there are far more of the latter type Christian service organization. (Such organizations would have been the first choice for study in an effort like this if they were not so difficult to examine on a comparative basis.) This particular organization already had a reputation for being very effective in the terms proposed in this study, so it provided a particularly apt subject for comparative purposes.

## The Character of the Field Studies

The seven organizations chosen then became the subjects of closer scrutiny. They allowed me to visit their national offices to observe their operations, examine documents and records, and interview their staff. The visits generally consumed about four working days.

Prior to my visit, each organization sent me a large and varied sample of the materials I requested: charters, bylaws and mission statements; planning documents; any personnel manuals, policy manuals, and board documents they were willing to share; and public relations and fund-raising materials. Some of the organizations were willing to have me examine some of these documents on site—particularly papers from their boards—but could not provide copies for me to keep.

In the course of each visit I interviewed at length many, often most, of the members of an organization's senior staff. This usually included the CEO and almost always included the chief operating officers (or their equivalents) and chief fund-raising executives. In several instances, it was also possible to talk with board members and key volunteers. In addition, however, I sought and generally had time with a wide variety of lower-level employees, to get a better picture of the informal structure and operative values of these organizations, as well as the formal structures and espoused values. This turned out to be extremely important in several cases. (Logistics and finances made it generally impossible to visit staff posted at program sites, especially since most of those were overseas.)

Finally, after these visits, on several occasions I conducted follow-up interviews by phone with a number of people after I had more time to review documents and reflect on the original interviews. Particularly significant in this regard were opportunities in two cases to talk with organizational consultants who had been working with these organizations.

Through this process, I was able to pull together a fairly comprehensive and detailed picture of each of these organizations in action. These field studies—and in two instances, my exposure to or knowledge of the organizations prior to this research—provide the basis for a number of the illustrations and examples and some of the analysis in the chapters that follow.

## Honoring Confidentiality

The organizations that agreed to be subjects in these studies did so with an assurance of confidentiality. Their openness in sharing materials and their staff members' candor in interviews were striking. To maintain the anonymity of the organizations, I have given them fictitious names and changed or concealed identifying characteristics insofar as that is possible while still giving an accurate portrayal of the key features or issues under discussion. The organizations were remarkably generous, and their contribution to what follows is significant.

## Seven Case Studies

### International Christian Relief

International Christian Relief (ICR) describes itself as an "ecumenical, evangelical, Christian service organization." It engages in relief and development work in a number of countries, and its peers view it as one of the most effective organizations in this field.

ICR sees its work as "sharing God's love with the world's neediest people." In fact, the organization has created a remarkable priority-setting system that directs it toward pursuing projects in the countries and regions where people's physical and social needs are greatest; where the climate is least hospitable to Christian evangelism; and where few other non-indigenous Christian service agencies are presently working but significant opportunities exist to work with local, indigenous churches and Christians.

In 1990 ICR sponsored approximately fifty projects, and had income and an operating budget of roughly $12 million. Its financial statements indicate 85 percent of its income goes to program work, with administrative costs of 15 percent, including fund-raising costs of 8.5 percent. The organization derives 10 percent of its cash support from churches, 8 percent from deputation, 60 percent from small gifts (coming mostly from direct mail), 10 percent from major donors, and 12 percent from granting institutions. Almost all of ICR's contributed support comes from private sources, with a little more than half of that coming in the form of donated supplies or "gifts-in-kind."

ICR employs 30 people in its U.S. offices, and approximately 150 staff overseas. In addition, it involves more than 200 volunteers at its distribution center in the work of sorting, cataloging, repairing, and shipping supplies. Its offices occupy most of a large building on its parent organization's campus. The distribution center, a large warehouse facility, is located about three miles away.

ICR is not an independent organization but rather a division of another larger Christian organization originally founded to support a number of locally focused ministries. These include a school, a radio station, a counseling service, and a retirement center and nursing home. ICR is largely autonomous in decision making and has to be self-supporting, but is not separately incorporated and does not have its own board.

ICR started about thirty-five years ago as a project providing medicine for Christian workers overseas. The need to respond to a major natural disaster about twenty years ago brought about ICR's involvement in supplying other goods, and the operation began to grow significantly in size and scope. About ten years ago, ICR found itself badly overextended and went through a series of severe and painful cutbacks in programs and staff. This crisis led to the creation of the priority-setting system for project work. The last five years have seen renewed but slower growth.

In all its community-development projects, ICR works in partnership with local Christians and churches. An underlying purpose of all its efforts is "to strengthen local churches to do their own mission work." For instance, in the work it undertook in one Communist country, where a project was designed to help a community devastated by a natural disaster, ICR was able to provide Bibles and other literature to local churches, which they in turn used for outreach, evangelization, and leadership training.

ICR's gifts-in-kind program collects and distributes medicines, medical supplies, equipment, household goods, clothing, and agricultural supplies (especially seeds). It sends these on to field-workers in many countries. ICR's workers get first priority, but the majority of the material actually goes to workers and projects other than its own. A primary concern of this program is to provide "appropriate goods," meaning materials that are really needed and helpful to Christian workers abroad. Missionaries contact ICR to request supplies, not only for service work but for their own needs as well, ICR then sends on whatever it can from the stocks of donated goods.

ICR has an eight-person "leadership team" consisting of the executive director, operations director, and the directors of the various programs. The team meets once a week for worship and business and the occasional special seminars. The entire staff, along with staff members from the parent organization, meet once a week for a worship service. Twice a year, the ICR program staff goes on retreat with overseas-based division heads (from Africa, Asia, the Caribbean, and South America). Once a year, the leadership team goes on retreat to work on budgets and planning. One other time each year, the entire U.S.-based staff goes on retreat.

Commenting on one of the trickiest facets of running this operation, one executive said,

> ICR always struggles with the question of whether we're going to be a business or a family. This is a major and ongoing struggle. . . . It's particularly important to maintain a supportive atmosphere because we are dealing with emotional issues—suffering, wars, and famines—and we have a different kind of employee, people who are sensitive to these experiences. But we still have to concern ourselves with people's performance, with how well they're doing their jobs.

The recruitment and selection of home office staff are handled in conjunction with the parent organization's personnel department. For senior positions, the organization places advertisements in Christian publications, and otherwise works extensively through church networks. People agree to a faith statement before they can be considered for a position. Hiring authority is in departments. All department heads are being trained to use a very sophisticated process for personnel selection, developed by a widely respected human resources consulting firm. For the most part, the processes for selecting and handling personnel seem to have been working fairly well, as there have been few occasions when ICR has needed to let people go.

On the other hand, there is a clearly felt need for much more careful and regular attention to employee development. Development efforts vary from department to department, with some being more structured than others. According to the director of administration, "The intention is to work more consistently on employee development—including *spiritual* as well as instrumental matters—but it is not happening now. It did in the past, but we got away from it, and we need to make it happen again."

In visiting ICR's offices, one is struck by the strong professional culture of the organization. Most people seem to bring good training and experience and high performance standards to their jobs. The religious culture of the organization is also strong, but generally less obvious. What is obvious, though, after only brief conversations with the professional staff, is the significant tensions

and conflict between the professional expectations typical of such an organization and the personal expectations the staff have for it because it is religious.

## Love in Action

Love in Action (LIA) is another "ecumenical, interdenominational" service
agency that states it is "guided by Christian principles . . . to educate the public
about the plight of the poor and work for peace and justice." It was not among
the groups considered most effective by other Christian service organizations.

It is similar to International Christian Relief in a number of ways. LIA also
is involved primarily in overseas community-development work, and has an
overall operating budget very close in size to ICR's. It is also a young organization, founded in the 1970s, and it is similar to ICR in size.

The differences between the two organizations are striking as well. First,
LIA is an independent organization, having been started by two evangelicals
to address a particular crisis in the third world at a time when immediate relief
services were desperately needed. When that crisis had passed, though, these
individuals chose to continue the organization for the purposes stated above.
LIA's board now consists of the two founders, who are also both full-time, paid
staff members, and seven or eight other people they recruited. Staff members
say it can best be described as a "very passive" board.

Second, LIA operated on a very small scale, never establishing a firm
donor base, until receiving a large government grant in the early 1980s. At that
point, LIA expanded dramatically, increasing its staff manyfold. It still failed,
however, to establish a firm, private donor base. As a result, when those first
government grants expired a couple of years later, the organization had to cut
back severely. A few years after that LIA was able to secure two more government grants, which led to another dramatic expansion. The organization is
now close to the end of those grants, still lacks a significant private constituency, and is again going through severe, painful, and demoralizing cutbacks.
This pattern certainly raises the question, as one staff member put it, of "whether
we are really a para-church or a para-government organization."

Love in Action, like ICR, had an operating budget of about $12 million last
year. Two important differences stand out, however, when one compares the
organizations' financial statements. First, more than $8 million of LIA's income
and expenses (two-thirds) are in the form of "material aid" of gifts-in-kind;
only $4 million is cash support. Second, of the cash, more than $2 million
comes from government grants.

These are especially significant matters for two reasons. First, in the case
of the material aid, we do not have a situation like that at ICR, where all goods

are received, processed, and then shipped by ICR's own staff and volunteers. Rather the materials are received by a freight expediter who sends them overseas for LIA (using government "ocean freight" funds), without any significant evaluation, sorting, or processing by LIA. A portion—perhaps a large part—of these goods is almost surely of little or no value where they end up, but LIA counts the full dollar value of all of them as income and again as program expense.

The implications of this become clear when one realizes that LIA's administrative expenses would go from 10 percent to over 30 percent, and fund-raising costs would go from the 4 percent figure the organization claims to more than 12 percent of total budget if one subtracted the value of this material aid. Furthermore, if one applies even the fund-raising costs to which LIA admits to the cash support it raises from private sources—subtracting material aid and government grants—those costs amount to almost fifty cents on every dollar. Frankly, if one looks closely at the way LIA operates, *all* of its figures for fund-raising and administration are suspect.

Second, there are strings attached to the government support LIA accepts. Despite its evangelical origins and its continuing claim to be "guided by Christian principles," LIA cannot make faith commitment a criterion for hiring because of the conditions of its government grants. All references to religious beliefs in all job descriptions—not just those directly related to the projects the government funds support—had to be removed as a condition of those grants.

One might assume LIA can still hire with faith commitment as an unspoken criterion, and clearly many of the present staff are avowed Christians who came to LIA because of its claim to be motivated and guided by Christian principles. But it is striking that 80 percent of the staff I interviewed did not speak of worship, staff devotions, or prayer as significant factors in the organization's life—whereas the great majority did in all but one of the other organizations I studied. The sentiments of many staff members seemed to be echoed in the observations of one who said, "Honestly, there is little or no emphasis on the spiritual aspects of our work."

Love in Action may never have been as "witness-oriented" as a number of other organizations, but it is fair to say that someone observing the organization now would be left to wonder what marks it as a Christian agency in any noteworthy way. Its choice of programs appears to be driven more by what funds are available than by any clear, coherent sense of mission. Its publicity and fund-raising literature make infrequent and often only indirect references to Christian motivations for and values in the work. There is no explicit effort to work in partnership with indigenous Christians and churches in its project work abroad. And its staff offers comments like, "No, LIA does not reflect Christian values in its operations."

The stark contrast between the experience and operation of LIA and those of some of the other organizations examined raises some pointed questions about what makes a Christian service organization Christian, and how that character can be sustained in the face of various pressures that may undermine it.

## Denominational Service Committee

The Denominational Service Committee (DSC) was begun seventy years ago to provide a channel for members of one small, distinctive denomination in North America to reach out in service to members of that same denomination in another part of the world where they were facing severe hardship. Following that first project, the organization lay dormant for about five years until another similar crisis occurred which brought the members of the denomination together for another major relief effort. In the aftermath of their second project, the members of the denomination were convinced that, despite some large theological and cultural differences among them, it was valuable to have a single service agency through which they could unite in service and witness to the world. A more formal structure for the organization was created, which has continued for the last fifty-five years.

The mission statement of the DSC today says that it exists "to demonstrate God's love through committed women and men who work among people suffering from poverty, conflict, oppression and natural disaster." It goes on to say the workers "minister in the name of Christ," striving for "peace, justice and dignity of all people by sharing [their] experiences, resources, and faith in Jesus Christ." The DSC is the *only denominational* service organization viewed by the population of other Christian relief and development agencies as among the most effective.

The first thing that strikes one about DSC's statement of mission is how clearly it brings people into the foreground of its work—it is "through committed women and men" that this demonstration of God's love will take place. This philosophy is reflected in the projects of the DSC, which are always designed to be small enough in scale to facilitate personal contact. The organization has turned down opportunities to take over larger projects that would have brought significant funding with them, on just these grounds. The object of the DSC's work is never simply to build a well or to teach people soil conservation, but rather, as one staff member put it, to "empower and develop people, to nurture leadership" in the communities in which they work.

This distinctive focus on the personal is also evident in the life of the organization, in that it has always seen one of its primary purposes, according to its executive, as "providing opportunities for [members of the denomination] to live out their faith, making a witness by giving service in the name of

Christ." This has led directly to the extraordinary support the organization enjoys among the members of the denomination. A large number of the members of the denomination have had direct experience with it as volunteers. Roughly 75 percent of the staff are members of the denomination, and at least 70 percent of the DSC's funds come from individuals and congregations within the denomination.

In fact, the members of the denomination look so surely to the DSC to be the service arm of their church that sometimes the funds and volunteers come without the DSC's even asking. One program staff member who works with the DSC-sponsored groups that respond to natural disasters told of the DSC receiving $400,000 in contributions to help clean up after Hurricane Hugo, before the organization even sent out an appeal. In addition, thousands of members came as volunteers under the DSC's auspices to help with that effort.

This view of the connection between denomination and agency is reciprocated in the DSC. Several staff members spoke of how the organization views itself "as a part of the church," or even "as a servant of the church." One long-time volunteer and board member said, "There is a spirit—the mind and spirit of Christ—that pervades the organization; not that we spend a lot of time verbalizing it, but we speak of it unapologetically. And we seek good volunteers, trying to find ways that we can allow committed and caring people to put their gifts into service."

"The church" of which the DSC sees itself a part is not narrowly defined. People who are not members of the denomination are welcomed as volunteers and staff as long as they are committed and active Christians and can affirm the theological stance of the DSC. In the selection process, references with the applicant's own congregation are checked carefully to assure that the person will be comfortable working daily in the context of an organization that is clearly and actively Christian.

In fact, another striking feature of the organization is the way it makes use of volunteers from a variety of backgrounds. In some ways, the distinction between volunteer and staff blurs in the DSC. Volunteers for the DSC range from people who come for a day to people who commit to two- and three-year terms of service. (Long-term volunteers are provided a stipend and medical insurance, but they are still essentially volunteers.) A third of the 180 staff people working in DSC's headquarters are volunteers, and it is not uncommon to have volunteers supervising paid staff. Moreover, volunteers do virtually all of DSC's fund-raising.

This is possible because of the exceptionally strong ties between churches and the committee. The DSC's approaches to fund-raising are remarkably unsophisticated. Outside of two regular fund-raising letters sent out by DSC's executive each year, and special appeals for special needs, the fund-raising is done through congregations and regional denominational structures. There are, in fact, a whole range of special events occurring every year that generate funds for the DSC, and many congregations run ongoing projects—thrift shops and other efforts—to raise funds for the organization.

All this supports a budget that, in 1991, surpassed $35 million and supported projects in more than fifty-five countries. Even excluding more than $10 million worth of material aid—all of it collected, processed, and shipped by DSC staff and volunteers—90 percent of donations went to program work. Fund-raising costs run less than 3 percent, at most.

One more interesting facet of the DSC's approach to resource development is its continuing focus on its own people as a donor base—despite having a reputation that would readily allow it to expand that base—and its refusal, on principle, to build an endowment. I asked several people about this. Their response was that, in the first case, "We wish to draw our support from the people who we represent. This requires us to remain accountable to them." Similarly, in the second case, being dependent for support on the church *as it is today* requires DSC to be responsive to the church's *current sense of mission* in service. In addition, many felt it is wrong to keep funds back in the face of pressing needs, as it is a tenet of faith that God will provide for the work God wants done.

It is not, perhaps, surprising that the DSC would be named as one of the most effective organizations in the terms the survey questionnaire set, as it represents a religious tradition that sees service as the most authentic form of witness—where, as an old adage puts it, one "must walk the walk as well as talk the talk". That theological and cultural foundation accounts for much of the special character and strong support of this organization. Yet DSC too has faced threats (and opportunities) that could have undermined the clarity of its mission and strength of its organizational culture. Examining its evolution in relation to changing circumstances offers some interesting suggestions about how to allow for the creative growth and transformation of a Christian service organization without sacrificing its essential character.

## The Sectarian Charitable Society

The Sectarian Charitable Society (SCS) also represents a small, distinctive denomination, and is also about seventy years old. Unlike the Denominational Service Committee, however, it is not viewed by its peers as one of the most effective international relief and development agencies. In overall size, it is rather similar to the DSC, with roughly the same size budget and a similar number of employees, although the latter comparison is difficult because of the DSC's use of volunteer "staff."

The most obvious and pronounced difference between these two organizations has to do with the relative closeness of the agencies to the denominations they represent. The SCS is no longer accepted as representative of the denomination by the majority of the members of the denomination. In part, this derives from the different nature of the divisions within the denomination that gave birth to the SCS; many of the more "evangelical" members never identified with the SCS's service-oriented mission. However, even between the SCS and a large portion of its traditionally supportive constituency, tensions have mounted in recent years, as the SCS has become more and more a professional development agency and less and less an organization that seeks to provide opportunities for the members of the denomination to practice and express their faith through service.

Indeed, a very small portion of the SCS's staff members are members of the denomination it represents, and such membership is not a significant factor in hiring. In fact, the hiring process generally does not explore an applicant's faith commitment or religious practice. Staff members are expected to agree with certain philosophical stances now typical of the denomination that gave the SCS birth, but they do not have to agree with—or even understand—the theological tenets on which those stances are based.

The topmost staff positions in the SCS have been consistently filled by members of the denomination in recent years—the bylaws require the CEO to be a member—in an effort to retain some semblance of denominational control. Yet even this has now created more problems than solutions. Since the ranks below this top level have long been filled with those who often do not understand the basis of the SCS's original values and decision-making processes, efforts by top management to reaffirm those values—under pressures from the denomination—have often caused serious divisions and tensions in the organization.

In fact, members of the denomination, especially in the last ten or fifteen years, have tried to put pressure on the SCS to move back toward positions more acceptable to a majority of its traditional constituency. This would (presumably) entail hiring more staff members from the denomination, taking stances on social issues that are more "balanced" (or less "radical," or just less "political," depending on your perspective), and developing programs that provide more opportunities for participation by members of the denomination—especially younger members. The denomination's efforts have largely failed, however. This may be in part because the SCS is largely dominated—as are many large nonprofits—by its highly professional staff. But it is also probably a function of the fact the denomination has very little leverage over the organization in terms of resources.

The truth is that the SCS is largely free of dependency for financial support on its parent denomination. Probably 70 percent of its funds come from the functional equivalent of an endowment—planned giving instruments, "annuity and life-income funds"—or from individuals and organizations outside the denomination. (It is hard to determine an exact figure absent a complete breakdown of individual donors.) So the SCS has little stake in being accountable to the denomination and runs minimal financial risks in alienating members of the denomination.

This financial freedom is, ironically, largely a function of the SCS's success. The SCS has been highly effective in developing an endowment (or the equivalent thereof) and was a leader among religious organizations in developing and using planned giving instruments. It has also long had a highly sophisticated, general fund-raising operation which has succeeded in broadening its donor base well beyond the denomination.

Finally, what is at issue in an examination of the SCS is not whether it is a good service agency. Most people, including many of its critics in its own denomination, acknowledge it runs valuable and efficient programs in terms of the delivery of practical services. The question is whether it clearly represents the Christian tradition, or in this case a particular and fairly distinctive branch of the Christian tradition, in that work.

Is just doing good works enough? Perhaps not. It depends on one's perspective. One chief executive—not the CEO of the SCS—commented in an interview,

> It is not enough that we do good work. There are lots of do-gooders out there, and I don't want to put them down because some of them help people in important ways. But if that's all we're doing, it doesn't justify our existence. We're here, and our donors think we're here, to be about building up the kingdom [of God], to point people to the power of God's love by the way we as Christians care for their needs.

Now it is unlikely that anyone in the SCS would ever have used this kind of evangelical language to describe its work. Still, at its founding and for some time thereafter, the SCS clearly was intended to provide an avenue for members of the denomination to express their faith in service, and to "point people to the power of God's love." These no longer seem to be central purposes for the SCS, and examining the SCS's life as an organization offers some interesting insights into how religious service organizations drift away from the witnessing aspect of their missions.

### Gospel Outreach International

Gospel Outreach International (GOI) is a very large agency for an independent Christian service organization, and a very successful organization in conventional terms. It was one of those identified as most effective by its peers. Roughly forty years old, it employs more than 700 people in its U.S. offices and operations, and it relates to a sister organization that actually carries on the work overseas and employs many more. When people hear the name "Gospel Outreach International," they generally picture the work of both organizations, as the distinction between the two would not be clear to anyone not intimately acquainted with the organizations' structure. In fact, GOI is now basically only a fund-raising organization, although it carries on some program work in the United States. Its sister organization relates to other Gospel Outreach organizations in other countries, and together they carry on relief and development projects all over the world.

According to its mission statement, GOI's purpose is "to glorify God by enabling people, through giving and serving, to follow Jesus Christ, Lord and Saviour, in meeting the spiritual and physical needs of the poor throughout the world." The clarity and directness of this statement are striking. GOI's service is intended as an expression of faith. Interestingly, along with the mission statement, there is a "vision statement" provided to employees, also emphasizing faith and works, articulating not only what the organization wants to do but also what it wants to be—how it wants to accomplish its mission. This statement says that GOI is "committed to the personal, professional and spiritual growth [of all employees]. We value each one as a person and as a part of a community of faith gathered for service."

The GOI personnel handbook picks up this theme in a different way, echoing comments that were made in another organization. The handbook describes GOI as "a Christian organization . . . as both a family and a business"; a family because the people "called together" to work in that ministry are part of the "family of God," and a business because it exists "to accomplish a specific purpose." It then goes on to note that "being a family does not excuse us from accomplishing our tasks" and "being a business does not permit the accomplishment of goals at the expense of people."

As a fund-raising organization, GOI appears to be rather effective in accomplishing its objectives. Last year it raised more than $220 million, including $68 million worth of gifts-in-kind. Of cash contributions received, $29 million (or 13 percent of total income) was spent on fund-raising, and $16 million (or 7 percent) was spent on administration in addition to fund-raising. These are reasonable costs, although because of GOI's unusual structure, several cautions should be noted.

First, of the remaining 80 percent of the funds that are listed as going to programs, $97 million (or 44 percent) went to international work, which meant it was passed on to GOI's sister organization. We cannot know, from looking at GOI's financial statements, what additional "administrative costs" are taken there to operate that organization and specific projects. Thus, the true administrative costs involved in running the international projects could be considerably higher than shown.

In addition, GOI shows $17 million going to "public awareness and education." Typically, these are expenses for producing and distributing periodicals, or producing and airing television shows, that talk about the work GOI does and the problems it is trying to address in that work. GOI—and most Christian relief and development agencies—appropriately see educating the public and their donors about problems of poverty, oppression, and injustice in the world as an important part of their mission, but questions about the best ways to do that and how the costs of those efforts should be assigned are significant. For instance, many of the television shows that talk about these issues, whose costs are assigned to "public education," are also primary fund-raising tools. Some agencies bury fund-raising costs in the "public education" category, making them "program" rather than "administrative" costs in order to make themselves look better to potential donors.

In any case, while GOI seems quite successful in terms of accomplishing its goals, the most obvious question that arises in examining this organization is whether this success comes, in fact, despite the words in the personnel manual, "at the expense of people." This is an organization with a remarkable reputation for "burning out" its people, a reputation corroborated in interviews with the present staff. At the professional levels of the organization, turnover is rapid and frequent. Many of the people interviewed commented on very high stress levels and overwork.

Some people attributed this to being understaffed because of efforts to keep administrative costs down. Others suggested it was an outgrowth of an organization that is vested in its own reputation as "high-powered," and is always pushing to accomplish things quickly and with the highest standards. Several facets of organizational structure and policy encourage interpersonal and interdepartmental competition, apparently geared toward boosting productivity; few facets encourage collaboration and community.

This situation appears to create a great deal of frustration—professional, personal, and spiritual—for some employees, which is heightened by the dissonance between GOI's internal dynamics and its emphasis on partnership and collaboration in the ministries it supports. Besides the fact that all this is incongruent with the organization's stated intentions as a Christian agency, one also wonders what the practical and financial costs are of the employee turnover it generates.

Another feature of GOI that bears comment is a result of its unusual structure, which largely separates fund-raising and program into two separate organizations. I saw in several other organizations the tensions, sometimes destructive, between the fund-raising elements and the program elements. The pressing question in a number of these organizations was whether they were going to be "funding-driven" or "program-driven." That is, was the organization going to select programs on the basis of a clear sense of mission and then seek funds to support those efforts, or choose programs in terms of what the organization can see others are willing to support financially?

One strength of GOI's structure is that it may largely defuse this tension. GOI's sister organization selects programs to pursue with its partners because of the way the programs fit the mission and goals, and then asks GOI and the partner agencies to fund them. Obviously, there is consultation around what kinds of programs are easier or harder to fund, and what kinds of resources are more readily garnered. But this kind of arrangement makes it less likely that new programs that are not in keeping with the organization's mission will be started simply because some fund-raiser has identified a potential donor.

On the other hand, this makes the fund-raisers' work more difficult in some respects because they are less involved in the actual work they are trying to support, and so lack a first-hand understanding of it and direct inspiration from it. Several people on GOI's staff spoke of the problem of feeling a step removed from the actual ministry, and this problem is more intense for those in functions—like data processing—that are further removed from either donors or ministry.

In the end, the most prominent question arising from an examination of GOI may have to do with how large a Christian organization can become while still retaining a Christian organizational culture that is satisfying to employees. GOI seems to have adapted several structural features that undermine its stated intentions for the kind of workplace it wants to be. Some of these appear to derive from the organization's assimilation of conventional secular expectations about how successful businesses are run. Others may be simply a result of its size. Perhaps there are other models from secular businesses for creating smaller, more manageable work environments and still retaining the necessary integration (for example, Ackoff, 1981) that GOI would do well to consider.

Regardless, its present configuration and operations offer a variety of insights into the possibilities and problems of managing Christian service organizations.

## Caring for the Children

Caring for the Children (CFC) emerged from the survey process as the fourth organization rated most effective by other Christian relief and development agencies. According to its "statement of corporate purpose" it was formed—approximately forty years ago—to "extend love and compassion by ministering to needy children, releasing them from the bondage of poverty and enabling them to become . . . through support, education, training and guidance, Christian in faith and deed; responsible members of their families, churches, and communities; self-supporting and able to share with others in need; and able to maintain their own physical well being." More simply stated, CFC understands itself to be engaged in a "Christian ministry of child development."

Last year CFC raised and spent almost $40 million on projects in twenty-seven countries. All of that support came from private sources—CFC accepts no government grants—and only about 10 percent was in the form of gifts-in-kind. Almost 150,000 children were "sponsored" and benefited by CFC's efforts, and many more children were helped, for when a school, clinic, or other program is developed in a community, other children (in addition to those who are sponsored) may take advantage of some services offered.

CFC understands itself to be an "interdenominational, ecumenical, Christian organization"; however, its ecumenism embraces primarily the evangelical Christian community. The faith statement one is expected to affirm as a member of CFC's staff is that of the National Association of Evangelicals (which is, in fact, the faith statement most of the organizations studied use for these purposes). And there is no question but that its focus on bringing Jesus Christ—as well as educational, health, and social programs—to the children it serves reflects CFC's evangelical character.

Still, while some may think of a tendency to be closed off from and distrustful of the secular world when they think of evangelicals, a visit to CFC gives a wholly different impression. The organization was entirely open and helpful to me. I had free access to virtually all records; its officers, including the CEO and chief operating officer (COO), gave me exceptional amounts of time for interviews; and everyone I interviewed was candid and forthcoming.

Several aspects of CFC are immediately noteworthy. One is the sense of commitment and common focus that seem to permeate the staff. Every person

I talked with, from senior executives to secretaries, could tell me about the history of the organization, describe the considerable range of its programs, and talk in detail about its philosophy of and approach to the ministry of child development. In addition, there was a visible respect and genuine warmth between staff members that seemed to be rooted in their sense of sharing both a ministry and a common faith in which that ministry was rooted.

Another striking feature of the organization was the clarity and rationality of policies and procedures that had been formulated to ensure the organization stays focused in that ministry and pursues it in keeping with previously articulated principles. So, for example, one can see obvious relationships between the commitment to an integrated, wholistic philosophy for a child-development ministry that CFC has articulated; the manner in which the organization designs and implements projects; and the manner in which it raises funds for those projects.

Thus, the CFC policy book says, "We believe in ministering to the whole person. People are neither 'soulless stomachs' nor 'stomachless souls.' " In planning projects the organization always tries to work in partnership with local Christians to strengthen the local church, and then to provide a variety of programs—for instance, regular school programs, health education, and religious education—to touch many aspects of a child's life. And in seeking support for these projects, CFC chooses to use "child sponsorship" as a fund-raising tool because this provides a mechanism that, beyond raising funds, also creates a relationship between a caring adult Christian and the child wherein the adult can contribute emotional support, counsel, and prayer, as well as money, to support that child's development.

Third, the organization is consistent, even zealous in its concern for maintaining absolute integrity in all its financial dealings. CFC's policy book says all its financial policies are based on 2 Corinthians, 8:20–21, "We want to avoid any criticism of the way we administer this liberal gift. For we are taking pains to do what is right, not only in the eyes of the Lord but also in the eyes of men." This concern for integrity is manifest in a number of ways. For instance, CFC has chosen not to assign any expenses to "public awareness and education" in its budget, even though the organization has produced a number of videos on the circumstances of women and children in the third world as educational tools, which make virtually no mention of CFC's work much less ask for money. The director of finance explained, "We know some groups use that category to hide administrative and fund-raising costs. We want to be above any suspicion about that."

Another manifestation of this concern is CFC's handling of gifts-in-kind. Again, the organization knows this can be used to inflate operating statements to make organizations look more efficient than they are, and it also knows these goods are often not provided in a way that is truly useful to development work. They can sometimes be valuable, however. So, CFC does two things. It accepts gifts-in-kind only when they are really needed in CFC projects, and it has a policy that these gifts can never account for more than 15 percent of overall contributions in any year. Finally, CFC runs an internal statement without the gifts-in-kind so the organization knows what its fiscal situation really is at any point.

Finally, the concern for efficiency evident in every aspect of the organization is impressive, but so is the thoughtful way in which efficiency is pursued, so that it does not become an end in itself and undermine other goals. The controller of the organization commented that CFC has to be very careful in fiscal matters because it already has to deal with the fact that "child sponsorship" is a relatively costly way to raise funds. On the other hand, CFC is committed to this approach for other reasons, having to do with the quality of the ministry it offers. Thus, it has tried to make itself as efficient as possible in other ways.

This effort has included a great deal of formal planning, particularly in the areas of data processing and financial management. Because of such planning, the organization is handling four times the financial work it did ten years ago, with only twice the staff, and almost ten times as many sponsored children with only a fourfold increase in staff. (This is an operation in which economies of scale are not great.) In addition, the serious investment CFC has made in staff development has been fruitful.

Despite all of its attention to efficiency and planning, however, CFC remains an obviously and intentionally religious organization. Most staff people are there because they identify strongly with the ministry the organization undertakes and want to be part of it. Furthermore, all of the staff people I interviewed talked about the importance of staff devotional activities and the significance of prayer in their work.

These elements of the organization's life reinforce an organizational culture created by the careful selection of staff members for their spiritual commitments as well as professional competency. Applicants for a job with CFC are not merely asked to sign a statement of faith; they are asked to write their own. (This is also the practice in the Denominational Service Committee.) And two of the references, which are checked, are from the pastor and another member of the applicant's congregation.

The evidence of the practical effectiveness of CFC's work is quite remarkable. One example given me was that, during the recent cholera epidemic sweeping through parts of South America, there has not been a single case among children and families connected with CFC projects, despite the fact many project sites are in areas where the epidemic has been most intense. CFC staff attribute this to the health-education components of their project work.

In light of that record, I inquired as to why CFC did not try to reach out to a broader support base to enable it to extend and expand its work. The organization gave two reasons for being cautious in this regard. First, the staff said they have known for years they could expand operations rapidly; they have chosen a policy of slow growth to ensure program quality. The records indicate a growth rate between 8 percent and 15 percent each year for the last decade. The CEO said, "We were concerned with the effects of growth on sound oversight of program quality, and on our ability to absorb and orient new staff to the essential values of our organization." CFC has placed both program quality and organizational integrity above opportunities for growth.

Second, the staff said that, while they want to reach out to a larger part of the evangelical population, they did not think it was fruitful to try to include most people outside that group. That is because of their view of the child-sponsor relationship, which they see as being as much spiritual as financial, and as providing a ministry to the donor as well as the child. The director of communication said, "We like to have Christian people as sponsors because we believe that can have a ministry to their child through their letters and prayer. We also believe these children can have a ministry to their sponsors." And the COO described CFC's mission by saying, "We have a mandate to minister to needy children there, and caring people here. All our [staff] people understand that and are encouraged to ask themselves how they are serving *both* these groups."

The COO's observation about what was asked of staff people led me to ask how CFC avoided problems with staff burnout. Clearly, the staff were very dedicated to the work, and the needs they were trying to meet were ever pressing. Furthermore, this staff got an extraordinary amount of work done. Yet no one I interviewed spoke of being stressed out or overworked. The COO's reply was that this was a place where the president of CFC both stated the organization's values and set an example. Everyone was told that the organization affirmed the priorities of "God first, family second, and the work of the ministry third." The president exemplified those priorities in the way he handled his job, and policies were enforced—for instance, around compensatory time—to make these the operative values of the organization.

In fact, CFC seemed to have profited from careful and enlightened leadership in many respects. Everyone spoke well of the president, and even when people cited some weakness in his performance, they did so with respect for his ability to choose other people around him who could make up for it. Everyone also spoke well of a helpful, active, and committed board.

Caring for the Children offers a remarkable example of a highly effective, values-expressive Christian service organization. It offers us a number of insights on how to address issues of management in Christian service organizations.

## Christian Community Services

Christian Community Services (CCS) is the one community-based Christian service agency with a local service focus included in this study. It is an agency with a national reputation for being extremely well managed, highly effective in service delivery to the local community, and strong in its Christian witness. It is in the unusual situation of carrying on a strong program of evangelism as well as service, and still being supported by corporate donors in its community, apparently because it is among the most effective agencies in caring for the homeless in that community, providing youth services, and running a highly regarded substance abuse program.

CCS was founded sixty years ago by representatives of area churches "to provide food, clothing, shelter and spiritual aid to the homeless and needy." It belongs to a loose-knit network of similar organizations found in many cities across the country. Strongly evangelical in its theology, it has been providing services and Christian outreach to those in need in the city where it is located for many years. Originally, its clientele was primarily male indigents, often with alcohol-abuse problems. In recent years, that clientele has grown to include a much broader range of people.

While CCS still runs a shelter that is the largest in its community, providing up to 400 beds on an emergency basis, it also now operates out of four other sites. These include its administrative headquarters, warehouse, and youth center; a family shelter; a special building for its substance-abuse programs and counseling offices; and a thrift store that both provides work for people in CCS's programs and income for the operation. The men's and family shelters do not just provide emergency housing, but also are the site for a number of programs to help those in need of aid get "back on their feet"—getting sober, recovering emotional stability, acquiring job skills and counseling, finding affordable housing, and coming to faith in Jesus Christ.

All this activity is supported by a budget of over $4 million, which pays for a staff of roughly 110 people, augmented by over 500 volunteers. This represents enormous growth over the last twelve years. In 1979 CCS employed only sixteen people, with a budget of $300,000.

If one is curious about the integration of service and witness in this context, the original mission statement of CCS commands one's attention. It states the organization's purpose is "the preaching of the Gospel of Jesus Christ by carrying on . . . mission work in this city, . . . and to carry on such work as may be necessary or convenient for the spiritual, moral and physical welfare of those with whom it may work." It goes on to note that "any phase of the work other than direct evangelism shall be kept entirely subordinate and only taken on so far as necessary or helpful to the spiritual work."

For some, this kind of language may evoke images of people offering others meals only as a ploy to get them to listen to a sermon. And it is true that those who come to the CCS shelter can get a meal ticket free, instead of paying one dollar, if they sit through services first. But to see this as some sort of trickery is to misunderstand the vision and faith that inspire the CCS people to provide the services they offer.

Perhaps the most striking feature of the approach to service that the programs and workers of CCS seem to embody is the sense that commitment to caring for people's physical and commitment to caring for their spiritual needs are inseparable. This view is captured in what the director of the men's program said, when he told me, "We give these men clothes and a meal and a place to sleep, and whatever we can, but all these things are given to give them hope, and to point them to Jesus Christ." The director was himself an alcoholic whose life had been turned around, forty years earlier, when he was given shelter and a chance to hear the Gospel at a similar institution in another city.

This sentiment, that really to help people one must give them faith, was repeated in a variety of ways by staff people in other programs many times in the course of my visit to CCS. The director of another program observed, "There are many things we can and should do for these men, *but what they need most is hope*. When we give them Christ we give them that, and their lives really begin to change."

To build a staff that is capable of working within this philosophy of service, CCS makes an active faith commitment a first consideration in hiring. In fact, in the shelters and programs that work with the homeless, many of the lower-level staff are people who came through the CCS programs and did well. Since all of these programs include a "discipleship" element, as well as counseling and other elements that help the participants stabilize their lives, that means these "graduates" will come with the kind of faith commitment CCS is looking for in addition to an immediate understanding of the clientele's problems. The director of the men's program said, "We value having these men [who have been through the program] on staff because we know their faith commitment, and we know they know how we do things and why."

In addition, at the professional levels, for directors and chaplains for these programs, CCS has a preference for people who have an experiential base with the problems they are addressing, as well as professional training. The director of the shelters told me that, when he was looking for someone to direct a new substance-abuse program, he "wanted someone who had been through that [a recovering addict or alcoholic], who also had the drive to get some training." When he could not find someone like this, with both theological training and counseling skills, he opted for someone who had the experience and theological perspective, and then sent him for the training in counseling.

Of course, raising $4 million a year to support all these activities is no small task, and contributions account for 90 percent of CCS's income. Last year, CCS spent about $500,000 to raise those funds, and the integration of witness and service are evident in fund-raising as well as in the program.

The director of development looks on CCS's fund-raising efforts as an important extension of the organization's ministry. He says, "Development [in this context] is a ministry where we create opportunities for God's people to be involved in God's work." He believes, in addition, that development efforts serve important functions for CCS as it tries to serve the church "first, by educating people about homeless and hurting people; second, by educating people about the practice of stewardship; and third, teaching people how to care in a practical, meaningful way."

Building on this understanding, one of the ways the director of development changed CCS's fund-raising efforts—he came to the organization two years ago—was to place more emphasis on religious themes. He took an effort to develop a large group of regular givers, which had focused on the practical needs to be met, and rebuilt it around a story from the New Testament, focusing on the opportunity to give as an expression of discipleship. This reframing of the fund-raising enterprise in more *explicitly religious* terms, in keeping with CCS's overall character, has been very effective, quadrupling the income from this group of regular donors in just two years.

CCS works with people who are often in desperate need, which places extraordinary demands on staff. I asked the chief executive how he dealt with this, and he spoke of the need to create an atmosphere in which people feel supported. He regularly visits all the sites to get a sense of what is going on and what demands the staff face. Regular worship, retreats, and opportunities for professional and spiritual development are part of the organization's activities. The chief executive avoids excessive overtime and keeps a "regular" schedule, making clear that he expects the staff to do the same. Finally, everyone is encouraged to see CCS as "a body" (building on the scriptural theme), with each part having its part to play, and no one being expected to carry the whole load alone.

He indicated his own work is made easier by the support of a strong board. He helps recruit and train people for that board, but they then take a free and active role in oversight of the organization, especially with respect to resource development, human resource management, and program development. The CEO sees the board as a strong asset to the organization in its growth over recent years.

Last, CCS has specific expectations and understandings about administration. The business manager told me he sees the administrative staff's role as being purely supportive. He believes the organization's focus has rightly been on programs, refining existing ones and creating new ones as needs in the community become apparent. The administrative side of the organization has been developed "simply to provide service to the programs so they can do what they should do." This, he believes, has kept the administrative machinery of CCS appropriately small, and allowed the organization to grow with flexibility.

## Summary and Conclusions

What has just been presented is, obviously, the barest of summaries of observations from many days visiting each of these organizations and many more studying their materials. There are far more fascinating aspects and details of each of them than can be presented in a brief precis, and additional points of comparison and contrast among them that will be brought out later.

Still, this summary tells us that there are a number of significant issues and questions with which all these organizations wrestle, which revolve around common themes and relate to certain administrative functions. Questions about whether they are going to be more like a family (or church) or a business; whether they will choose programs and structures based on their own sense of mission or the availability of funding; whether the mission they articulate is going to be defined more by their need to serve the church (or constituency that founded or now supports them) or by the particular needs of the people they might assist—these are all questions that all the organizations seem to confront. Moreover, in dealing with these issues, the functions of the management of personnel and organizational culture, the approaches to fund-raising and resource development, and the executives' and board members' roles in leadership and planning seem, in various combinations, to be crucial factors in determining organizational effectiveness.

These are the matters we explore further in the chapters that follow, drawing examples and illustrations from the organizations described here. We will turn first, though, to a general overview of the roles and functions of management in Christian service organizations.

# 6

## Management of a Ministry

### *The Function of Management in Christian Service Organizations*

WHAT IS MANAGEMENT, and what are its functions in the operation of any organization? According to James Stoner and Charles Wankel, "Management is the process of planning, organizing, leading and coordinating the efforts of organization members and of using all other organizational resources to achieve stated goals" (1986, p. 4). This definition is deceptively simple and straightforward. One might even think, in light of such a definition, that management can be something of a science, reducible to formulas that simply have to be used in the right combinations and adapted to the circumstances of different organizations. Of course, anyone who has ever been responsible for running an organization will know that this is, unfortunately, not true. Management is rarely, if ever, so simple.

Peter Drucker, whom many see as the father of modern management, says that, while "the work of a manager can be analyzed and classified . . . management can never be an exact science" (1954, p. 9). This is because some of the elements of management in the definition above—for instance, "leading"—involve human relationships and subjective judgments that are unpredictable and impossible to quantify. Furthermore, usefully adapting any set of management concepts and techniques to specific circumstances frequently requires capacities for vision, discernment, and intuition that cannot be taught.

Indeed, images of the work of management prominent in management literature today—"thriving on chaos" (Peters, 1987), or "permanent white water" (Vaill, 1989)—indicate the high probability that disorder is more common than order in the experience of many organizations, or at least in organizations' relationships to their environments. This same literature also tells us, as did the organizational theories discussed earlier, that tending to those environments with all their vagaries is at least as important for management as dealing with the interior of an organization. This further erodes the likelihood that management can be a purely rational endeavor. This literature suggests that management is becoming an increasingly complex function in a rapidly changing world.

Both our examination of organizational theories and the data that emerged from the studies of Christian service organizations in action confirm the complexity and difficulty of managing those organizations. The business of "planning, organizing, leading and coordinating" the activities of many staff people working on different tasks in different countries, and of "planning, organizing, leading and coordinating" the efforts to explain their work to those who might be interested and able to support it, is not a simple business. There are, nevertheless, some central concepts and issues that emerge from those studies to highlight key concerns for Christian service organizations, and that may usefully serve as organizing principles for further inquiry about how these organizations—and others like them—should be managed.

From those studies and our consideration of organizational theories arise three issues that require management attention and on which we can profitably focus this inquiry. One has to do with defining organizations' missions and, closely related, defining effectiveness. The second has to do with assuring (and defending) "organizational integrity"—making sure that an organization is and can continue to be what it claims to be. The third has to do with the way Christian service organizations prepare themselves for their (hoped-for) future, especially in terms of accumulating resources and planning.

## Articulating a Mission and Defining "Effectiveness"

One excellent nonprofit manager I know says that all the serious dilemmas in operating nonprofit organizations relate to what she calls "the three M's: mission, management and money." "The problem," she says,

is that people tend to concern themselves with the wrong 'M' first. They tend to see most things in terms of money; thinking about what their organization could do if only it had more money, or what it cannot do because it doesn't have as much money as they wish. But in fact, that is usually the last thing they should worry about. I believe that if an organization can define and articulate its mission in terms that are clear enough and compelling enough, and put in place structures and processes for achieving its goals that are obviously appropriate, then raising the money it needs will not be a problem.

This manager does not mean to say, I am sure, that fund-raising is unimportant or can be taken for granted, but rather that the most important elements for management to focus on in nonprofit organizations are the articulation of their mission and the development of organizational capacities, structures, and procedures that will make the achievement of the mission possible. Absent those elements, no amount of money raised will make an organization "successful," and raising any amount of money is likely to be difficult.

If my friend's thumbnail analysis of the tasks of nonprofit management is correct, then a number of interesting and significant questions follow. The first has to do with the nature of an organization's mission, and how it is determined.

## Mission Statements

The view that defining an organization's mission is the first and most crucial task of management—in any context—is shared by many. Peter Drucker says, "It is the first responsibility of top management to ask the question 'what is our business?' and to make sure that it is carefully studied and correctly answered" (1954, p. 50). Drucker, writing about for-profit organizations, says the way to determine the "correct" answer for this question is by studying "the want the consumer satisfies [when buying] a product or a service" (p. 50).

For nonprofit philanthropic organizations, however, mission determination by this method is problematic. First, there is the question, Who is the consumer? Is it the person who uses the service provided or the person who pays for it, the contributor? For philanthropic organizations, these are usually not one and the same. Second, even if we agree to define the consumer as the recipient of the service, we still need to ask whether missions should be defined by the needs of society or individuals (as they would make demands on these organizations), or by the intentions of the individuals who create and support these organizations, so long as the organizations are genuinely serving public purposes?

If we accept the idea that missions should be defined—that is, the organizations' agendas should be set—by the needs to be met, then the missions are going to be subject to change as needs change, or some organizations are going to go out of business. In fact, some organizations redefine their mission over time, and others fold. In the first instance, there is the noteworthy example of the March of Dimes, which started as an organization dedicated to finding a cure for polio. When its mission was achieved, it had to find another cause or go out of business. (As a number of the organizational theories we looked at earlier would predict, it found another cause.) In the second instance, there are many smaller—especially community-based—service organizations that are born and die as the problems or conditions that they are created to address emerge, change, or even (occasionally) are resolved.

For most organizations a change of mission is a purely practical matter, without normative ramifications. When a business decides to change the field within which it will work or the type of product or service it will sell, so long as its obligations to its stockholders and stakeholders are met, there is little ground for objection. Again, even when nonprofits change their mission, so long as they still serve the public good in a manner appropriate for them and acceptable to their stakeholders, few serious objections can be raised. However, when we look at religious organizations, the situation may be different.

When we look at how the missions of Christian organizations are defined, we discover a new factor, unique to this sphere, for many Christian organizations will claim to be involved in the work they have undertaken as a matter of "calling." They will claim, at the least, that their mission is a response to a divine mandate found in Scripture, and may well claim that it derives from more immediate religious inspiration, from a "burden laid on the heart" of the founder(s), to carry on a specific ministry for a specific group of people. Clearly, if some organization's mission derives from such sources, altering that mission has profound moral and spiritual as well as practical implications.

One lesson in the Bible is that one cannot just walk away from God's call to service or alter God-given responsibilities of discipleship once they have been accepted. From the lives of the prophets to the lives of Jesus' disciples, we see in the Scriptures a long history of God's relationships with those who choose to walk in faith, a record of relationships that tells us that, when people acknowledge and accept a call to ministry, they are obligated to stay with it, unless God releases them from it. (For example, see the Book of Jonah.) It is fair to assume that organizations that choose to place themselves in the same tradition of discipleship exist under the same obligations.

In this context, we should note that two of the most effective organizations in the study, Gospel Outreach International and Caring for the Children, began under such circumstances. In both instances, they were started by evangelists who, on preaching trips abroad, were confronted by the plight of the poor in the countries where they traveled. In both cases, these men found themselves "with a burden"—by their own understanding, from God—to do something about what they saw. So they founded these organizations with their stated missions to carry on their ministries. In both cases, the founders have since died, but for the organizations founded to carry these "burdens" and entrusted with these ministries to change their missions to do other work given these origins would be to take an action with serious spiritual and moral as well as practical significance.

The definition and articulation of an organization's mission can be seen—in this perspective, should be seen—as management's most important work.

For these purposes, we must include in "management" the board or trustees, for in practice the definition or clarification of mission should be a primary responsibility of whatever group is finally accountable for an organization and its actions, which is legally and ethically the board or trustees. If a basic task of a board or trustee body is to set policies and review programs to ensure that they all work together toward the attainment of the ends for which an organization was formed, then obviously that body must understand and be able to state clearly what those ends are.

Why is it so important to be clear about an organization's mission? Russell Ackoff says,

A mission is a very general purpose that can endow everyone in an organization and all they do with a sense of purpose. A mission can mobilize an organization into concerted action. It can be to planning what the Holy Grail was to the crusades: a vision of something strongly desired accompanied by a commitment to its pursuit. (1981, p. 107)

If we accept Ackoff's claim, it appears that the key to formulating or articulating a mission, for a philanthropic organization at least, lies in framing the statement so that it is broad enough to indicate, for society or the world, the real value and significance of the work to be done, and yet specific enough to engage and interrelate the interests of the different kinds of participants the organization may need to attract—for example, staff people with different backgrounds and expertise and, perhaps, a wide range of contributors. What is more, in both these aspects, the question of the manner in which the mission is articulated as well as the substance of the statement is crucial because, to give the organization legitimacy and attract the participants needed, a mission statement needs to make a *compelling* case for the organization and the work it wishes to undertake.

Yet, in addition to these functions of a mission and mission statement, which have to do primarily with relating an organization to its external environment, the mission statement has a critical internal function as well. Again, as Ackoff describes it, "A mission statement is much more than a specification of a role for a system [organization, in society]. A mission is a purpose that integrates the variety of roles that a system plays" (1981, p. 107). In the discussion from which this observation comes, Ackoff is primarily concerned with the different roles any one organization may play in society—as service provider, employer, consumer, and such. However, by addressing this reality, a good mission statement may also illumine the different facets within an organization's operations that need to be integrated in its life and work, and may suggest how that integration is to be achieved.

Obviously, this is of special concern for Christian service organizations if they wish to combine service and witness. How can their mission statements highlight this unique element in their work, and help those responsible for carrying out that work remember this integration is part of their task? The mission statements, or statements of corporate purpose, of a couple of these organizations provide us some examples.

Perhaps the most striking example of this is one we have already considered, that of Christian Community Services. Recall that while the organization was founded to "preach the Gospel of Jesus Christ by carrying on . . . such work as may be necessary or convenient for the spiritual, moral and physical welfare of those with whom it may work," its mission statement goes on to note that "any phase of the work other than direct evangelism shall be kept entirely subordinate and only taken on so far as necessary or helpful to the spiritual work." In other words, CCS is committed to providing a Christian witness and practical services, and the operation must be organized to ensure that witness and service always go hand in hand. Or, as a recent annual report puts it, CCS believes it is to be "as James 1:22 says, [a] doer of the Word."

Similarly, the mission statement of the Denominational Service Committee says it "seeks *to demonstrate God's love* through committed men and women who work among people suffering from poverty, conflict, oppression and natural disaster" (emphasis mine). The mission is an integrated commitment to witness and service. Explaining its work in a related document, the DSC says, "We strive *to embody the values and insights of [our] faith community* in our ministries" (emphasis mine).

Finally, the statement of corporate purpose of Caring for the Children says the organization was formed to "extend love and compassion by ministering to needy children" and goes on to spell out the practical and spiritual aspects of this commitment. What is unique about CFC's mission statement, however, is that it extends to include donors, believing they also have a commitment to "people . . . with a burden to care for children," which may be met by "increasing their [the donors'] awareness of the needs of children; offering a viable opportunity for response; and extending to them [the donors] a response of compassionate appreciation, love, and prayer." Here an integrated vision of mission is complete, encompassing *all* the participants in the process, those who provide support for the services to be delivered as well as the primary recipients.

The two organizations studied that were not viewed as most effective by their peers have, in the case of the Sectarian Charitable Society, no mission statement, and in the case of Love in Action, a mission statement that claims but subordinates the facet of making a witness. In the first instance, it seems plausible that the fact that SCS never tried to articulate the place and functions of the values-expressive elements of its work has contributed to the erosion of those elements. In the second case, it would seem LIA's present mission statement is (at best) a half-accurate portrayal of the organization's character. Recall its own employees say that "there is little or *no* emphasis on the spiritual aspects of [its] work" (emphasis mine).

However eloquent a mission statement may be, though, it cannot assure that an organization will do good work. We noted before that one crucial reason for trustees to be clear about their organization's purposes is that they are the ones who are finally responsible for assessing whether their organization is attaining those purposes. In other words, one value of a good mission statement is that it can provide a foundation for assessing an organization's effectiveness, for making the judgments that the trustees have a responsibility to make and act on if improvements are needed. But the concept of "effectiveness" is an ambiguous one, and one we should examine further.

## *Defining and Measuring Effectiveness*

What do we mean when we say an organization is effective? This is never an absolute judgment. To know what it means, we need to know who is making the judgment and on what grounds. As W. Richard Scott suggests, when someone says an organization is highly effective, to understand that claim we need to know "what types of criteria [for measuring effectiveness] are [being] proposed by what constituencies, and what types of indicators of effectiveness are proposed with what implications for organizational assessment" (1987, p. 319).

In addition to having a clear statement of purpose or mission then, management—including a board or trustees—should also be concerned with defining performance standards for the organization in its efforts to fulfill its mission, and with understanding what set of outcomes of the organization's work can fairly be seen to provide an adequate indication of success or failure in this regard. This is important for several reasons.

First, unreasonably low performance standards may lead to an organization's never attaining its goals or even making serious progress toward them. Unreasonably high standards may lead to serious demoralization and other problems for an organization and its staff. Consider the case of Gospel Outreach International: why is GOI's staff so stressed?

The director of personnel hypothesizes that the stress is largely a result of the unrealistic expectations that permeate the organization. "Seeing the faces of the starving poor," he says, "there are people on [GOI's senior] staff that respond by setting goals that reflect their sense of urgency rather than a clear perspective on what it is possible for GOI to do." Then, many people on that staff, coming to this work out of a sense of identification with those in need, and with the calling to minister to them that GOI articulates as its mission, feel like they can never do enough. Add to this the senior executives' sense that administrative costs must be kept down, not just to look good to donors but also out of a sense of moral obligation to put as much of the money raised as possible toward programs, and you find a tendency to be understaffed and to do much less for staff development than is needed. The result is serious problems.

What appears to be happening is that inappropriate criteria for effectiveness have been established for GOI's performance. What is more, not only are the goals unrealistic, they are also being shaped by the wrong indicators. Criteria that are easily quantified, like the percentage of costs going to administration, the number of new donors, the percentage of donors retained, the number of new projects, and the number of people served, appear to have become the *only* criteria *really* considered in assessments of the organization's performance. Not that these measures are unimportant, but they have to be balanced by other considerations.

For example, none of the present measures tells much about how effective GOI is in "glorifying God by enabling people through giving and serving to follow Jesus Christ," even though this is the first objective in GOI's mission statement. In fact, the present criteria may be guiding GOI to behavior that has precisely the opposite effect, driving people out of the organization who want to "glorify God through giving and serving," and leaving them cynical about that mission. The director of personnel described the exit-interview comments of employees who had resigned, which included such remarks as, "GOI is like an orange juice squeezer. They drain all that you have to give, and then they just discard you." One has to ask if such results bespeak good stewardship, whatever the high motivations of senior executives that set the policies that cause them. What are the costs to GOI in recruiting and training replacements, given a high level of turnover in professional staff, and what are the costs in lost productivity?

A second problem with allowing inappropriate criteria for effectiveness to dominate organizational assessment is evident in the GOI case. The wrong criteria, instead of measuring an organization's attainment of its goals, may distort those goals. Thus, a Christian service organization that has come to review its work largely in terms of increases (or rates of increase) in numbers of projects or people served, growth in its donor base, or growth in its income, may also begin to find that its primary operative goals are no longer to serve as much as they are to grow. One staff member at GOI commented that he worries about the organization's "reputation for power, flash, and glitz. We spend way too much money on flash and glitz," he said, "and there may be a tendency to compromise our principles, . . . to be first in the field, to make the most powerful appeal."

It is interesting to contrast this with an organization like CFC, which has eschewed rapid growth and a high profile to ensure program quality and continue to work through and empower indigenous Christians and churches in its work. What are the effectiveness criteria CFC employs? This organization is concerned with administrative and fund-raising costs, with the character of its relationship with its donors, and with its donors' relationships with the children they help. CFC takes quantifiable measurements of its work, looking, for example, at health statistics and improvements in literacy, school attendance, and employment. It also, however, asks about how the congregational life of the local church and that church's witness in its community have been strengthened.

Another question to be raised about defining effectiveness, as Scott (1987) again points out, is, From whose point of view is this judgment to be made? In an industrial organization, what management views as appropriate criteria for measuring the effectiveness of an organization—for example, profit margins—may not be a good measure from labor's perspective; labor may prefer to look at increases in jobs available and improvements in wages and working conditions. Do similar incongruities exist among the various participants in Christian service organizations?

If one of the primary reasons people work for or give to these organizations is that they identify with the organizations' espoused goals, then there are likely to be fewer and less-pronounced incongruities between the various participants' views of what constitutes effectiveness for them. Rather, the most likely place for incongruities to arise is between those within these organizations and the broader public, which may not always understand or agree with the organizations' goals. Thus, for example, when an organization like CFC chooses to use a more expensive fund-raising mechanism to support its work, increasing its administrative costs, because of the benefits in terms of spiritual growth that may accrue to donors and children through the use of this mechanism, it is decreasing the possibility it can persuade people who do not already share its Christian perspective to support its work.

Fortunately, in CFC's case, the organization has already decided it does not wish to try to expand its base of support in that way. However, an organization's interest in presenting itself positively outside its faith community can have potentially damaging—or, at least, mission-altering—effects when the organization is not so clear about its goals and processes. Look again, for instance, at Love in Action's treatment of gifts-in-kind. In its desire to appear efficient to potential donors, it has taken to accepting, handling, and accounting for these donations in a manner that raises serious questions about its integrity and almost certainly wastes valuable resources.

## Key Questions about Mission and Effectiveness

How shall the management—including the board or trustees—of a Christian service organization define, clarify, and articulate that organization's mission, and subsequently consider and define what constitutes effective performance for that organization? These tasks are among management's most important responsibilities. I propose here a list of key questions, which are fairly simple but have profound implications, that boards and managers and anyone else concerned about the life and performance of Christian service organizations should consider when thinking about their missions and effectiveness.

1. *Whom does this organization wish to serve?* This emerges as a key question when we see how much the definition of a Christian service organization's mission may be altered when the organization is seen as serving the church as well as the people outside the church whose particular practical needs it is trying to address.

2. *How does this organization intend to serve these people?* Is it simply trying to meet some concrete, practical need, or also (as the staff kept saying at CCS) to "give them hope?" If the mission includes giving hope, does that require preaching to those served? Or is providing the example of Christian love and a Christian life (presumably, with a willingness to explain one's motivations if asked) sufficient? If the second is sufficient, how important is the "collective witness" of the way the organization operates and its people work together within it, in addition to workers' individual efforts? Is what the organization *is* as important as what it does?

3. *What does the organization need, and what must it be, to be able to render the service desired?* What participants—staff, volunteers, contributors—are needed? What type of people must they be, not only as professionals but as persons? What quantity and type of resources are needed? What kinds of incentives and opportunities can and should the organization offer to induce people to provide that support?

4. *How will the organization know if its mission is being fulfilled?* What results, changes, or outcomes will be visible among those served, those who support the organization, and those who work for it if the mission is being fulfilled? How will the organization itself look and act if it is being true to its mission?

I believe that, if the board and managers of a Christian service organization can answer these questions to their own and their supporters' and participants' satisfaction, they will be able to articulate the mission of their organization with clarity and power. They will then be ready to make a reasonable and helpful assessment of how effective the organization is in fulfilling its mission.

## Assuring Organizational Integrity

Two of the seven organizations in Chapter 5, and many other agencies in the religious and nonprofit worlds, offer examples of organizations that started out to do and be one thing and ended up doing and being something else. Organizations, like people, evolve over time, sometimes for better and sometimes for worse. The patterns of that evolution and the factors that affect it can be fascinating (for some examples, see Kimberly and Miles, 1980).

As I argued before, however, evolution and change in Christian service organizations may not be viewed as a strictly value-neutral occurrence. Frequently, these organizations were created and exist to serve a specific need or to carry out a specific ministry for a particular religious body; to cease doing that, or to change radically the way they do it, can amount to breaking faith with their founding and supporting constituencies. Furthermore, if the claims of some of these organizations are true, that they have undertaken the work they do as a result of divine guidance or direct inspiration, then to abandon or alter their corporate purpose—absent additional guidance or inspiration—represents another, in religious terms even more serious, betrayal.

Finally, a number of these organizations that appear to change their course and character, that may be seen devoting the majority of their energy and resources to matters outside of, sometimes even in conflict with, their espoused missions, also seem to be unaware of their altered behavior. At the least, there are striking disparities between the real thrust of their operations and the statements of purpose and descriptions of mission they still offer in their publicity and fund-raising literature—statements and descriptions that seem to date from earlier times. In these cases, one is confronted with a basic lack of integrity between an organization's public face and actual operations, which amounts to a deception (albeit sometimes unintentional) of its supporters.

Given this reality, one of the important questions the management of Christian service organizations must deal with is, How can we ensure this organization's integrity of purpose and character while maintaining the flexibility, creativity, and responsiveness we need to address human needs in a changing world? To answer this question, it is important to understand the forces

that provoke and promote organizational change and evolution and that sometimes create dynamics that may undermine organizational integrity.

We should begin by observing that some evolution and change in organizations is inevitable and healthy. As a Hewlitt-Packard grows from a business
run out of a garage into a huge, multinational corporation, it is going to have
to revise its structure and operations many times. So, too, an agency like Caring for the Children will have to change as it grows from working with a few
hundred children in one country to serving tens of thousands of children in
dozens of countries.

There have been many studies about how organizations need to change in
order to survive, as they move from their founding through various stages of
growth. One set of ideas in organizational theory called "population ecology"
focuses especially on how these issues affect the numbers, births, and deaths
of various types of organizations (see Hannan and Freeman, 1977; Aldrich,
1979). A number of these studies—as well as common sense—tell us one cannot run a small, new organization the same way one would run a very large,
established one.

As growth and change occur, though, it is easy for the sense of mission
and the character of an organization, which were essential to achieving its original goals, to erode or evolve in inappropriate directions. The earlier review of
organizational theory and the study of Christian service organizations suggest
that the primary causes of this relate to the attainment of two types of resources
that these organizations have to secure from the outside: that is, people and
financial and material support. In the first case, the people themselves are a
likely source of change. In the second case, the ways in which the organization
has to go about—or sometimes merely thinks it has to go about—securing that
support are the potential problem.

### Human Resources and Organizational Integrity

Obviously, questions about what kinds of people are needed—with what
skills, what backgrounds, what values and attitudes—and how the organization attracts them to participate in its work are vital questions for any organization.

For a long time, the organizational theorists and managers represented by
the "scientific management school" (Taylor and others) assumed that people
generally did not want to work, or at least would not usually identify with the
goals of work organizations (businesses), and were motivated to work primarily or solely by economic incentives. Organizational structures and procedures
were designed on those premises. This is one reason for the extensive empha-

sis on hierarchy, control, and motivation in most organizational and management theories. Even as later researchers and theorists from the "human relations" school (for example, Mayo and Barnard) began to highlight the importance of social factors for workers' performance, this did not significantly alter
the management emphasis on "control," because there was still pervasive
doubt that workers' efforts would be directed, however motivated, toward an
organization's goals. Finally, other theorists and researchers (Argyris, 1957;
McGregor, 1960) began to point out that there are many factors affecting work
motivation and organizational loyalties, and consequently suggested management should be more concerned with enriching and enlarging the possibilities
for workers' involvement in their jobs and an organization's work as a way of
motivating and sustaining productive contribution than with controlling and
limiting workers' behavior.

Most perspectives on management still seem to assume that significant efforts will have to be made to get workers or other participants in organizations
to align their efforts with organizational goals. I have suggested, however, that
Christian service organizations may be a notable exception to this, that many
of the staff members—and certainly most of the volunteers—choose to work
in these organizations because they identify with the organizations' espoused
goals and want to contribute to the ministry intended to achieve those goals.
Where this is true, participants may be expected to give their energy and efforts more consistently to activities that are in keeping with organizational
goals. How true this may be, though, depends largely on how participants are
recruited and selected, and on how they are directed and supported in their
work once they have been brought into the organization.

Charles Perrow provides us a very useful framework for thinking about
how to ensure that participants' efforts and behavior will contribute to the fulfillment of an organization's mission, as opposed to undermining or altering
that mission. He observes that organizations may employ "three types of controls—direct fully obtrusive ones such as giving orders, rules and regulations;
bureaucratic ones such as specialization and standardization and hierarchy,
which are fairly unobtrusive; and fully unobtrusive ones, namely the control
of the cognitive premises underlying action" (1986, p. 129). The most effective
Christian service organizations in the study rely heavily on—and in a variety
of ways try to reinforce—the last type of "control" to ensure that their participants' efforts will contribute to mission fulfillment.

By hiring people with a deep Christian faith, who share an organization's
view of the importance of combining faith and works, service and witness,
they are bringing in participants who share "the cognitive premises" underlying the organization's intended actions. (Chapter 7 looks more closely at the

processes used to select and support personnel in this way.) In addition, the most effective Christian service organizations reinforce participants' commitments and attention to those premises in the work situation by activities and procedures that lift up those ideas and values that are of central importance. So, in these organizations we find the heaviest emphases on worship and prayer as part of the work, on articulation of basic values and beliefs in discussions of organizational priorities and plans, and on essential religious themes and images in public relations and fund-raising material.

This effort to hire for and reinforce faith commitments and Christian values in the work is important because there are other "cognitive premises" that participants may bring to these organizations that can operate at cross-purposes with those commitments and values. Most significant and insidious in this regard—because the conflicts are so subtle—are some staff members' professional commitments and values.

The Christian organizations we studied said a technically well trained and professionally devoted fund-raiser may find it difficult not to think consistently in terms of increases in dollars raised and new donors added to the list, even if pursuing these goals may lead to neglecting building the kinds of relationships with donors that enlarge an organization's Christian witness. A community-development expert and hydrologist may have trouble remembering that the point of a project is finally to give people competence and control over their own lives, and the sense of hope and faith those bring—rather than just to provide a village with water—if that person is not hired with an eye toward commitment to these human and religious values as well as for technical competence.

One of the organizations considered less effective by its peers has clearly moved away from the explicit articulation and practice of its religious values, undermining its witnessing capacities, in part because over the years it has chosen to take on increasingly technical projects requiring staff with increasingly sophisticated technical expertise. This has made hiring people—particularly members of its own denomination—who can understand and represent the distinctive religious values it originally intended to bring to its work very difficult. This same organization also decided to pursue an "affirmative action plan" on the grounds that having people in it who represented the kinds of people to whom it provided services was more important than continuing to try to provide opportunities for service to members of its founding denomination. This has also contributed to the erosion of the organization's religious character—and many other problems.

In Chapter 4, I observed that no matter how closed and self-sufficient an organization may be in other respects, it will always have to import one resource from the environment: people. Studying the Christian service organizations and the insights of organizational literature indicates that, for the purposes of maintaining the focus and character of a Christian service organization's mission, issues concerning the recruitment, selection, and socialization of those people into the organization are crucial. Chapter 7 looks more closely at how these challenges can be met. I observed at the beginning of the present chapter, however, that the manner in which Christian service organizations pursue the other resources they need, financial and material resources, can also have serious, often deleterious consequences for organizational integrity. Let us look further at that claim now.

## Material Resources and Organizational Integrity

The possibilities for erosion or subversion of an organization's mission may be even more obvious in relation to the pursuit of material resources than in relation to the selection of personnel. The most dramatic illustrations of this in my studies revolved around questions of whether or not to use government funds, given the various strings attached to them. More subtle but equally important are the instances in which organizations may alter program choices or designs, or fund-raising techniques, in order to draw more material support.

The problems with respect to government funds are fairly straightforward and very serious for Christian service organizations. For international relief and development agencies, the issue usually involves the acceptance of funds from the United States Agency for International Development (US AID). US AID funds are granted to religious groups for community development work only on condition that no evangelism be done as part of the project supported; further, religious belief and practice cannot be grounds for the recruitment and selection of personnel—not only in the project supported but essentially across the operations of the grantee organization. Such conditions are incompatible with any Christian service organization whose mission includes witnessing to its faith tradition as well as delivering a practical service.

Nonetheless, two of the organizations described earlier accept US AID funds (and material). They offer two interesting examples of different, unsuccessful ways of trying to reconcile the conflicts inherent in that decision.

Love in Action is largely dependent on government funds. Its history demonstrates the practical as well as ethical and spiritual problems that go with that choice. LIA's history is one of severe organizational instability, with dramatic expansions and devastating cutbacks triggered by the receipt and loss of those grants. The results have been staff people hired and let go on fairly short notice, and the remaining staff generally demoralized. Because of the constantly changing financial picture and the lack of continuity in staffing, there is virtually no continuity in program—with effects one can only guess at on the populations served.

On top of all this, there is the fundamental question of what type of organization LIA is: as one staffer put it, "para-church or para-government?" Another key staff member claimed that "accepting government funds affects the way we do our mission, but doesn't compromise it." Indeed, he said LIA was still making religious commitment a factor in hiring. If that is true, then the organization is violating the promises they made to the government in accepting those funds—hardly an impressive display of Christian values, or even basic honesty for that matter. In fact, however, there was no evidence that the statement was true, and a good deal of evidence to the contrary, which means that LIA is, in essence, presenting a false face to donors and potential donors about its Christian character.

Gospel Outreach International presents a more complex but also troubling case. Clearer about the religious, in fact evangelistic, elements of its mission from the outset, GOI has not had its whole operation subverted by its pursuit of government funds. Still, one can—and should—ask if its integrity has not been seriously compromised by that process.

GOI set up a "separate" corporation, whose mission does not include evangelism, to receive and transmit government funds and material aid to community-development projects run by GOI and others. As the law requires that this organization be independent and meet the requirements described before—no consideration of religious commitment in hiring, no mention of religion in job descriptions—that is how this "separate" corporation is described in official documents. But, in actuality, the board of GOI is also the board of this corporation. All its staff are hired through the same processes as GOI's staff, and their job descriptions include the same language as GOI's, including the requirement that they must be committed Christians capable of affirming GOI's faith statement. In other words, this arrangement is a ruse. Again, we must ask how such a practice can possibly reflect adherence to Christian values—"therefore everyone of you must put off falsehood, and speak truthfully" (Eph. 4:25)—being mindful of the admonition that Christians are to "avoid even the appearance of evil" (1 Thess. 5:22).

It is probably important to say that not all acceptance of government funds necessarily brings such problems. One of the organizations looked at receives substantial grants in aid, in the form of grain, from the Canadian government, and these come with no strings attached. Moreover, Christian Community Services receives surplus foodstuffs from the U.S. Department of Agriculture, which go to good use in feeding the hungry in CCS's shelters and in no way interfere with its evangelistic efforts. But the fact remains that, in most cases, accepting government funds to support the work of Christian service organizations requires compromising the character of that work; the most effective of such organizations generally refuse to take those funds.

Not that appealing to private sources is always without problems. A number of the people who nominated Caring for the Children as one of the most effective agencies spoke especially of how "it absolutely refuses to compromise any aspect of its programs for the purposes of broadening its donor base." The survey respondent in this instance was talking about CFC's requirement that children in their programs attend church. Clearly, many people who might be impressed by the practical effectiveness of CFC's projects, who might be potential donors, would be put off by this aspect of CFC's efforts. But CFC will not compromise what it sees as an essential aspect of its witness, as well as its service, to draw those people in as donors.

On the other hand, we can look at another organization, which is much larger than CFC and seeks to continue to grow and expand its donor base, whose literature has clearly toned down its evangelical language over the last several years while this growth has been occurring. Is there a relation between the goal and the change in language? It seems extremely likely that the effort to reach beyond the evangelical community, to broaden the organization's donor base and sustain its growth, led to these choices about how to package information and appeals. It is hard to know whether the evangelistic aspects of programs are being diminished as well—several staff people I interviewed said this had happened—or if this organization too is moving to a point where the kinds of work it really does and the kinds of work it says it does are going to be significantly different.

The point here is that the kinds of resources Christian service organizations pursue, and how they pursue them, have implications for the life of these organizations that are more than financial. The choices made and policies implemented may help sharpen and sustain the organizations' missions, or undermine and subvert them. It is thus critical that matters of material resources, like matters of human resources, be considered in broader contexts.

On the other hand, these are also matters with plainly practical implications. Whether Christian service organizations can carry on their ministries at all depends on their inducing the right kinds of people to work for them, and others to contribute to them. The future of each organization depends, in part, on its ability to raise here and now the material resources it needs. Yet, each organization's future also depends finally on its ability to position itself to establish its legitimacy and reputation as an effective agency in both providing service and making a witness to the faith tradition it represents, thereby securing the loyalty of persons from that tradition (and others) who want to see that work go forward. Indeed, the other key set of issues that many of the organizations studied were wrestling with had to do with how to prepare for that future.

## Preparing for the Future

### Endowment Funds and Future Options

One of the themes fund-raisers frequently evoke relates to the challenges their organizations face in moving into the future. Resources are sought not only to address present needs, but in many cases with the intent of ensuring that an organization's anticipated needs will also be covered. This is a primary impetus for the building of endowments in colleges, for instance.

Christian service organizations seem less inclined toward this kind of fund-raising. Faced with overwhelming demands for services in the fields in which they labor, most of these organizations find the idea of holding something back for a "rainy day," much less to create investment income, simply immoral. In the relief and development business, every day is a rainy day, if not literally a monsoon, for the people you are trying to help. Of the six relief and development agencies in the study, only one—the Sectarian Charitable Society—had anything like an endowment (generating between 15 percent and 20 percent of its income last year), and one other, Caring for the Children, is hoping to build an endowment.

Most of the study organizations can articulate specific reasons for not creating an endowment. For a number of those that responded to questions about this, the rationale just cited—that whatever monies they can raise need to go to current programs—was offered most often. In addition, one director of development observed,

> Quite frankly, it would be very difficult for [us] to raise that kind of money; it is difficult enough to raise funds for development work, as opposed to relief work. It is the immediate needs, generally the most dramatic needs, the pictures of starving children, that most readily draw the dollars for us. . . . We find it very difficult, too often, to make people see the real need for investment in long-term development efforts. Raising funds to endow those kinds of efforts would be extremely difficult.

One wonders if this is not one place where denominational affiliation may be an advantage. Church people with strong and long-standing ties to a particular denomination are probably more inclined to think "institutionally" in their religious life and to think about providing gifts that create and support enduring organizations as part of their church. This may be one factor in the success of the SCS in creating its endowment, for it is an organization with ties to a denomination with a noteworthy history of institution building. On the other hand, this advantage, if it exists, may be fading away for SCS and others, for if survey research is right and current trends hold, there are going to be fewer and fewer people of this type.

One organization expressed a specific concern that the presence of an endowment would release it from the support of, *and thus its immediate accountability to,* its primary constituency. There are actually two issues here. First, anyone who has worked with religious organizations, especially congregations, will recognize that the existence of an endowment often has a dampening effect on their spiritual vitality. There is some connection between the practices of regular, sacrificial giving on the part of members of a religious body to support it, and the vitality of that body. Religious bodies that are living on "the dead hand of the past" often seem lacking in that spiritual vitality. This may be true for religious service organizations as well.

Second, and probably more important, an endowed organization has greater freedom to ignore the wishes and desires of a supporting constituency because it is less dependent on those people. Again we see the relationship between resource dependencies and power. What if the leadership of the organization wants to ensure that it will remain accountable to its constituency, as a part of the church reflecting their wishes in its work, not only now but in the future? It is on these grounds that the Denominational Service Committee has refused to create an endowment. One executive observed that DSC "wishes to draw its support from the people who we represent. This requires us to remain accountable to them."

CFC has a different view, and says it wants an endowment to be able to put more money into programs "in the long run." The organization is just beginning the attempt to create an endowment, and the purpose for that endowment would be to underwrite administrative costs. The chief operating officer says, "The dream is to reach a point where we could tell the donors that every dollar we raise goes into programs, because our administrative costs would be completely underwritten by endowment funds." Given the observations offered by development officers in other agencies about the difficulties of raising those kinds of funds, it will be interesting to see how CFC fares in this realm.

### Anticipating the Future—To Plan or Not to Plan

Beyond the effort to secure resources that will be available to an organization in the future, or in connection with that effort, some Christian service organizations undertake formal planning, strategic and long-range. Others do not. The question of whether the organizations will, or should, engage in formal planning activities is both significant and interesting, because the justifications offered for planning or not planning are not just pragmatic. In some cases they are also spiritual and theological.

Some organizations that are heavily involved in formal planning, like CFC, insist this activity is part of their commitment to good management and good stewardship. In CFC's case, the planning efforts seem to have increased organizational efficiency without in any way eroding the organization's spiritual character. CFC's commitment to planning reflects its intention to be exemplary in its implementation of the best management practices within a Christian context. CFC's president described this view, saying, "We're not required to be as good as secular organizations in our management; we're required to be better—because this is God's work, and if we're going to do it to God's glory, we ought to do it as well as it can be done."

On the other hand, some of the organizations that have eschewed formal planning not only question its usefulness, they also doubt that it can be undertaken without undermining something important in the organization's character. So, when I asked the chief executive officer of the DSC, a very well run operation in which no formal planning process has ever been undertaken, why this was the case, he said, "There is a real aversion to MBO types of things. Partly that is a matter of personality; partly it's out of a belief that we should be a 'responsive' organization, listening—[especially] to our overseas partners." The assumption is that such planning would lessen the organization's flexibility to respond to new circumstances and needs with new approaches or programs. It is also evident, however, that the very notion of formalized planning seems at odds with some (perhaps many) staff people's view of what it means to be a "Spirit-led" organization.

In conversations with other managers and trustees of religious organizations, it has been apparent to me that skepticism about the compatibility of formal planning processes and religious values and inspiration is, though not universal, widely shared. This is especially true when a theological tradition emphasizes the significance of the "leading of the Holy Spirit," as opposed to a reliance on interpretation of earlier revelation.

Of course, whether formal planning processes are useful and compatible with organizational values depends on the context in which they are undertaken and how they are designed and implemented. For organizations whose activities are centered around responding to natural disasters and social upheavals, planning for their actual activities is difficult. Nobody knows when or where to expect the next hurricane. On the other hand, the organizations can plan for organizational growth and change: first, to try to ensure their capacity to respond to the needs in the world they hope to meet as those needs arise, and, second, to try to ensure that their organizations can continue to be what they want them to be—in terms of their organizational cultures and character—through whatever changes in size and structure and activity are required.

Some of the most helpful literature on strategic planning makes the point that it may not be the plan that emerges from a planning process that is most helpful to an organization. Rather it may be the way that engaging in a planning process can teach people to think strategically that is of lasting value (Bryson, 1990). Indeed, some of this literature talks about "planning as learning," and argues that we should "think of planning as learning and of corporate planning as institutional learning" (De Gues, 1988, p. 70). If this is true, there is no good reason why planning processes undertaken in a Christian organization, depending on how they are designed, cannot involve everyone in the processes in spiritual as well as practical learning, both about the organization's mission and character and about opportunities and threats for which the organization should prepare itself.

If planning efforts are to have that effect, however, they must be more than rational; they must also be spiritual. Planning that is in keeping with the traditions these organizations represent will have to acknowledge that the organizations need to look *not just to logic and strategy, but also to revelation and inspiration* as they try to determine their own futures. Chapter 9 looks more closely at questions about how Christian service organizations now use, and might use, planning.

## Summary and Conclusions

This chapter began with a brief consideration of the functions of management in general, arguing that in our rapidly changing world, while some aspects of management can be profitably analyzed and quantified, the work of management taken whole is as much art as science. This is also true, perhaps even more true, for the management of Christian organizations. Still, I suggested there are three sets of issues and functions on which we can focus to structure a fruitful inquiry about the business of management in Christian service organizations, relating to what appear to be some of their most difficult operational dilemmas: (1) defining the missions and the meaning of "effectiveness" for these agencies; (2) assuring their integrity; and (3) preparing them to meet their own futures.

I argued that defining, clarifying, and articulating mission was the first and most important function of management, taking "management" here to include boards and trustees. We considered the benefits that follow from a clear statement of mission or organizational purpose. We noted, though, that even if the mission is clearly and compellingly articulated, it is not enough if management cannot also say what constitutes effectiveness in the pursuit of that mission, what outcomes serve as accurate and appropriate indicators of success in achieving organizational purposes. We examined problems that may arise where the criteria for organizational effectiveness are unreasonable or inappropriately formulated, and I proposed key questions for managers of Christian service organizations to ask themselves about mission and effectiveness.

Next we turned our attention to the questions of assuring organizational integrity. Having demonstrated that changes in mission have moral as well as practical implications in Christian service organizations, I suggested that one of the crucial dilemmas these organizations face is the struggle to ensure that whatever evolution they experience does not represent a betrayal of founding or supporting constituencies, or of divine calling. Examining some of the forces and dynamics that engender organizational change, particularly those dynamics that arise from the selection and socialization of participants and the pursuit of material resources, we looked also at problems that can be created when these issues are not dealt with thoughtfully, carefully, and creatively, and some ways organizations avoid those problems.

Last, we turned our attention to key questions Christian service organizations face in preparing for their futures. We considered whether they can and should try to create financial bases—like endowments—that go beyond meeting current needs and, if so, what some of the consequences may be. We examined the matter of if and how these organizations may use formal planning processes and, again, benefits and problems with engaging in such planning.

The illustrations in this chapter suggest how the experiences of the Christian service organizations studied may provide useful insights into principles for addressing these and other functions of management. The studies highlighted the importance of three particular concerns of management for the operations of Christian service organizations. We will turn to an examination of those three areas in Chapters 7, 8, and 9, looking in greater depth at the lessons these organizations may have to teach us about possible principles for the management of Christian service organizations.

# 7

# Sustaining a Christian Organizational Culture and the Management of Human Resources

## Two Views of Organizational Culture

A ROUND THE BEGINNING of the 1980s, management writers and consultants discovered—or rediscovered—the notion of "corporate" or "organizational culture" (see, for example, Deal and Kennedy, 1982; Peters and Waterman, 1982). I say possibly rediscovered because much of what Chester Barnard (1938) describes as the most important "functions of the executive" can readily be seen as activities designed to create and sustain what these writers now call organizational culture. Still, people like Deal and Kennedy and Peters and Waterman make a number of interesting claims about the character and value of "organizational culture."

In their widely read book, *In Search of Excellence* (1982), Peters and Waterman claim that, "without exception, the dominance and coherence of corporate culture proved to be an essential quality of the excellent companies" (p. 75). This is a particularly striking finding from my point of view, in that I would make very much the same claim about "excellent" Christian service organizations. However, I would make that claim while understanding "corporate culture" in a rather different light, and would add that, as a variable for predicting excellence, the "substance" of the culture is as critical as its mere presence or strength. So, for example, some Christian service organizations have strong "organizational cultures" in the sense that Peters and Waterman use that phrase; they emphasize service quality, administrative efficiency, and innovation in fund-raising. But they fail to emphasize and reinforce the religious motivations for and assumptions in their work. These organizations' peers do not view them as excellent, at least in the wholistic sense asked about in the survey, because the function of promoting specific moral and religious values has been largely lost or subordinated in their work.

When Peters and Waterman and Deal and Kennedy speak of corporate or organizational culture, they talk some about values. They talk primarily about material or production-related values, not moral values, and certainly not spiritual values. Even more important, these writers seem to see as the key components of culture, the traits, structures, procedures, and rituals that appear to recur in an organization's life to give participants a stronger shared sense of identity. They pay much more attention to these phenomena than to the assumptions, beliefs, or ideals that may generate the phenomena. This focus is manifest in the title of Deal and Kennedy's book, *Corporate Culture: The Rites and Rituals of Corporate Life.*

For these writers, organizational culture is important because management needs to unite participants in a common purpose. In particular, organizational culture relates to the need to provide participants in for-profit organizations with a motivation for aligning themselves with organizational goals that is deeper and more encompassing than purely economic motivation. It relates to the need to involve participants in shared activities that serve to reinforce their commitment to organizational goals (as management has defined them) and to that sense of shared identity. There are at least three problems with this formulation of organizational culture.

First, it is superficial. Descriptions of organizational culture framed in terms of traits and behavior patterns may provide a misleading picture of an organization's true character. In different organizations, the same traits, procedures, or rituals may be the outgrowth of very different assumptions or preferences about organizational goals and functions and individuals' roles. For example, an organization in which people seem to relate to each other easily and informally may be one in which open and substantial communication about professional concerns across levels and departments is desired and encouraged and has become the rule; or it may be one in which virtually all conversations are held on an informal personal level because professional roles and duties are so strictly circumscribed that there is almost no occasion (or permission) for dialogue about particular tasks or one another's responsibilities. In the latter case, conversations that could involve people speaking from authority and standing on formality, conversations that could so be fraught with tensions, would not be likely to occur. Similarly, an organization may have a wide variety of rituals that involve people in shared activities, but still lack any real sense of community.

Second, a superficial view leads to false expectations that organizational culture can be easily changed. Experience says this is not true. For instance, if an organization is one in which people tend consistently to think of their goals, responsibilities, and achievements in individualistic terms—and they have been brought into and survived in this organization because they can perform well in such a context—transforming this organization into one that focuses on collective responsibilities and actions will not be easy. Rhetoric about collegiality and shared vision is not likely to help much, and changing reward systems and structures to facilitate more cooperative behavior is something current participants in the organization are likely to resist strongly, if they are able to do so. Organizational cultures tend to be durable.

Third, where this is not understood, an inadequate understanding of organizational culture may readily contribute to manipulative behavior on the part of management. In some cases, such behavior is merely unproductive or counterproductive, in the ways suggested above. In other cases, it may raise ethical difficulties.

In the instance of unproductive manipulation, we could consider the case of an organization wherein there is very little opportunity for participants in support roles to have much input about the development of policies or activities they have to help implement. Each person does his or her part with little or no understanding of others' parts, and with very little sense of ownership of whole projects or the mission in which they are involved. Staff morale tends to be low, as people work largely in isolation, and there is no feeling of community. The organizational culture of this agency is highly individualistic and task-oriented, but it seems the quality of its work could be greatly improved if there were more genuine collaboration.

Now suppose that senior executives, seeing staff unrest and recognizing problems with work quality, believe something should be done to encourage collaboration and to create a sense of community and raise morale. They might plan more social activities and opportunities for staff development. Still, absent more consultation on the part of senior executives with those "below" them (or even one another) about how specific tasks might be better planned and implemented, and more opportunities for staff to work together around common endeavors, these other activities and plans may serve only to deepen the other participants' cynicism about senior managers' understanding and appreciation of their contributions.

In an instance of manipulation leading to ethical questions, consider an organization whose managers' investment in community-building and purpose-affirming rituals has led to what amounts to an ongoing practice of deception and, ironically, self-deception. One Christian service organization I know requires—according to its personnel handbook—attendance of *all* staff members at weekly worship services. This organization also, however, fails in a number of ways to demonstrate an attitude of Christian care for its employees, and has a number of policies that encourage them to see one another as much as competitors as collaborators. One consequence, among others, is a diminished sense of Christian community in the organization as a whole, and in that context there is little enthusiasm for participating in the weekly worship.

So, despite official policy, less than a third of the staff attend the weekly worship. Rather than enforce or abandon the policy, though, the management has instead chosen to reduce the number of chairs in the room where worship is conducted, creating the appearance that the service is well attended. Why it is important to maintain this false appearance—except, perhaps, for a few visitors—is hard to understand. This rather odd practice appears to be an example of commitment to a ritual because of an understanding that the ritual somehow embodies the organization's culture; the continuance of the ritual raises questions about organizational integrity.

In contrast to the views that equate patterns of behavior or rituals or structures with an organization's culture, Edgar Schein defines culture as "the deeper level of basic assumptions and beliefs that are shared by members of an organization, that operate unconsciously, and that define in a basic 'taken-for-granted' fashion an organization's view of itself and its environment" (1985, p. 6). He also says, "this deeper level of assumptions is to be distinguished from the 'artifacts' and 'values' [by which he means espoused ideals] that are manifestations of surface levels of the culture" (pp. 6–7). He claims a culture then must belong to and be a product of a distinct group. "Culture, in this sense, is a *learned product of group experience* and is, therefore, to be found only where there is a definable group with a significant history" (p. 7; emphasis in the original).

Schein's view has some elements in common with those of the authors just examined, in that he does want to look at behavior. Claims to values or assumptions that are not manifest in behavior are of dubious credibility. In Schein's perspective, patterns of behavior are important as potential indicators of the "substance" of culture, that substance being the "basic assumptions" he speaks of and fundamental "values" as we have been using the term in this document—"preferences for end states serving to shape choices and actions"—which undergird and give shape to an organization's existence and activities. Schein claims "overt behavior is always determined by cultural predisposition" (p. 9).

What Schein wants to caution us against is superficial analyses of culture, analyses that fail to give due weight to the complicated and powerful relationships between basic beliefs and behavior, and between the operative beliefs and assumptions within an organization and those beliefs and assumptions present in the surrounding society. Schein cites three problems that result from such inadequate understanding of culture. The first is a failure to understand the "dynamic consequences" of culture; especially, that is, that it *cannot be made up and it is very hard to change*. The second is an overemphasis on the process of culture, that is, looking too much at how it is manifest rather than at the substance of it. The third problem is a tendency to confuse parts of the culture with the whole (pp. 44–47).

Where Schein clearly differs with the views previously considered is in his claim that examinations of regular behavioral patterns, norms in group attitudes, prominent espoused values, the philosophy of an organization, rules for intraorganizational operations, and the climate of an organization all yield inadequate or incomplete understandings of organizational culture. Instead, he contends, we must look at behaviors, attitudes, and espoused values *in conjunction* with basic beliefs, fundamental assumptions, and operative values if we want to understand the way an organization is actually answering the question, What is our function in the larger scheme of things? (p. 54). It is this question that the formation of culture finally answers for any group, according to Schein.

This, of course, is ultimately the question we are asking about Christian service organizations in American society; and we want to see how they answer this question for themselves. If we can assume—on the basis of our previous examination of the historical, sociological, economic, political, and theological influences that shaped and still shape these organizations—that the function of these organization is (or should be) both to provide needed practical services and to promote spiritual and moral values, we should then ask what kinds of basic beliefs and assumptions and patterns of behavior such organizations should hold and demonstrate to fulfill that function. The organizations studied certainly offer some helpful insights in this regard.

## Fundamental Beliefs of Effective Christian Service Organizations

If Schein is right, and organizational culture is "the deeper level of basic assumptions and beliefs that are shared by members of an organization, that operate unconsciously, and that define in a basic 'taken-for-granted' fashion an organization's view of itself and its environment" (1985, p. 6), what basic assumptions and beliefs can we expect will be shared by members of effective Christian service organizations? As the question was posed earlier, we need to ask, What makes this organization, what it does, and the way it does it "Christian"? The study of the seven Christian service organizations suggests at least five basic assumptions and beliefs, no doubt with numerous corollaries that may derive from them, undergird the character and work of the most effective Christian service organizations. Let us look at these one at a time.

First, effective Christian service organizations seem to view their work as "ministry." Ministry here is activity and involvement with others that are intended to make God's presence and God's love visible and tangible to others. Each of the effective organizations studied speaks of the purposes of its work in terms that fit this description of ministry. This is evident not only in mission statements and the comments of senior executives (espoused values), but also in the way people in these organizations treat one another, those they provide with services, and donors (operative values). For example, coworkers treat one another with respect and care as a rule, whatever their relative positions in these organizations; those served are invited to help shape the programs that serve them, regardless of their religious or educational backgrounds or social status; and donors are always dealt with honestly and openly, and invited to contribute more than just money—their ideas, their prayers—to the work at hand.

This commitment to make the work they do a ministry in the fullest sense is evident in many ways in the behavior of the most effective organizations. There is International Christian Relief's commitment to undertake all its work in partnership with indigenous Christians, giving them a major role in designing any projects to be attempted, and its commitment to maintain its volunteer operations in working with material aid because providing that opportunity to volunteer is part of ICR's ministry to the churches in its own area. There is the Denominational Service Committee's refusal to take on projects whose scale prohibits the kind of personal interactions among participants that are essential to ministry—not just from their staff to the clients, but also from the clients to their staff. There is Caring for the Children's insistence on using a fund-raising mechanism that is less efficient but creates opportunities for donors to be more fully involved in the spiritual substance of the work—allowing spiritual benefits to flow to both the children served and the donors.

These are examples of how the most effective Christian service organizations consciously design their operations to try to highlight the religious essence of their work. This intention is also reflected in the best organizations in internal practices and the articulated reasons for them. For instance, I was told at CFC that the weekly devotional practices do involve all staff members—in worship services some weeks; in smaller prayer groups other weeks—and "serve not only to refresh and renew the staff and build bonds among us, but also, most importantly, remind us of whose work this finally is."

Second, effective Christian service organizations appear to view caring for practical and spiritual needs as one business, seeing Christian service that is not mindful of both kinds of needs as not truly adequate for either. This is closely related to their vision of their work as ministry, yet another factor that stands out in an examination of the most effective of these organizations is the depth of their integration of faith and works. In the view of those who run and work for these organizations, truly "faith without works is dead" (James 2:17), but works that do not point to the source of hope and faith are not adequate. As one of CCS's annual reports put it, their basic understanding of themselves and their organizations is as "doers of the Word" (James 1:22).

The correlation between espoused and operative values is telling. It was certainly striking at Christian Community Services, where almost every staff person I talked with used similar phrases about how important it is to "give these people [their clientele] hope," and then combined the actions of serving these people and witnessing to their own faith in every program and opportunity. Likewise, when one talks to the people who plan and oversee CFC's programs, one finds that they truly cannot see how to give the children they work with a future if they do not give them a faith to sustain them as well as practical survival skills and material aid.

By way of contrast, organizations not viewed as most effective seemed quite willing to set aside the commitment to articulate as well as enact their faith where that made securing funds for programs easier. The managers of one of these organizations maintained their workers still had a "walking witness" or "witness of lifestyle" that was very important, and that may be so. Clearly, individuals' willingness to put themselves in hardship to help others may make a strong statement about values of service and caring. But if those making the "walking witness" cannot talk freely about their beliefs, it may say little about the source of those values or how they can be sustained.

Significantly, one also has to note that these are organizations where, despite being Christian in name or mission statement, the staff members seldom worship together and do not mention worship as significant in the life of the organization; where some staff members apparently have no active involvement in the life of a congregation; and where the fund-raising materials employ less explicitly Christian themes frequently or water them down. Looking across the life of these organizations, one finds that in many ways they see faith and works as quite separable.

**Third, the most effective Christian service organizations seem to understand themselves to be truly part of the church.** This means that, in addition to their intentions to serve some population outside of the church, or at least outside of the particular Christian denomination or constituency they represent, these organizations also intend for their work to serve their own specific Christian constituency in some clear way, and they can describe how they believe this should work. This service may take the form of providing members of their constituency with opportunities to engage in active service. It may take the form of educating them about specific problems of poverty, injustice, or oppression in relation to their faith, or about the roots of those problems and possible ways the members of that constituency can get involved in addressing these as an expression of their faith. It may take the form of addressing the needs of society in such a way as to reflect positively on the Christian tradition represented, to remind others in society of the power and worth of the moral and spiritual ideals and beliefs in that tradition.

These intentions and functions to serve the church may be most obvious in the case of denominational organizations whose ties to a particular faith tradition are immediate and easily traced. For instance, the Denominational Service Committee works hard to continue to provide opportunities for members of its own denomination to have the kinds of experiences in service in which their faith can be expressed and they will experience spiritual growth. Feeling pressures from the groups with which they work in the field, and knowing how easy it is to drift into having more and more professionalized programs that would eliminate such opportunities, the DSC is consciously trying to stay accountable and responsive to its own constituency, including choosing to remain financially dependent on this constituency.

Denominational ties are not necessary for an organization to understand its mission and functions in this manner, though. An interesting parallel exists in this regard between Christian Community Services and the DSC. CCS, though nondenominational, has a fairly well defined support base in the evangelical community in its own area and sees itself as serving that constituency—as well as its clients—in a number of ways. In its work, CCS is representing that evangelical constituency in a positive light to the rest of the community by showing how Christian beliefs and values lead to action for those in need. It chooses and operates programs that create opportunities for members of its constituency to get involved in CCS's ministries by volunteering as well as giving. CCS refuses to accept support that requires it to compromise its evangelical beliefs in any way. And it sees its fund-raising and public relations work as helping educate its own constituency about the needs for service work and urban ministries.

Also, like the DSC, CCS is choosing to remain financially dependent primarily on that constituency. Almost 90 percent of CCS's funds come from small givers, which creates some cash-flow problems—80 percent of those funds are received around Christmas or Easter—and concerns about financial vulnerability. Still, CCS sees this funding situation as good for it. Why? Because, says the business manager, "this widow's mite approach to funding . . . puts us right where we ought to be. If we are not doing what we should do, we'll know it. But, if we are doing God's work in God's way, then God's people will respond. They have been very generous to us so far." In other words, this keeps CCS accountable to its supporters, and that is where it wants to be to stay faithful to its calling and mission.

**Fourth, effective Christian service organizations seem truly to believe that God will provide whatever resources are required for doing God's work.** This is not to say there is a kind of naive faith here that good intentions are all that is needed to secure resources, or that there is a failure to comprehend the importance of persistent and creative efforts in fund-raising. It is to say that these organizations tend to see fund-raising as a means to an end and do not allow it to become an end in itself. They all would agree with the statement of the administrator at CCS, "If we are doing God's work in God's way, then God's people will respond."

The most important manifestation of this faith in the most effective organizations is that they have been and remain program-driven and not funding-driven. They choose programs because the programs fit with their missions, because they provide an appropriate opportunity to achieve the organizations' goals, to meet the needs they say they exist to meet in ways that express the values they say they want to express—not because this is what the foundations or US AID is interested in funding this year, or because these are the kinds of efforts that are easy to package for direct mail or television.

This does not mean that the organizations are unaware of the potential advantages or difficulties of funding various kinds of programs, nor that they should not be conscious of and creative about how to present the work they do so it may be most appealing to potential donors. It does mean those kinds of questions are secondary in decision making about program selection and substance; the primary questions are about how programs fit—or can be designed to fit—with an organization's calling to fulfill a particular mission.

Perhaps the best illustration of this is not a single case but the entire system for making decisions about program selection and design. International Christian Relief's priority-setting system is, in essence, a vehicle to ensure that ICR's programs are all chosen and implemented in accordance with its mission, and that funding cannot distort those choices. By establishing this system, which incorporates the priorities articulated in its mission into a "filter" through which potential programs must pass, ICR has made it impossible to select programs primarily for funding potential, at least not without violating a very clearly understood set of rules.

To implement such a system is to act in faith that it will be possible to raise funds for programs selected and shaped in this way. ICR's system was, in fact, implemented in response to a crisis that came about when programs were being selected and shaped according to potential donors' interests and yet had led ICR into serious trouble because, as donors' interests changed, ICR was left with many projects that could no longer be funded. This caused major organizational instability and situations in which promises were broken and serious problems created. Both those to be served and staff people were hurt, being left without promised services and without jobs, respectively.

For ICR, being funding-driven led not only to a betrayal of the organization's mission and values, but also to operational outcomes that threatened its existence. Meanwhile, the new approach, based on faith that, with dedicated fund-raising, "the right work" will be supported, has been rather effective so far. It has helped establish ICR's reputation as a very effective agency, and ICR has since been generally stable and able to raise sufficient funds to support the projects it has undertaken under this new arrangement.

**Fifth, the final basic assumption or belief that seems to mark the organizational culture of effective Christian service agencies is that their participants believe that serving and caring for one another are as important as serving and caring for others.** As the president of Caring for the Children put it, "We have a major challenge in living up to our commitment [to care for people], not just for children 8,000 miles away, but also for the people at our elbow."

This type of sentiment was, in fact, the most often repeated when I asked the staff members of these organizations what marked their organization as a Christian working environment. Again and again, in the most effective organizations especially, people replied, "We care for each other." Or, "There is a lot of openness, a lot of trust, a lot of support." Or, "By far the majority of people here are seekers after the kingdom of God, with a commitment to love other people above all things." Most of the people who managed and worked in these organizations wanted it to be true that, as it says in an old hymn, "they will know we are Christians by our love."

This means that, for management, caring for the welfare of those who work for the organization must be a top priority. This does not mean that salaries or benefits need to be excessive, nor that participants will not be expected to perform their jobs as well as they can. Rather, as the president of CFC observed, the goal is to have an organization wherein *"nurture of the staff . . . is balanced with accountability* to our task, to the people we are working with in programs, and to our donors." What this means, to borrow the phrase from Gospel Outreach International's handbook, is that "being a [Christian organization] does not permit the accomplishment of goals at the expense of people."

The evidence that this basic assumption is present and manifest in the behavior of an organization appears in a variety of ways. One is simply the "feeling" of an organization. What is the tenor of people's interactions? How do people feel about working together? Is there a sense of interpersonal warmth in the organization? This is an admittedly qualitative judgment, but I can say with absolute certainty that, in at least three of the most effective organizations in the study, the sense of mutual affection, respect, and support among staff members was pervasive and palpable to an outsider present.

Another significant piece of evidence has to do with the quality of intra-organizational communication. How easily and comfortably do people communicate across divisions or functions, and across levels? Is that communication easy whether the focus is professional or personal? Where people are sharing their work because they share a common faith and a sense of mission, and they have a genuine respect and affection for one another, their communication will generally have this quality about it.

A third and very important manifestation of this commitment to care for one another are the practices of communal worship and people praying for one another. Christians who truly care about one another—or who, in fact, may not like each other but still *want* to care for one another—will worship together and pray for one another. This was the other most frequently mentioned characteristic of effective organizations when staff members were asked what marked their organization as Christian. They spoke repeatedly of how people treasured the opportunities for prayer and worship in the organization's life.

In all these ways, and too many others to mention here, organizations that have a truly Christian culture will clearly be places where people care for and respect one another. This is not to say they will be perfect. A number of people, even in the most effective organizations, commented on the fact that these organizations are not without office politics and territorial disputes. But they also commented that the politics and disputes tended to be handled differently, that participants, assuming they could work at reconciliation on the grounds of a common faith, were more willing to seek an honest airing of their differences and committed to finding a resolution that was fully acceptable to all parties involved.

These five basic assumptions or beliefs appear to be present and operative in effective Christian service organizations. As Schein suggests, they provide the foundation for other manifestations of culture that are more readily observed, the "artifacts" of culture on which Deal and Kennedy and Peters and Waterman tend to focus—norms for behavior, rituals in the organizations' lives, espoused values about faith, and practice in the organizations' work. If the presence of such cognitive, ideological, and theological bases of organizational behavior is required to create and sustain patterns of behavior and structures that are essential to these organizations' Christian character, the questions that arise next are, Where do these come from, and how does an organization keep them? How does one develop and sustain a Christian organizational culture?

Our discussion about closed and open systems and organizational boundaries included the claim that the one resource every organization has to import from its environment is participants, people. The studies of the Christian service organizations suggest that, in the recruitment, selection, and development of participants, we find both the keys to creating and sustaining a Christian organizational culture and the most important factors in eroding such a culture. The management of human resources is a crucial function in this respect, a function I want to examine in this light.

### Managing Human Resources to Sustain a Christian Organization

The first and most obvious way basic assumptions take root to establish an organization's culture is that they come to the organization in its first human resources, its founders. As Schein notes,

> Organizations do not form accidentally or spontaneously. . . . Organizations are "created" because one or more individuals perceive that the coordinated and concerted actions of a number of people can accomplish something that individual action cannot. . . . Founders usually have a major impact on how the group defines and solves its external adaptation and internal integration problems. . . . They typically have strong assumptions about the nature of the world, the role that organizations play in the world, the nature of human nature and relationships, how truth is arrived at, and how to manage space and time. (1985, pp. 209–10).

The founders bring an organization its first set of basic assumptions and beliefs, and, to the degree that the founders are successful in getting others who join the organization to share those beliefs, they establish a stronger and more coherent or less strong and less coherent organizational culture.

We have seen that culture defined in this way "is a learned product of group experience" and common history. This means, first of all, that the greater the degree to which the founders' assumptions and approaches to the organization's work prove successful in the organization's experience, the more likely they will come to dominate the ongoing life of that organization. Yet, it also suggests that the more that those who come to the organization later bring similar assumptions from other experiences with them, the easier it will be for them to contribute to the organization's work.

The implications of this for Christian service organizations are straightforward. First, the stronger the founders' commitment to the kinds of assumptions and beliefs described above, and the more successful the organizations when they act on those assumptions and beliefs, the more probable it is the organizations will have strong organizational cultures with a markedly "Christian character." Second, if they want to sustain that strong Christian character, one of the most important things they can do is recruit new participants to the organization who are already inclined on the basis of previous experience to share those basic assumptions and beliefs.

This second statement merely confirms the observations of Charles Perrow (1986, p. 129) we cited in Chapter 6, that one of the most effective ways to ensure that participants in an organization will contribute to fulfilling its mission is to select them with an eye toward the degree to which they share the "cognitive premises" underlying the action of the organization. More simply, if, for example, one wants to create and sustain a social service agency with a clearly evangelical Christian tenor, then the most important thing one can do is hire evangelical Christians with a strong interest in social service.

This conclusion is borne out by the examples of the Christian service organizations studied. The most effective consistently gave the most attention to recruiting and selecting staff for religious commitment as well as professional competence. Those that were less effective, where the witnessing aspect of the work had eroded, gave very little attention to whether or not new participants actively demonstrated the faith commitments that originally underlay the organizations' work.

## Selecting Staff for Values Commitments

The determination of whether someone shares the assumptions and values underlying an organization's mission may not always be easy to make. How does one know with any certainty what basic assumptions and beliefs a person holds? The Christian service organizations we studied moved through three levels of inquiry in efforts to answer this question about potential employees. Those with the strongest, most clearly Christian organizational cultures took their inquiries about applicants for jobs (and in some cases, about volunteers) to the third, and deepest levels. Those with weaker cultures took inquiries only to the first level.

The first level of inquiry is simply to state one's own beliefs and ask the other people if they agree. This is what most Christian service organizations do when they ask potential employees to affirm a "statement of faith." Since most of the organizations examined have evangelical roots, they use the faith statement published by the National Association of Evangelicals, which largely parallels the Nicene and Apostles' Creeds except that it adds some affirmations about the infallibility of Scripture. The only organizations that did not require potential employees to be able to affirm this statement (or one like it) were the Denominational Service Committee and the two less effective organizations.

The difficulty with this approach is that, for many Christians who grew up repeating one of the creeds regularly in church, these statements may not be very meaningful in one sense. Millions of people who affirm the same faith statements still have quite different understandings of what it means to be a Christian in terms of how they live their lives and relate to others, both inside and outside of the church. Potential employees' willingness to affirm one of these statements may not tell an organization much of value about their basic assumptions and beliefs—that is, how they will fit into the organization's culture.

Recognizing this, two of the four most effective Christian relief and development organizations take the process to a second level. They do not merely ask the applicant to sign a prepared statement, they ask him or her to write his or her own faith statement. This, their human resource directors told me, is not always insightful—sometimes they get what is simply a paraphrase of one of the creeds—but it often is helpful. The statements applicants write, according to one director, "give us a much better picture of the applicants' beliefs."

Finally, these two organizations as well as one of the other most effective relief and development agencies and Christian Community Services—interestingly, the organizations with the strongest and most clearly Christian culture—take this inquiry about their applicants' basic assumptions and beliefs, about their faith and character, to a third level. They ask people who are part of the applicants' faith communities about how the applicants live out their faith. Each of these organizations requires references not only about the applicants' professional history and aptitudes, but also about their practice of their faith. So inquiries are made of a person's pastor and at least one other member of their congregation to find out about how they function in a Christian community, demonstrate their faith in their personal lives, and contribute to the life of their own church. As the director of human resources for Caring for the Children put it, "Maturity in their faith is a key consideration in the selection of candidates. We feel if they are not firmly spiritually anchored, we cannot hire them."

As for recruiting, it should be noted that all the effective organizations re-cruit people first through churches, church networks, or networks of Christian organizations. They may publicize positions in Christian periodicals, but very rarely use general circulation media, and then only for local advertising for the lowest-level positions. As the director of administration at ICR said, "When it comes to looking for people to work for us, I've always thought that if you're looking for Christians the best place to look is in the church."

It was interesting to note how many of the staff people at the effective organizations were recruited through notices posted in their own congrega-tions, or in church or denominational publications. This probably accounted for 70 percent of the staff interviewed in the study. At Christian Community Services, many program managers and executive staff members came through the network of similar organizations and related institutions. Here and in the other agencies, information about openings often was spread through word of mouth, as many staff members know people who do (or did) similar work for other agencies.

In any case, this is one more informal way in which the pool of applicants for positions in these organizations tends to be prescreened for the likelihood they will share the assumptions fundamental to the work of these Christian organizations. And a number of the administrators spoke of (and demonstrated in practice) a patience born of faith about filling positions, trusting that Prov-idence will play a role in the best people finding their way to the organization. For example, the business manager at CCS said simply that, when there is an opening, they put out the word through their networks and then "try to pray and wait for God to bring the right person to us."

## Supporting and Sustaining Those Commitments in Worship

The careful efforts of effective organizations to ascertain whether those they are hiring are already in unity with the basic religious tenets and vision underlying their work clearly are highly significant to the creation and mainte-nance of the strong organizational cultures that sustain the focus of that work. Yet they do not simply hire these people and leave it at that. They take great care as well to socialize and support the people in adherence to their underly-ing values.

This means specific attention is given to orientation and staff development efforts that reinforce those values and reward structures that do so as well. These efforts include some of the rites and rituals on which some observers of organizational culture focus. However, these rituals are not made up de novo for the organizations' purposes, but emerge directly from a desire to affirm the underlying Christian assumptions and values on which the organizations' work rests.

Opportunities for worship, prayer and spiritual fellowship, and learning are essential parts of the effective organizations' ongoing activities. The commitment to making worship and prayer a part of their activities—not just the activities of individuals—further develops and sustains a Christian organizational culture in several ways.

First, in the words of one effective organization's handbook, the practice of corporate worship is "a reminder of who we are and Whom we serve." In other words, it is a prominent and important symbol of the organization's intention to be Christian. The expectation that organizational participants will share in the experience of worship is certainly one of the first things most people would look for as a mark of a Christian organizational culture.

Second, worship and prayer deepen and strengthen the relationships among the staff, rooting them in a common recognition of their shared religious hopes and loyalties. The sense of this may be best captured in the very candid comments of a manager in one of the most effective organizations,

> What stands out here is the prayer, support, and sharing among the staff, and that makes a huge difference in the quality of the working environment. For example, when you have a professional relationship that is strained, when you've come to think that the person who works down the hall is really a jerk, but then they share a personal trial and ask you to pray for them, that creates a different relationship. You're reminded how you need to treat people. I'm sure I'm a better manager because people here pray for me every day.

Third, the occasions of worship can become occasions for shared learning about both spiritual and more practical concerns in the life of the organization, and a time when new inspiration may come to those seeking to solve problems. Several staff people interviewed spoke of having the ideas for solutions to organizational problems or difficulties in the workplace come out of the readings, a message heard in worship, or prayer.

Finally, these occasions of worship and prayer may be particularly important for developing the sense of involvement in an organization's ministry and projects for staff whose direct involvement—for example, administrative support or data processing—is minimal. These are times when they hear about "the victories and the defeats" field-workers have experienced, and are invited to pray for those people and their work. In two organizations, these are times when staff people take on a ministry of prayer for the organizations' donors who have let it be known that they need that support. In the organizations where such activities are part of the practice of corporate worship, administrative support staff (and others) spoke of how important and fulfilling they found them. The activities strengthen the staff members' sense that, even if their primary role is packing boxes or processing checks, they too are engaged in and part of a ministry.

To allow for this kind of experience to emerge from the practices of worship, the most effective organizations seem to arrange a variety of activities. All have a worship service that involves all employees at least monthly, and they also have arrangements for smaller group worship activities, often by department or working groups (which builds community within these groups), and for various prayer fellowships, chains, and networks. Finally, what is important to see is that, in the effective Christian service organizations, worship is placed alongside work as central to the life of the organizations.

### Supporting and Sustaining the Staff in Its Work

In addition to their efforts to sustain and focus staff members in the underlying spiritual and moral values of an organization through worship, the effective organizations also attend to what some might call more pragmatic concerns for staff nurture and development. Caring for these peoples' professional development is not only in the organizations' self-interests, it is also an important reflection of a wholistic Christian commitment to caring for staff as people. This involves both structural and programmatic matters.

On the structural side, to give the staff members a sense of fulfillment and satisfaction in their work, in addition to giving them opportunities to be engaged in the spiritual aspects of the ministry, the effective organizations try to ensure their roles and tasks are structured so that a sense of control and accountability is present. These organizations have designed or arranged the work of individual participants in ways congruent with the observations of Lawrence and Lorsch that

> there seems to be an important connection for the individual between working in an organization structured to deal effectively with its task and his feelings of personal satisfaction and growth. Organizations so structured that members can deal realistically and effectively with their tasks will provide powerful sources of social and psychological satisfaction. (1967, p. 17)

Thus, in Caring for the Children, each person dealing with "sponsor relations" stays with a particular sponsor to deal with whatever issues may arise in that sponsor's relationship to CFC or to his or her sponsored children. The organization's structure and culture encourages employees to pursue with any other staff member—in finance, programs, or wherever, regardless of position—any questions they need to ask to help a sponsor and his or her children. Each person has a sense of satisfaction in having an ongoing and full relationship with a number of sponsors and their children. The staff are directly accountable for those sponsors' satisfaction with the program, and empowered to do whatever is necessary (within reason) to get their job done.

This offers a marked contrast to Love in Action, where different staff members seemed to be juggling several, often unrelated, programs. The person dealing with donors seemed hard pressed to get good information about questions about programs. The finance staff seemed unable to get needed information from the program staff in planning for budgeting. There seemed to be general confusion about roles and responsibilities. Staff members told numerous stories about being assigned tasks but not being given the authority or resources to get them done, and about being held accountable for the failure of programs that other staff members undermined by refusing to follow through on commitments. There seemed to be neither consensus among managers (and staff) about goals and plans, nor anyone in charge to impose some order.

Another structural issue relates to compensation. The salary incentive and reward systems in all but one of the effective organizations reflect an assumption that the ministry of the organization is a collective responsibility. Accordingly, compensation is related to levels of training and responsibility rather than prestige or rewards for individual performance. There are clearly two assumptions at work here, which were in fact articulated for me by executives in each of these organizations.

One is that people do not come to work for these agencies "for the money." They come for the other rewards and satisfactions. This means they must be reasonably compensated, but generally not at a level fully competitive with the for-profit or government sectors. The second assumption is that, since compensation is not in this sense a competitive reward for performance, neither should it be set up as a competitive reward within the organizational structure, especially one that may break down the sense of community. Thus, where elements of compensation are related to performance, they are structured to reward collective performance, not to set people up in competition against one another.

The only exception to this is Gospel Outreach International, which explicitly states it will provide economic rewards—essentially an individual merit pay system—for performance, and even offers a rather curious attempt at a scripturally based argument for this. This is noteworthy because GOI is also the only organization among those judged most effective by its peers that seems to have serious problems with stress and dissatisfaction among its staff, and the organization with the least sense of Christian community among the participants. Indeed, an organizational consultant working with one department remarked that he was astounded by the amount of "fear" he found in the organization around performance and communication issues. There appears to me to be a connection between these problems and the structures at GOI that encourage and reward competition between departments and between individuals.

In addition to such structural issues, the effective organizations devote resources and staff time to personnel development programs. Each of the effective organizations budgets significant funds each year for staff development for each staff member. One of these organizations appears not to make sufficient accommodation in terms of releasing staff members' time so they can take advantage of these funds; several staff members there spoke of "mixed signals" from supervisors about whether there was really support for this kind of activity. All the other effective organizations, however, actively encouraged and supported staff development—personal and spiritual as well as professional.

For example, Christian Community Services sends all professional staff to at least one conference (for professional development) and one retreat (for personal and spiritual development) each year. This is in addition to bringing a number of resource people in to provide workshops and training. Caring for the Children provides up to $500 per employee per year to support additional education and training, and encourages staff participation in religious retreats and conferences. The Denominational Service Committee provides retreat opportunities that staff people help plan, and provides for their participation in those activities.

The point is that all the effective organizations make a serious commitment to nurturing and caring for their staff. These activities are not merely self-serving, though they clearly benefit the organizations in terms of improved skills and greater loyalty among the staff; they also represent a genuine expression of the organizations' Christian caring for their employees. In addition, not surprisingly, the organizations that seem to have the strongest Christian culture are those that are most explicit about including spiritual development in their personnel development activities and programs.

### Including the Volunteers

Before we leave the subject of organizational culture and the management of human resources in Christian service organizations, we need to look briefly at the place and management of volunteers. All the issues, principles, and applications of principles we have considered pertain to volunteers as well as staff, though usually not in the same way.

For instance, in an organization like the DSC, which frequently treats and uses volunteers in the same way as salaried staff, the questions of selection and support are as significant for volunteers as for staff. The DSC uses the same procedures and structures for selection and support for both. But for ICR's use of volunteers in the gifts-in-kind program, the same concerns for selection do not apply. Nor would it be possible or desirable to apply them in the selection and support of the short-term volunteers who help a number of these organizations raise funds through special projects.

There are types of volunteer involvement that raise related issues, though. For example, CFC uses volunteers in fund-raising in two ways that have led the organization to impose selection criteria and processes—and in one instance, a support mechanism—similar to those it uses for staff.

First, CFC does a great deal of outreach through Christian musicians who talk about the work of the organization at the intermissions of their performances and provide literature about CFC's work at the close of those performances. The artists that are invited to do this, however, have to be sponsors of children themselves, have to be oriented to CFC's programs (often including a trip overseas, at the artists' expense, to see those programs), and have to be people CFC is sure understand and agree with CFC's faith statement and mission.

Second, CFC is now using more volunteers who travel to churches on its behalf to present programs about CFC's work and recruit new sponsors. Again, however, not just anyone can do this. CFC is recruiting these people from among longtime sponsors who, it is sure, understand and fully agree with its mission. In addition, CFC puts them through a special orientation and flies them into its headquarters once a year for a special retreat for fellowship and further training.

It is fair to say the rule of thumb that may apply in volunteer development relates to how fully the volunteers will be involved with the core of an organization's work, and whether they will be representing the organization to others. Where they will be heavily involved with others in ongoing activities or have a significant role in representing the organization to others, the effective organizations apply the same kinds of selection criteria for volunteers as they would for staff.

On the other hand, when providing opportunities to volunteer is part of the organization's service to the church, and volunteers will be handling only short-term assignments or responsibilities with little effect on other workers or the public, the organization may find it important to keep access to volunteer opportunities relatively open. Such opportunities may even become vehicles for outreach, involving people who are not fully understanding of or in sympathy with an organization's values and assumptions, but who may come to be so as a result of this involvement.

## Summary and Conclusions

This chapter begins with a look at two different views of corporate or organizational culture. One perspective equates culture with the traits, norms for behavior and attitudes, patterns of behavior, rites and rituals, and atmosphere discernible in an organization. The second view maintains that these things are only the surface manifestations or artifacts of culture and that the substance of culture is the basic assumptions and beliefs the people within an organization share about the world and their place in it and about the function their organization should serve in the world in that light.

In this second view, patterns of behavior are still important because they may provide evidence about what basic assumptions and beliefs are at work in an organization's life; but true comprehension of the culture of an organization requires looking at both the patterns of behavior *and* the assumptions and values that underlie them.

Holding this second perspective to be valid, I outline five basic assumptions and beliefs manifest in the life of the effective Christian service organizations studied, and offer examples of how these become evident in the consistency between espoused values and structures and daily operations of these organizations. The key assumptions and beliefs are: (1) the effective organizations view their work as a ministry; (2) they see caring for practical and spiritual needs as inseparable concerns; (3) they see themselves as part of the church; (4) they believe that God will provide the resources they need as long as they are doing God's work; and (5) they believe caring for those within the organization is as important as caring for others.

If one accepts the view that the basic assumptions and beliefs participants hold are the defining elements of organizational cultures, the question that arises is how the desired assumptions and beliefs can be established and maintained in an organization to create and sustain the "right" organizational culture. For Christian service organizations wishing to integrate service and witness, the culture must be Christian as well as professional. The keys to successfully establishing and maintaining such a culture, it was argued, are, first, the assumptions and beliefs of an organization's founders, and, second, its recruitment, selection, support, and development of human resources.

We looked at the ways effective Christian service organizations in the study selected and recruited staff members for their fundamental values and beliefs as well as their professional aptitudes. We examined how the organizations supported and reinforced those values and beliefs through corporate worship and prayer. We also examined how they oriented, socialized, and supported staff in their professional roles, considering both how programmatic, personnel-development efforts can contribute to this, and how the structures of these organizations and the design of specific jobs can further enhance (or undermine) the professional and personal performance and satisfaction of these staff members. Finally, we considered how these issues and concerns may and may not affect the handling of volunteers.

The picture these organizations provide us suggests that the establishment and maintenance of a strongly Christian corporate culture is one of the most important tasks for the management of effective Christian service organizations. It also suggests that the way these organizations handle the selection, support, and development of human resources is a critical aspect of that task. The examples they provide us offer some very helpful insights into the best ways to manage the human resources of such organizations to secure and sustain a staff that is both professionally competent and personally and spiritually capable of carrying on an effective ministry of service and witness.

# 8

# Fund-Raising and Resource Development

*Securing Support for God's Work*

### Money and Ministry

THE GATHERING OF resources, especially money, can be a source of difficulty for Christian service organizations. Not only can it be hard to do, but the processes by which it is done can generate troublesome dynamics within organizations and may even lead to the subversion or erosion of their character and mission. The choices the organizations make about how and from whom to raise resources have implications concerning to whom they want to be accountable and in what ways, how closely they want to be tied to representing a particular constituency, and how much freedom they want for expressing their religious witness and calling in the ways they deem best, as well as how much money they will have to pursue their work.

In our examination of organizational theory, we saw that "resource dependency" can be a problem for any organization because it may result in those outside of an organization, those who can control its access to resources it needs, having power over it. Donors, foundations, and other agencies that provide the resources a Christian service organization needs may be able to exercise some control over it. This means that, when a Christian service organization is thinking about raising funds and securing material aid for its projects, it should be thinking not only about how much it needs (or desires), but also where these resources should come from in terms of who then may be in a position to exercise influence over the organization.

On the positive side of this equation, the organization should also be thinking of whom it can influence, and how it may do this, by the way it raises funds. As observed in previous chapters, the ways in which these organizations raise and manage material resources make statements about the values they see as most important, and may offer a significant witness about their essential religious beliefs and assumptions. For example, those who, to secure resources for their programs, are willing to give up their freedom to incorporate religious elements into those programs say something about how important the religious elements and facets of witnessing really are in their perspective. On the other hand, those who decide what programs to undertake on the basis of their own sense of calling and mission, then make a commitment to secure the resources necessary to support this work, may offer testimony to their faith that God will provide what is necessary to do God's work.

In this last belief and the understanding that they exist to serve the church as well as the world—which we observed before appear to be basic to the culture of effective Christian service organizations—the most effective of these organizations have a basis for looking at fund-raising and resource development in a different light. They do not see fund-raising and resource development simply as an activity that is an unfortunate, perhaps even unpleasant necessity to support the ministry they do in projects and programs. Instead they see fund-raising as an undertaking that, if done properly, can become a part of their ministry. Believing this can and should be the case, that for effective Christian service organizations the work of resource development is an integral part of efforts to serve and make a witness to both the world and the church, I want to do two things in this chapter.

First, I want to suggest, on the basis of some historical and theological considerations, what positive effects the efforts to raise resources for ministry might and should have. These efforts can contribute to fulfilling the aspects of missions that involve making a witness to the finest values and ideals of the Christian tradition they represent. We need to ask what beliefs should be given expression in fund-raising and what values and beliefs should not be given acceptance or prominence in these efforts. Second, I want to look at how the effective Christian service organizations in the study implement approaches to resource development that are effective in both raising the resources they need and giving witness to the values they want to promote.

What follows is an exploration of organizational, cultural, ethical, and spiritual implications of fund-raising, *not*, for the most part, technical or instrumental aspects. The information obtained in my studies of the seven Christian service organizations does not provide a sufficient basis for comparing the relative financial effectiveness of their various approaches to fund-raising. The claim it can and does support is that none of the organizations that have designed their resource-development efforts specifically to enhance the way these may extend their witness—and avoided some conventionally acceptable approaches for spiritual and moral reasons—appear to have suffered financially for those choices. Indeed, some may be clearly profiting for staying so "spiritually focused" in their resource-development efforts, in that this focus has made them more distinctive in an increasingly crowded market of Christian organizations seeking donor support. They may thus be better able to attract and retain the support of committed Christian donors in the long term.

All of those organizations that were identified as most effective in the survey process are doing well, financially as well as in terms of making a witness. Moreover, the one that has obviously compromised its principles and its capacity to make a witness in its effort to secure more resources has not, in the long run, profited for it. In fact, the reverse appears to be true. In any case, we turn now to an examination of the spiritual and moral principles that should undergird and be manifest in fund-raising for Christian purposes and organizations.

## Altruism or Self-interest: To What Do We Appeal?

Jesus told his disciples, "No one can serve two masters; one cannot serve God and mammon" (Matt. 6:24). Christian service organizations are, for the most part, established to serve God by serving God's people—all people—as an expression of God's love. They do not have the luxury, however, of avoiding all involvement with mammon. To feed the hungry, give drink to the thirsty, clothe the naked, and care for the sick (see Matt. 25:34–36) requires money and material resources. These organizations must find ways to secure the resources to carry out their work.

Obviously, there are many different ways to ask for money or support for an organization. Different types of appeals are intended to engage different kinds of motives. To what kinds of motives should religious—in this case, Christian—organizations be appealing if they want their fund-raising and resource development to extend their efforts to glorify God and spread the "good news"? In light of earlier discussions in this volume, we should also consider to what kinds of motives it is appropriate for these organizations to appeal if they want to meet society's expectations for them as philanthropic agencies and as part of the church. In other words, there are two sets of ideals or values that the fund-raising efforts of Christian service organizations should honor to have integrity in the context of their own traditions and to meet the expectations of the public. The first set of ideals and values has its roots in theology and history.

### Theological and Historical Considerations

The Bible has no chapter on fund-raising. Nevertheless, since the beginnings of the Jewish and Christian traditions, there have been collections of money for various and sundry purposes and projects carried out by religious leaders, the temple, the church, and other individuals or bodies representing the Judeo-Christian tradition. From references in the Old Testament to the first collections for "the service of the Tent of the Meeting" (Exod. 30:11–16) and instructions about the practices and purposes of "tithing" (Exod. 23:10–11; Lev. 19:9–10) to references in the New Testament about taking up "a collection for God's people" (1 Cor. 16:1–4), there are many passages that articulate and illustrate the rationales and approaches that should characterize giving, and consequently appeals for, funds motivated by faith. I have explored this subject in greater detail elsewhere (Jeavons, 1991), but summarize here what these passages tell us should mark giving and fund-raising that honor Christian ideals.

A survey of the literature of the Judeo-Christian tradition suggests this tradition expects that giving for what we call charity or philanthropy will be motivated by one or more of five types of emotions, ideals, beliefs, or commitments: (1) fear or guilt or both, (2) a sense of belonging or obligation to a specific community, (3) a sense of fairness or reciprocity, or obligation to justice, (4) a desire for self-aggrandizement, and (5) love or gratitude. It is interesting to note, by way of confirmation of the insights of the Scriptures, how empirical evidence from a very different source supports this analysis and schema of motivations. There is a striking correspondence between this list of rationales or motives for giving, which emerges from careful exegesis of biblical texts, and an analysis and list developed by psychologists studying motivations for volunteering (see Clary and Snyder, 1991).

The first Old Testament reference to raising funds for religious purposes is the passage in Exodus (30:11–16) about support for "the service of the Tent of the Meeting." In this passage, God commands each Israelite to contribute support for this edifice of worship and religious services, paying "the Lord a ransom for his life." This passage is complex, and capturing the nuance of the Hebrew in English is problematic, but it appears that what we have here is a payment of "atonement money." In essence, this is a fund-raising appeal—the term "appeal" may be too weak here—based on guilt.

This is the only time such an explicit appeal to guilt or fear appears in the Old Testament, but it was common practice in those times, in that culture and others, for religious leaders to make appeals for contributions as payments for guilt or to assuage the anger of the gods. Unfortunately, this is not a practice that died out in antiquity. In any case, such an understanding of and rationale for religious giving rarely appears again in the Bible, and is even ridiculed in later passages (see, for example, Amos 4:4–5).

Indeed, the rationales for giving that are most pervasive in the Old Testament emphasize, first, the obligation of every member of "the people of God" to contribute to the common welfare and support of the covenanted community and, second, the obligation of the people of God to "act justly and love mercy" (Mic. 6:8). So, on the one hand, we find a set of passages that emphasize the need for each person in the Israelites' community to contribute financially to support that community's religious life and rituals (for example, Num. 18:21, 25–29; Lev. 27:30–32), and, on the other hand, passages that highlight the importance of contributing to the support of the members of community who are in need (for example, Exod. 23:10–11; Prov. 14:31). Occasionally, we find passages that bring these two themes together (Deut. 14:28–30). And in this tradition, the point is clearly made that whoever enhances the quality of the community's life in either of these respects brings blessings on him- or herself as well as the community (see Deut. 26:12–15).

To frame this in more modern terms, the behaviors we call charity or philanthropy are seen in the Old Testament as matters of justice or righteousness. Within the context of the prominent concern for the vitality and integrity of *community*, which is at the heart of the Old Testament, righteousness is whatever contributes to the proper ordering of the community's life, and justice is a function of reciprocity, treating others as one would hope to be treated oneself. This last concern is especially crucial, because it dictates the need to extend compassion, and the Jewish practice of giving called *tsedakah*, beyond the immediate—in this case, ethnic and religious—community.

At its origins, thus, the Judeo-Christian tradition lifts up and affirms a sense of belonging and obligation to one's own community and a moral obligation to uphold standards of justice and mercy, even for those not of one's own community, as honorable motivations for giving. Moreover, it promises that giving and service so motivated will bring God's blessings for oneself as well as the community. It does not, however, suggest seeking those blessings should become the motivation for giving.

The teachings of Christ build on this tradition. In the shifting frame of reference that distinguishes the New Testament from the Old, though, teachings on these and other subjects focus more on individuals and less on community. At least in the Gospels, much less is said about obligations to a particular religious community and its traditions, and Jesus' teachings sometimes even devalue such notions (see Mark 2:27, or 7:9–13).

In Jesus' teachings, we find a continuation of the expectation that people should give out of a sense of reciprocity—"do unto others as you would have them do unto you"—but he also extends the idea, subtly and radically. "If you love those who love you, what credit is that to you? And if you do good to those who do good to you, what credit is that? . . . Love your enemies, and do good, and lend expecting nothing in return" (Luke 6:32–36). Then Jesus sent his disciples out to preach, serve, and heal with the simple exhortation, "Freely you have received, freely give" (Matt. 10:8).

Teachings like this, when applied to matters of giving and serving, shift the focus of the discussion from obligations to opportunities. Considered in the light of the passages wherein Jesus emphasizes the importance of losing one's self in caring for others as the way to finding one's true self, the perspective is one that assumes people can be induced to give and volunteer to serve others by appeals to the love and gratitude they will feel and want to express for the love and grace of God they have experienced. And, of course, it is also believed there is a wonderful spiritual and practical paradox in all this—that is, the more people give of themselves, the more deeply they will experience God's grace and love.

Part of what is evident here is the assumption of the inevitable integration of faith and works. The assumption is that those who have experienced and so believe in the love and power of God will demonstrate it by living a life that expresses that love to others and reflects a trust in God. Besides the Gospels, other documents of the early church reflect this view when they ask questions like, "If anyone has the world's goods and sees his brother in need, yet closes his heart against him, how does the love of God abide in him?" (1 John 3:17).

Jesus encouraged his disciples to lives of giving and service. He told people to admit and acknowledge their own guilt, but so that they could come to terms with their failures or sins and move on to accept God's grace and begin new lives in wholeness, not so that the guilt could become a motivation for other actions. Indeed, a critical message in the Christian tradition (at its best) is that "perfect love"—that which one can come to know in God's grace, and which motivates true charity—"casts out fear" (1 John 4:18). Charitable appeals that play on guilt or fear are inconsistent with Christian values.

Also inconsistent are appeals directed to the human instincts for self-aggrandizement. This approach may be much harder to avoid because it has become so much a part of modern fund-raising practice. Still, it should be obvious that religious teachings that exhort one to lose one's self in service are incongruent with fund-raising practices that name buildings after donors (see Matt. 6:1–4). In the perspective of faith, motives are not unimportant. If they were, why would the apostle Paul, who can be seen as the church's first fund-raising executive, congratulate the Corinthian Christians "that they were not only the first to give, but the first to have the desire to do so"(2 Cor. 8:10)? It was Paul who also gave us that line most often quoted by church treasurers, "God loves a cheerful giver" (2 Cor. 9:7).

Taken altogether, the Scriptures emphasize the potentially positive, affirmative, even celebratory motives for giving. They indicate that requests for the support of God's work ought to be made in terms that appeal to people's sense of community with other believers, or to their commitments to God's call for justice and mercy, or to the opportunities that giving and serving provide for expressing and sharing one's own experience of God's love. They certainly denigrate, and even warn against, more self-serving motivations and manipulative appeals that would play on the negative feelings of guilt or fear as inconsistent with the spiritual foundation of Christian faith and practice.

Even a cursory review of the history of the church reminds us that organized Christianity often failed to honor the ideals of faith in its own behavior. Funds were raised for medieval cathedrals, and a host of less attractive projects, by crass appeals to potential patrons' desires to be glorified, and by the most despicable efforts to play on the fears of the peasantry in the sales of indulgences. If any Christian fund-raiser needs an object lesson about what the use of inappropriate techniques for fund-raising can do to a religious organization—techniques that, however efficient they may be in bringing in money, violate basic moral and spiritual principles—he or she should look carefully at what those excesses brought. The collapse of Catholic hegemony and the development of Protestantism in Europe were in no small way connected to these excesses in fund-raising, and the great cathedrals that were built with those funds now stand mostly empty, symbols of architectural and engineering genius, perhaps, but not of vitality in the church.

Recent decades have brought a number of scandals around religious fund-raising practices in the United States. Though only a few organizations have been involved, their activities have tended to reflect badly on the whole Christian community. Again, Christian service organizations need to uphold the highest standards of integrity and accountability in financial matters if they do not want to see further erosion of the trust and credibility on which all depend to raise the support needed to do their work.

Even more important, though, in consideration of the spiritual and scriptural ideals and values for giving (and more generally for dealing with money) articulated in the Christian tradition, Christian service organizations should look on the work they need to do in resource development as an opportunity for extending their ministry to potential donors and for serving the church by embodying those ideals in their fund-raising. They should make their appeals in ways that reinforce the altruistic motivations and values that are at the core of Christian living. In this they honor not only some essential ideals of the Christian tradition, but also some important expectations the general public seems to hold for the church more broadly.

## Societal Expectations

Wuthnow offers a rather compelling argument (1988, especially pp. 57–69) that, after World War II, the church's role in the public's eye changed so that the public came to expect that one of the church's primary roles in American society should be the teaching of values needed for the support of a good society—a curious role in which the church is confined, in one sense, to addressing individuals in the private sphere, but its activities are seen as necessary to support the moral order of the public sphere. In addition, Wuthnow goes on to point out that, in more recent decades, the general public has increasingly identified the church with special interest groups—like Christian service organizations—representing particular constituencies within it. Given these circumstances, the way in which Christian service organizations represent or promote specific values, especially altruism, in their fund-raising activities has direct bearing on how they meet, or fail to meet, public expectations.

American society expects religion to promote altruistic values and behavior. It holds this expectation also, though somewhat less firmly, for philanthropic organizations generally. The expectation definitely applies to Christian service organizations, because they are part of that set of philanthropic organizations and because of their connection with the church.

The statistics we looked at in the Introduction and in Chapter 2 tell us that, in fact, participation in religious life does generally serve these purposes. People who are involved regularly with worshiping communities or religious congregations are more inclined to give and volunteer. But does religious fund-raising reinforce the promotion of these values? That depends on how it is done.

Christian service organizations need to be mindful of these issues because, if they adopt some of the approaches to fund-raising employed in the secular world, they will promote and reinforce quite different values. Many of these approaches are based on the premises of economic theories and modern marketing, which assume that only those fund-raising appeals addressed in some fashion to people's self-interest are likely to be successful. But if religious organizations should be promoting altruistic values and behavior, they must begin by demonstrating such values and behavior, and by uplifting and appealing to those values in others, when they seek support for the work they do.

Finally, for religious and practical reasons, it is clear that the resource-development efforts of Christian service organizations should concern themselves with more than raising money. They should be mindful of how these efforts give witness to religious ideals and reinforce altruistic values by the manner in which support is solicited and generated. Their appeals for aid should appeal to positive motivations like people's sense of empathy for those in need, their sense of belonging and obligation to faith communities committed to serving all God's people, their gratitude for God's providence in their own lives, and the fact that opportunities to give may provide occasions to express and grow in faith and grace. These appeals should not play upon potential donors' guilt or fears, nor appeal to their interests in self-aggrandizement, nor create a sense of pity for those in need. Such principles were evident in the ways the effective Christian service organizations studied designed and implemented their fund-raising efforts; they saw their fund-raising as an extension of their ministries.

## Fund-Raising as a Ministry

In what ways can resource-development and fund-raising activities become a kind of ministry?

They start to take on this character when they are designed to promote and reinforce the altruistic values and ideals central to Christian faith and practice. When they appeal to and offer people opportunities to act on those motivations and beliefs, and so experience the satisfaction that comes of such behavior, they become ministries.

Second, they become a kind of ministry when, in this way and others, these activities serve the church as well as the organization or programs seeking the resources. For example, fund-raising endeavors become a ministry when they are designed to teach the Christians they reach about the nature of and reasons for human suffering in various parts of the world—far away or around the corner—that those who believe in a loving God should want to alleviate, and about the possibilities for responding to those circumstances as people of faith. When they help Christians who are potential donors understand the meaning of stewardship in their own lives in light of these problems and possibilities, they become a ministry.

Finally, they become a ministry when they fit the description we offered previously of "making God's presence visible and tangible to others." This may occur in a number of ways in the kinds of relationships created with donors.

Illustrations of all these possibilities can be drawn from the fund-raising and resource-development activities of the effective Christian service organizations in the study. We have noted that these fund-raising activities have also been effective in the more conventional, pragmatic sense for these organizations. That is to say, each of these organizations has been relatively successful in securing the resources it needs to do the work it desires. It is not to say that any of them is completely satisfied with the level of support it raises, although we saw that a couple of them have actually limited their growth rate or refused to take on funded projects out of concerns for ensuring the quality and integrity of their organizations and programs. Nevertheless, each of them has been successful in securing sufficient funding to maintain a desired level of work on a relatively constant or growing scale over the years. What we want to look at here is how they have done this while also making these resource-development efforts an integral part of their Christian witness and ministry.

### International Christian Relief

International Christian Relief's resource-development efforts embody the principles described above in a number of ways. This organization claims that a central element of its mission is to strengthen the capacity for and commitment to mission work in Christian communities both at home and abroad. One of the items ICR sends to inquirers and potential donors is a statement of the "Theology of Mission for ICR." The statement offers a carefully constructed and compelling argument for the importance of more Christians and churches becoming more fully engaged in service and mission work. Simply by putting this before a large number of Christians, ICR does the church at large a real service. By including this statement with fund-raising materials, ICR makes it clear that its work, and even the requests it is making for support, cannot finally be reduced to financial calculations. It is trying to encourage others to think about membership in the church, money, and mission and service in more integrated ways.

This statement says ICR's goal is "to strengthen the church by linking the church in the U.S. with the church in the two-thirds world through the sharing of resources and personnel to enable these churches [both in the U.S. and abroad] to carry out more fully their anointed task." ICR's fund-raising activities reflect this intention in a number of practical ways.

The use of a "modified deputation" process to raise support for workers in particular projects serves this purpose. Through this arrangement, specific congregations (or other groups of Christians) in the United States get more fully involved with and educated about needs for mission and service abroad. Those supporting field-workers receive regular communications from them as well as visits when the workers are home on leave, in addition to educational material from ICR explaining the needs for, philosophy behind, and outcomes of these projects. However, while this arrangement places primary responsibility for the support of particular projects on particular groups, some continuity and constancy in the work in the field are guaranteed by ICR's support of the "modified" deputation arrangement even if there are failings or changes in the backing of the U.S. supporters. This would not be the case in a traditional deputation process.

In addition, ICR works with congregations to conceive of other ways in which the congregations might take on sponsorship responsibilities for particular projects. The organization will work with a congregation to create a project that expresses its calling to mission and meets a felt and genuine need somewhere in the world under ICR selection guidelines. In these efforts to create full partnerships between different bodies of Christians and between other groups and ICR, we see relationships being built that make a witness to the Christian experience of God's presence and grace. These relationships are founded on a recognition of and respect for each party's talents and gifts, each one's commitment to faithfulness, and each one's experience and vision of God at work in the world. At their best, these relationships give testimony to others about the power of faith to move people and bring them together to do good works for the benefit of all God's people.

Besides the deputation process and the work with congregations, much of ICR's fund-raising is done by direct mail. In such campaigns, questions of what motives and emotions are appealed to become highly significant. The problems relief and development agencies face in the field are often dramatic and heart-rending, but that does not mean the fund-raising related to their work should be also. There are at least two issues here.

First, dramatic pictures of people in abject poverty and great suffering may pull on potential donors' heartstrings, but the question arises whether they pull too hard, at least if used often. Fund-raisers for these organizations, at the end of a year when there had been an unusual number of natural disasters and a major war to generate "innocent victims," talked about their concerns the American public is suffering from "compassion fatigue." They worry that people have seen so many pictures of wide-eyed, starving children with bloated bellies that these pictures have little impact anymore.

In addition, such tactics, while potentially effective for appeals for emergency relief, may make raising support for development work harder. Potential donors who have grown used to dramatic, emotional appeals for their dollars may be harder to move with more reasoned arguments about the need for support for efforts that might prevent—or at least lessen the likelihood or severity of—famines, floods, and other types of disasters that produce starving children.

Second, the question has to be asked whether these kinds of appeals do not dehumanize the very people they intend to help. What kinds of emotions and reactions do descriptions and fund-raising appeals that represent people as utterly powerless, stripped of all dignity, without any potential to help themselves, evoke in those to whom the appeals are made? Often pity, sometimes condescension, or even, in some circumstances, guilt. Not only are these inappropriate emotions for a Christian organization to be trying to evoke in potential donors, but to depict people in this way is also to fail to see and understand them as children of God, with an inherent dignity that no set of circumstances can take away. This is particularly important if relationships of equality based on a common faith are to be built, relationships in which it is important that those providing the resources be open to learning from those who are being helped.

Reporting as well as fund-raising efforts that depict victims of poverty, oppression, and natural disaster in this negative manner have become so common they have engendered a response from some elements of the relief and development community. The organization Bread for the World has issued a statement decrying what it calls "hunger pornography" (Bread for the World, 1991). It notes, "hungry people often are portrayed with what is called 'hunger pornography.' This type of coverage emphasizes the helplessness of 'the hungry' (rather than 'hungry people'), dehumanizing them further by dropping the word 'people.' " This phenomenon is observable in the graphics as well as the words some organizations use. The ways in which the potential recipients of aid are pictured (literally) are important.

ICR's appeal letters and accompanying literature always describe and picture those whom it would help in ways that highlight their dignity. Project descriptions emphasize, again, aspects of partnership, noting what those receiving help are bringing to the projects; and letters from workers speak of what they are learning from those they are helping. These workers—as well as those of other organizations—often speak of the quality of the faith of those whom they are helping or with whom they are working, in ways that make clear the workers understand they have something to learn about living a Christian life from the people of other countries.

ICR's appeals stress the opportunities that giving to its work represent for expressing and growing in one's own faith, rather than simply stressing how desperate the needs are. Needs are often desperate, and ICR's appeals offer a blunt and pointed portrayal of these needs, trying to make that clear. Still, much of its fund-raising literature emphasizes how "giving . . . brings life, joy and hope." A brochure that lists what people can do to help highlights "prayer, studying what the Bible says about aiding the poor, volunteering, and being a good steward," as well as giving money, as important ways to contribute to

ICR's ministry, making clear all these efforts must ultimately grow out of and contribute to the life of faith.

Similarly, being true to its evangelical roots, ICR stresses in its fund-raising how the work it does is spiritual as well as practical. A good example is one recent appeal for support of a medical facility that treats victims of leprosy (as well as other diseases). After telling a story that illustrates how crucial that treatment can be to the welfare of families in that country, the postscript on the letter says, "Every victim of leprosy we treat also experiences a glimpse of God's love—many for the very first time. Often, the spiritual transformation that comes from that love is even more exciting than the physical cure."

## Gospel Outreach International

Gospel Outreach International is certainly taking on the task of serving the church through education. A number of its publications appear to stress "development education," providing very helpful analyses in a Christian context of problems that developing nations and their citizens face in poverty, poor health care, lack of education, and other difficulties. These publications speak of the need for Christians to be involved in solving these problems, basing arguments on Christian ideals and values of compassion, caring for the neighbor, the poor, the widow, and the orphans. They stress the need for these efforts to acknowledge the dignity and strength of those who are to be helped, emphasizing approaches that empower and equip them to shape and improve their own lives.

Like ICR, GOI stresses values of partnership. GOI also tries to focus its appeals for funds on the opportunities giving provides donors to express their faith, even while attempting to help potential donors understand how urgent the problems are it is trying to address. So, though stressing how large the needs are, GOI appeals are often finally phrased, as one brochure put it, in terms of "how much hope a dollar can buy."

One aspect of GOI's fund-raising that raises other interesting issues, however, is the "sophistication" of its efforts. As I reviewed a large number of mailings and publications, a comment by one of its staff members in the interviews came back to mind, "We spend way too much money on flash and glitz." A number of the fund-raisers interviewed commented on the decreasing returns organizations were experiencing on direct mail, and how difficult it was to create pieces that captured donors' attention. Looking at GOI's pieces, one wonders whether there may be too much focus on style relative to substance, and whether some of these pieces are "very sophisticated," or simply "gimmicky."

At what point do very sophisticated, modern marketing techniques obscure rather than enhance what should finally be a fairly simple message?

### Caring for the Children

In Caring for the Children's resource development work, the most striking element is the emphasis on creating vital relationships between the children to be helped and the potential donors. One executive at CFC told me, "CFC doesn't survive so much on fund-raising as on marketing. Primarily what we do is market the concept of sponsorship; the idea of a *spiritual* as well as practical linkage between Christians in the first world and children in need of Christian care [primarily] in the third world."

Donors are looked at as more than donors. They are solicited as sponsors with appeals that stress the opportunity they can have to share of their experience of God's blessings in their lives in many ways with children who are, in material terms, less fortunate. Yet, these appeals also suggest how the relationships they can have with these children become another source of blessings, a relationship in which they can learn more about the world, the work of faith, and how God's presence may be known differently in the lives of those who live in very different circumstances. One appeal says simply that this work creates a relationship in which the donor "can step across the distance dividing us [from people from different cultures], and meet another person for whom Christ died."

CFC's appeals also highlight how becoming a donor or sponsor is an opportunity to become part of the ministry, and to respond to God's calling and presence in one's own life. One brochure leads off, "Let God use you in a very special way." A magazine advertisement says, "Do something now! Some suggestions for *putting your faith into action*." Another brochure talks about the opportunity to "be a willing instrument."

Still, to attract sponsors, CFC has to show them how serious the needs of these children are; it attempts to do this in ways that explain the conditions of and reasons for the poverty that affects the children as well as the suffering they experience. The director of communications said, "When we are talking about the needs of children, we have to touch people's emotions as well as their intellect. But we would really like to help Christians [in the United States] see the world and understand the causes of poverty and suffering we are called to address."

In the cause of development education, CFC has prepared curricula for churches about poverty and the plight of children, to be used in Sunday-school programs. These are fine materials, one set for each of five age groups including adults. They are provided to churches free, and in the last session (of five) ask the students to think about what they might do to address the problems they have just learned about, and offer thirty possible responses—only one of which is sponsor a child through CFC.

In addition, CFC produces videos about the issues their work addresses, and not just about the plight of children but also about related issues—for instance, about the circumstances of women in the countries where CFC works, or more generally about the causes of poverty in the third world. These also are made available to churches at no charge and often are entirely educational in nature, containing no appeal for CFC at all.

The images in CFC's videos and literature always present those in need as people who, given some assistance, have the personal and spiritual capacities to help themselves. Again, the dominant themes are those of partnership; it is assumed that, even when the partners are children, they bring something of value to a common effort to improve their own and their community's situation. The stories one finds in CFC publications are of the courage, faith, and integrity of the people with whom CFC works, and of their ability to make their own lives better with some practical and spiritual support. CFC's literature states, "The value of the individual is a basic part of our Christian faith."

Moreover, the thematic emphasis on partnership extends into program design. One articulated intention for CFC programs is that they be "transparent . . . [so that] when the community looks at a project it will *not see* Caring for the Children. It *will see* members of the local church, reaching out to their own and others in the community" (emphasis in the original).

Finally, CFC demonstrates in a most impressive way how fund-raising can be turned into a ministry by the way an organization creates relationships with its donors. All its fund-raising requests include a place on the response instrument for people to make prayer requests, and these are taken very seriously. There is a chaplain on staff whose *primary* responsibility is to organize CFC's prayer ministries—part of the whole staff's worship practice—so that every request is met. This individual also corresponds with those requesting prayer.

Additionally, sponsors who fall behind in their commitments are not simply addressed with a series of requests asking them to pay. Rather they first receive a letter inquiring why they have fallen behind, and if this is a consequence of problems that they would like included in CFC's prayer ministry. There is an attempt to establish personal contact, and to follow through on any requests. In other words, donors and sponsors are treated with the same Christian care as the people whose needs CFC is trying to address in its programs.

In recent years, CFC has begun moving beyond the mechanism of sponsorship to become more fully involved in other forms of resource development as well. For instance, it is now trying to find major donors capable of helping it build an endowment to underwrite administrative costs. Still, in these efforts, the same attention appears to be given to build caring relationships, to appeal to motives of faith and compassion, and to invite these people to give as a form of personal participation in a ministry. It will be interesting to see if these emphases can be clearly maintained as the organization's fund-raising efforts diversify.

### The Denominational Service Committee

The Denominational Service Committee faces a rather different situation than the organizations discussed above because of its denominational affiliation. Its primary donor base is established as a result of that affiliation. Further, it has consciously chosen to stay close to that base, which, as the example of the Sectarian Charitable Society demonstrates, did not have to be the case.

In this context, the thing that is most striking about the DSC's fund-raising efforts in comparison to those of the other effective organizations is their relative lack of sophistication. This is clearly a function of the organization's denominational affiliation and the culture of the denomination. First, the DSC is not competing for new donors in an open market in the same way as the other organizations, so there is less need for and less of a tendency to move into fancy mailings, slick eye-catching graphics, and clever response instruments. Second, most of its present donor base within the denomination would be quickly and profoundly alienated if they saw those kinds of materials with the DSC's name on them.

One finds instead fairly simple letters from the DSC's executive on DSC stationery, explaining the needs for funds in terms of the needs, crises, and opportunities the DSC—as part of the church—can address in its work, and in terms of the opportunity members of the denomination have to be part of that work by giving and volunteering. The letters are sent to all members of the denomination twice a year, and occasionally in special circumstances, such as when there is a major disaster. These letters are accompanied by materials that are handsomely but plainly produced, and that explain particular projects or opportunities in more detail and with helpful graphics. In addition, the DSC communicates with its donor base through the denomination's congregations.

A periodical is sent regularly to donors, keeping them abreast of developments in the DSC's ministries, and indicating opportunities for involvement through prayer, giving money, or voluntary service. This periodical is attractively but plainly produced, and emphasizes educational material and stories from and about DSC projects and workers. In this way, it continues and rein-

worldwide mission effort, but rather is asking them to help care for those who are literally as well as spiritually their neighbors. Nevertheless, CCS's commitment to make its fund-raising efforts an important part of its ministry to the community and the church is manifest in a number of ways similar to those we have already discussed and seen reflected in the operations of the other effective organizations.

First of all, CCS's development activites are guided by an explicit statement of "Biblical Foundations for Development and Development Principles." This statement emphasizes those motives and approaches to giving and appealing for funds we saw are based in a wholistic reading of the Scriptures and an examination of the Christian tradition. Adhering to these principles, CCS's appeals highlight the possibilities that giving can become an occasion to grow in faith and deepen one's own experience of God's blessings. In its appeals, CCS tries to stress that it is offering "opportunities for God's people to get involved in God's work"—in this case, the work of caring for those most in need of a practical as well as spiritual experience of God's love. So, for example, CCS's appeals speak of opportunities to "give the gift of hope to the homeless" and "to touch the lives of those in need in Jesus' name."

As a further manifestation of this concern to root its development efforts in religious convictions, CCS stresses religious themes, talking to potential donors about the call to become "doers of the Word" and "good Samaritans." In addition, CCS's appeals lift up the connection between faith and works by lifting up the importance of prayer for all CCS's ministries. Each appeal asks for the potential donors' prayers, even if they cannot make a contribution, and each response instrument offers the donors an opportunity to make prayer requests that can become part of the CCS's staff members' ministry of prayer. Those requests are taken seriously.

This attention to building personal relationships with supporters is another way CCS's development work becomes a ministry. CCS, of course, has an advantage that many relief and development agencies lack, in that it can invite its donors to become participants, volunteers, in its ministries—and it does so. Many volunteers become donors, and some donors become volunteers. Members of the regular donor's club CCS has established are given frequent opportunities to visit the sites of CCS's work and observe the programs.

In this regard, CCS makes a conscious effort to involve not only individual Christians but also whole congregations. Its staff visits and speaks in congregations in the community regularly; and groups from these congregations are encouraged to participate in CCS programs—from leading worship in the shelters, to serving meals, to adopting homeless families coming out of these shelters to help them get established in new housing and a new, stable life. In these and other ways, CCS attempts to educate the churches in its community about the needs that God's people should be attending to and the opportunities for mission and service that exist for caring congregations.

One striking feature of CCS's donor base is the presence of a significant number of corporate givers. This is highly unusual for a religious organization, especially an evangelical one. CCS has not in any way downplayed or disguised its essential character to elicit that support, though it certainly places more emphasis on the quality and importance of the services it delivers to the community than on its religious message when it seeks such support. More than anything else, though, the involvement of the corporate donors indicates that a Christian service organization can succeed in drawing support from secular sources without watering down its witness, if the services it provides are important enough and are of such quality as to be acknowledged as excellent by any reasonable standard.

## Contrasts with Less Effective Organizations

Given the limited number of organizations in the study, and without more detailed information about particular fund-raising initiatives—specific mailings, broadcasts, and such—and the responses to them, it is impossible to draw any hard-and-fast contrasts between the effectiveness of the particular resource-development strategies and techniques of the more effective and less effective organizations. Of the two less effective organizations in the study, only one was experiencing serious financial difficulties. The other was doing relatively well, although questions could be raised about whether it had sacrificed some important elements of its mission or altered its character over time to achieve that financial security. Some general observations can be made, however, about differences in the tenor of the less effective organizations' fund-raising efforts.

First, both these organizations—Love in Action and the Sectarian Charitable Society—put more emphasis on appeals to individuals and less on working with congregations or groups than do the more effective agencies. This seems to reflect the fact that neither sees itself, really, as part of the church; and they are both then less helpful in terms of serving the church. This dynamic is also manifest in the fact that both spend more effort trying to reach donors and sources of support outside of the church—individuals or government—and so appear to downplay their religious origins and elements to run less risk of alienating potential supporters in secular humanitarian spheres.

Second, corresponding logically with the contrasts just noted, the appeals the less effective organizations put forward place more emphasis on the needs to be met and the suffering to be alleviated in the world, and less emphasis on the ways in which giving and supporting this work may offer an opportunity to give expression to faith, and can even become an occasion to grow in faith. Simply put, these appeals are more clearly requests to support particular projects (or organizations), and much less invitations to become involved in a ministry. Further evidence of this is that the SCS's appeals and literature never suggest the respondent pray for the work being undertaken; and LIA's appeals do so less often—and with less emphasis—than the other organizations.

Finally, though this is an issue where we are looking more at places on a gradient than at simple contrasts, there appears to be some contrast in the relative simplicity of appeals between the less effective organizations and the more effective ones. We noted before the possibility that GOI's mailings and productions may be too glitzy, putting more emphasis on style than substance. Still, a factor that seems to characterize the appeals of the more effective organizations is their emphasis on "just telling the story." Perhaps this is a further reflection of the assumption we noted before as present in these organizations that "God's people will support God's work." The sense one gets from a number of these appeals is that the organizations believe that, if they can just make the character and significance of their work clear enough, people will respond with support.

Reading the fund-raising materials of LIA—and of a number of other less effective organizations collected out of the survey process—I was often struck by how gimmicky they were. There were extra messages scrawled in different colors to emphasize different points about the organizations' work, or how important a gift was now. A number even included coupons that indicated gifts received in response to that mailing would somehow be "multiplied" by matching funds, or that referred to other, less obvious mechanisms to increase the value of the donor's gift, if it was received "immediately." Reading these mailings was more like reading a shoppers mailing from the local mall or some sweepstakes notification than a request to consider thoughtfully or prayerfully supporting important charitable work. It left one to wonder if the story to be told, the mission to be described, was not strong enough to merit a response on its own.

A more extensive and detailed study specifically focused on the fund-raising strategies and techniques of different religious service organizations might offer more substantial insights about the relationships between the quality of organizations' work, the theological premises that undergird that work and the constituencies that launched or support it, and various approaches to fund-raising employed. It might also offer useful information about the financial effectiveness of different approaches relative to these factors. I can only observe here that, among these organizations, these contrasts stood out.

## Other Issues

Two other issues and practices merit comment because they emerged with some prominence in relation to at least one of the organizations studied. Consideration of these issues does not necessarily raise a clear contrast between the most effective and less effective organizations in the study, but they still deserve attention.

*Truthfulness and accountability* describe the first of these issues. The point has been made elsewhere that these are the bedrock concerns for all philanthropic organizations and anyone concerned with the continued strength of philanthropic practice. When philanthropic organizations—including religious organizations—are not entirely truthful, open, and accountable to the public in their operations, they endanger not only their own future but that of the whole voluntary sector.

In fund-raising operations, the temptation to engage in what might be called sleight-of-hand may be particularly great. Almost all nonprofit organizations practice some form of cross-subsidization in their operations, using excess revenues from some programs to support others. This is not necessarily problematic. However, when specific programs are the focus of an appeal, and funds raised are regularly used for other purposes, then serious questions about organizational integrity arise.

One of the less effective organizations was constantly focusing on one of two programs in its appeals, lifting these programs up as exemplary of the kind of work the organization does and inviting donations to support this work. The programs being highlighted, however, were already fully funded, and *all* the donations—presumably with the exception of those earmarked and subject to audit—were going to other parts of this organization. While not illegal, this practice is certainly deceptive and in no way honors the Christian principles that this organization says guide its operations.

Another interesting and troubling example of problems with truthfulness is found in organizations simply misrepresenting their character. One organization in the survey sample declined to respond to the survey because, it said, "We are not a religious organization." This organization, however, incorporates the word "Christian" prominently in its name, and on this basis would generally be assumed to be motivated by and operating out of religious ideals and commitments. Again, this surely raises serious questions about the organization's integrity.

*The development of revenue-generating enterprises* by religious organizations is the second issue. This is the subject of an interesting study (La Barbera, 1991) that points out the potential for conflicts and problems the creation of such enterprises raises and examines some of the variables affecting that potential. Given the degree to which many nonprofits have entered into revenue-generating enterprises to subsidize their operations, I was somewhat surprised to see how little of this was going on among the Christian service organizations studied.

The organization in my study that had become most heavily invested in such a venture was the Denominational Service Committee, although this enterprise was started not as a revenue-generating venture but as an attempt to open up first-world markets and provide income to third-world artisans and communities. It has become a remarkable success story in terms of those goals, as well as in terms of bringing greater visibility and income to DSC operations. Still, in my interviews, it was clear that all the problems La Barbera and others have found with trying to incorporate a profit-oriented enterprise into a mission-oriented nonprofit are present here. These problems include tensions between those involved in the profit-oriented venture and those involved in the core organization, the possibility the venture will divert too much of the core organization's management time and energy from its primary mission, and even some potential for the new venture to affect adversely the entire organization's sense of mission.

The DSC appears a strong-enough organization and well-enough managed to deal with these problems creatively. It has already begun to discuss some of them. Still, the example helpfully illustrates the very serious dangers and potential pitfalls of Christian service organizations entering into revenue-generating ventures to subsidize other aspects of their operations.

## Summary and Conclusions

At the outset of this chapter, we looked at the place of money in the work of ministry, examining the scriptural and historical tradition of Christianity in delineating the ideals and practices that should surround the acts of giving and receiving. In that examination, we saw there are certain motivations that the resource-development efforts of Christian service organizations should uplift and appeal to in potential donors, such as people's sense of community, their commitments to justice and mercy, or their sense of gratitude for their own experience of God's love; and there are other motives that fund-raising should not play upon, such as desires for self-aggrandizement and feelings of guilt or fear. We noted this is also important in terms of the public's expectations of these organizations as part of the church and as philanthropic organizations. In both these contexts, these organizations are expected to nurture and reinforce altruistic values, not further reinforce the already-dominant expectations in our culture that people will always act out of self-interest.

Then we looked at how the resource-development efforts of Christian service organizations can become an integral part of their witness to Christian values as well as the source of support for the programs. This can occur primarily in three ways: (1) when such efforts promote and reinforce the altruistic values and ideals that are central to Christian faith and practice; (2) when, by doing this and by educating the church about the problems and opportunities in the world that Christians should be addressing, these activities serve the church as a whole in addition to the organizations or programs seeking the resources; and (3) when they fit the description previously offered for ministry—"making God's presence visible and tangible to others"—through the kinds of relationships they create with donors and between donors and recipients. We looked then at how these principles are exemplified in the practices of the most effective organizations in the study, noting some other issues those practices raise.

With so small a sample and the limits on the information available, it is not possible to paint a simple picture of the variables that may determine the effectiveness of fund-raising approaches in the more effective versus the less effective organizations. There were still, however, some notable differences in the general character of their strategies and techniques. First, the less effective organizations seem to put more emphasis on appeals to individuals and less on working with congregations or groups than do the more effective agencies. Second, the appeals of the less effective organizations seem to put more stress on the needs and suffering to be alleviated in the world, and less on how giving may become an expression of faith and an opportunity for spiritual growth. Third, the appeals of the more effective organizations tend to be more straightforward in telling their story, and involve fewer gimmicks.

Finally, we noted that there were two additional issues relating to fund-raising in these organizations that deserved the attention of managers. One had to do with the truthfulness of the organizations' appeals and representations of themselves. The approaches taken to securing resources must be beyond reproach and free of any deception. The other had to do with the potential problems involved in getting into revenue-generating enterprises to raise additional funds and subsidize other aspects of an organization's operations.

The crucial point of all of this discussion is to recognize that the resource-development effort of Christian service organizations can be a function that diverts an organization from its mission, or even undermines the mission; or it can be a function designed and managed to enhance and extend the ministry of the organization to those from whom it seeks support as well as those to whom it would provide services. For the most effective Christian service organizations, those that successfully integrate and offer both service and witness, it will be the latter.

# 9

# Leading and Planning

*Executives' and Board Members' Roles*

## Leadership and Management in Our Society

OURS IS A society much enamored of, yet often disenchanted with, leadership. In our organizational lives—as citizens, as participants in work organizations and voluntary associations, as members of religious communities—we often have high hopes for leaders. We expect them to be the people who find the answers to our society's most pressing questions and solve our problems, to make the organizations in which we work both profitable and pleasant environments, even to show us the way to wholeness or salvation. Yet these same people are often accused of being undemocratic or dictatorial when they try to take charge in situations for which they feel responsible; of being weak and indecisive when they refrain from taking charge in hopes of engendering more citizen (or worker or congregational) involvement in situations that should involve collective action; and of being simply ineffective if they cannot speedily resolve what are often intractable problems.

In the literature on leadership, there is very little agreement on how this function should be defined. Some writers speak of leadership in terms of the ability to get others to do things. Some speak of it simply in terms of the ability to make things happen. Others speak of leadership less ambitiously, in terms of the capacity to envision what should be done and direct people's attention to it.

Not surprisingly, there is also little agreement on what a "leader" is, and on what leaders do. After several decades of academic research on these points, scholars have for the most part agreed that leadership cannot be explained primarily in terms of the traits or attributes of individuals, nor in terms of their patterns of behavior. There is no statistical evidence to show that any particular set of traits is predictive of a person's ability to be a leader; nor does it appear to be possible to identify a specific set of behaviors that—regardless of the context—mark people as leaders and characterize their activities as leadership (Stoner and Wankel, 1986; Hershey and Blanchard, 1988; Robbins, 1988).

The research on leaders' behavior led to a recognition that leaders did different kinds of things to lead under different conditions, and produced a wide range of "contingency theories" about leadership (see above, and Burns, 1978; Gardner 1989). It also led to greater recognition of the factors that complicate or interfere with effective leadership in a world where, for the most part, assumptions that leaders have any inherent rights or authority to lead have largely disappeared, and people's expectations of leaders have grown more complex (see Bennis, 1976, 1989; Burns, 1978; Gardner, 1990). While these newer theories seem to have greater descriptive power, one wonders if they have not also come to define leadership in such broad terms as to provide little or no information about what we should expect leaders to do, or what we can do to prepare and equip people to take on leadership responsibilities.

Management literature muddles these issues further. Some management theorists would have us believe there is a relatively clear distinction between leadership and management, but others would say not. Some would have us believe that we can have adequate managers who are not leaders, but that the most effective executives must be leaders as well as managers. These distinctions tend to be made in terms of managers being people who do things to maintain the status quo, see that things get done right, and focus on how to attain purposes others set, while leaders are people who seek change, try to figure out the right things to do, and focus on what an organization's purposes should be. Such distinctions are clearly inadequate, given the obligations of managers now to help their companies stay competitive in rapidly changing environments (see Peters, 1987; Vaill, 1989), and given the evidence that the most effective leaders not only envision the end states an organization should seek but also help map the course to get there and empower people and organizations to make the journey (again, see Bennis, 1989; Gardner, 1990).

On the basis of my examination of Christian service organizations, I would argue three points. First, to be effective, these organizations must have excellent leadership *and* excellent management. Second, for these organizations, that necessarily includes having senior executives who contribute significantly in both respects, as leaders and managers. Third, this also includes having a board that contributes to both leadership and management functions.

## The Roles of Boards and Executives

There are probably few who will dispute the contention that excellent organizations should have excellent leadership and excellent management. There may be some, however, who would argue these are not both the concern of an organization's board.

A traditional view holds that a board's role is primarily concerned with leadership as that may be manifest in the governance function; that its functions should largely be limited to "setting policy," meaning articulating mission and objectives, and choosing a senior executive who can see that the board's intentions are implemented. Traditional advice to and expectations of boards have been that they should not involve themselves in management, if by that term one means the normal or day-to-day operations of an organization. This is reflected, for example, in Robert Greenleaf's work on "Trustees as Servants" (Greenleaf, 1977, esp. pp. 94–97), though he uses the term "administration" to describe the functions for which he warns against board or trustee involvement. Along with this, the idea has been espoused that leadership—in the sense of setting organizational directions and policies—is *solely* the board's prerogative. (Here, interestingly, Greenleaf disagrees.) Recently, there have been many challenges to these positions.

In a very helpful book on the work of executives in nonprofit organizations, Robert Herman and Richard Heimovics (1991) argue that two traditional but inadequate conceptualizations have dominated thinking about the roles of the boards of these organizations and their executives. There is either the "traditional hierarchical model in which [the executive is seen] as subordinate in all ways to the board"; or a model whereby "the board merely ratifies [the executive's] decisions. The board, indeed, becomes a rubber stamp" (1991, pp. xi–xii). Instead of either of these views, Herman and Heimovics advocate conceptualizing the board and executive roles as a true partnership in both leadership and management functions (1990, 1991). Other researchers and theorists support this perspective as well (see Middleton, 1987; Drucker, 1990a; Stone, 1991).

Drucker claims

> the work of the executive and the board does not divide neatly into policy-making versus execution of policy. Boards and executives must be involved in both functions and must coordinate their work accordingly. In a well-functioning nonprofit organization, the executive will take responsibility for assuring that the governance function is properly organized and maintained. (1990a, p. 7)

Melissa Middleton may best summarize the tension—potentially creative—in this situation:

> The board-management [board-executive] relationship is essentially paradoxical. For many important decisions the board is the final authority. Yet it must depend on the executive for most of its information and for policy articulation and implementation. The executive has these

emergent powers but also is hired and can be fired by the board and needs the board for crucial external functions. As with all paradoxes, resolution is not possible. Instead the relationship is dynamic. . . . (1987, p. 152)

Given such a context, what is crucial is that an organization's board and its executive reach real clarity about what their respective roles and functions should be, and that these give adequate opportunity for both parties to be involved *appropriately* in meeting both the leadership and management needs of the organization. Middleton notes that "lack of clarity concerning the expectations of board members . . . raises the possibility that [board] functions will be driven in part by [the board members'] personal and social needs" (p. 143) rather than by the organization's mission. In addition, Drucker believes that, where "board members are committed to the nonprofit's cause . . . [but] given no legitimate function and no real job to do, they will do mischief; they will 'meddle' " (1990, p. 9).

What then are the legitimate functions of boards and board members, and what "real jobs" can they "appropriately" be asked to do? In his book on *Governing Boards* (1989), Cyril Houle provides a helpful list of eleven "central functions" of a governing board (see pp. 90–94). These may be seen as focusing on five areas of responsibility:

- First, the board's role in articulating the mission and larger objectives of the organization, being involved in planning to aid in the achievement of that mission, and assessing the effectiveness of the organization's plans and efforts to that end;
- Second, selecting and working actively with a chief executive who can organize and guide the organization's efforts effectively;
- Third, establishing and reviewing broad policies to facilitate the organization's work, and assuring that the board is being faithful in its legal and ethical responsibilities for trusteeship;
- Fourth, helping secure the resources required to fulfill the organization's mission, and more generally concerning itself with the effective integration of the organization with its environment; and
- Fifth, setting standards for its own performance and appraising its efforts against those standards.

Obviously, a whole host of real and appropriate jobs for individual board members derive from this list of responsibilities. Individual board members' efforts, in fact, will be needed to cover such a range of obligations.

On the executive's side of the ledger, we find another set of responsibilities—some that parallel the board's, and others that are not in the board's port-folio.

- First, going back to our earlier discussion of organizational culture, I would insist that one "thing of real importance that leaders do is to create and manage culture" (Schein, 1985, p. 2), and that this is surely and pri-marily a responsibility of the executive, although a board may be able to contribute something in this realm as well.
- Second, as Herman and Heimovic's studies demonstrate, effective nonprofit executives "work to see that [their] boards fulfill their organi-zational and public roles" (1990, p. 171). More specifically, they "work with their boards to facilitate interaction both within the board and be-tween themselves and the board" (1991, p. 57).
- Third, executives must be actively engaged in representing their or-ganization to its constituents and its larger environment, and in garner-ing from those constituents and that environment the information and resources their organization needs. An active board can be very helpful here, as Middleton (1987) points out. Still, the chief executive is often the most prominent spokesperson for, and sometimes a symbol of, an orga-nization, and therefore the person to whom others look to find out about the organization, its work, and its mission. Moreover, while the CEO may not be primarily responsible for raising funds or collecting informa-tion, she or he often has to be involved in securing major gifts or grants, and is the person through whom much of the information the board gets will be filtered.
- Fourth, the executive is finally responsible for smooth operation of the organization, for tending to the general management of operations. The executive may tend to particular management functions personally, or—as is often the case—delegate those functions. However, while able to delegate functions, the CEO cannot ultimately delegate responsibility, which makes the selection of other managers and staff one of the execu-tive's most important responsibilities.
- Fifth and finally, one executive responsibility that may be seen as part of administration, but can be usefully examined on its own, is plan-ning. This deserves special attention because it is a function that can and should integrate what some want to distinguish as separate functions of leading and managing, and because it is the function that most obviously needs to involve both board and staff members to be successful—at least on an organizational scale.

Clearly, what the boards and executives of different organizations should do to be effective in their leadership and management roles is contingent on a number of variables. The most obvious relate to the size of an organization, its age, its field of mission or operation, and its ideological or values base. Whether an organization has few staff members or many, few constituents or many, and how large and far-flung its programs and operations are—these factors have a profound effect on the character and responsibilities of the board and the executive. Whether an organization is in an entrepreneurial stage or well established may radically alter the kind of executive it needs and the kind of board it is likely to have (Kimberly and Miles, 1980; Middleton, 1987). Certainly, the different fields within which organizations operate—with different requirements for programs and personnel, subject to different levels and types of regulation, addressing potentially very different clienteles and constituencies—may dramatically affect what kinds of boards and executives they need, and what their primary concerns are. Finally, the basic values and assumptions of the founders and supporters of an organization must influence the choices it makes about the character and responsibility of its board and executive.

Here we are particularly interested in Christian service organizations. Some of those studied are young, some old; some are small, some large. Most are primarily focused on relief and development work abroad, but a number have domestic programs and one serves a local community. Let us look then at the character and operations of boards and executives of those that were viewed as very effective and those that were viewed less favorably.

## Leading Christian Service Organizations

As the previous section has suggested, executives and boards both have roles to play in both leading and managing Christian service organizations. For simplicity's sake, here these two functions—assuming they may be usefully distinguished in other contexts—will be subsumed in an examination of leadership in these organizations. We consider first the functions and activities of executives, and later those of boards and board members. We will focus primarily on what executives and boards of effective organizations do, drawing contrasts with the patterns observed in less effective organizations when that seems useful.

### Executives' Leadership Activities

In the course of my fieldwork, I had extensive interviews with the chief executives of four of the seven organizations. Fortunately, in two of three organizations where I was not able to have such conversations, I was able to talk in depth with the CEOs' key assistants, and in the other case to talk to two board members about the CEO's role. Unfortunately, both of the less effective organizations were among those where the CEO was unavailable. Nevertheless, overall the process did offer a number of valuable insights into what effective executives do in their leadership roles, and suggested some contrasts between this activity and what is occurring in other organizations.

Articulating and modeling the values they wished to see operative in their organizations was something that most of the chief executives in the most effective organizations did quite clearly. This was a particularly striking feature of executive behavior in the organizations with the most clearly Christian organizational cultures. And, interestingly, offering some confirmation of the special importance of modeling these values, the CEOs of the effective organizations that were having difficulties with their corporate cultures seemed to represent those difficulties in their own behavior.

For example, Caring for the Children's president gives considerable time and attention to ensuring there is clarity about his organization's mission and values, and ensuring that other key personnel are equally committed to those values. He describes this as a "crucial" part of his work. He makes sure those values are described and discussed regularly in staff meetings focused on program work and planning, in board meetings focused on policy setting and evaluation, and in occasions for staff worship and fellowship—such as retreats. Just as important, though, he models those values in his own behavior; and staff people frequently mentioned this.

When asked about how overwork and staff burnout at CFC have been kept to a minimum, every staff member interviewed talked about how the president talks about the importance of balance between work, family, and other responsibilities, and how the president is active in his own church and refuses to let the responsibilities of his job overshadow or divert him from his responsibilities to his family. Asked about how they maintain such open and effective communication among staff members, most staff members mentioned the fact that both the president and the chief operating officer emphasize the importance of free and clear communication, are accessible to any staff member, and frequently take time just to get around the building and talk with other staff members. Asked about why everyone seems to have such a thorough understanding of and commitment to CFC's mission and programs, most staff members talked about how the history and character of the ministry of CFC are explained in orientation, how this is frequently a point of reference in discussions of their work, and how eloquent and passionate a spokesman the president is for that mission.

The chief executive of the Denominational Service Committee has been long involved with it as a volunteer, a board member and a staff person. He came to be CEO from a position as a historian and administrator at a denominational college. With this background, he has a strong sense of the history and values of the organization, and both articulates and models those values. In an organization that eschews hierarchy, it is impossible to distinguish his "office"—a partitioned space in a large room with many such spaces—from any other staff member's office. There is no formality in the way he relates to other staff members, who describe his administrative style as "very consultative." His involvement with his church and his commitments to family and responsibilities outside the organization clearly model what he hopes for in other staff members.

One finds a similar pattern in the president's activities at Christian Community Services. This organization is more hierarchical than the DSC, but the president wants there to be open communication, delegation of responsibility as far as possible to the levels of staff closest to a particular ministry or task, and a strong emphasis on CCS's religious witness in all activities. He says his own role is that of "coach. I prepare them, and then they have the authority to act." Among his primary tasks, as he sees them, are, "setting a tone; establishing expectations about values, ethics, and integrity in our work; and setting priorities for how we will work. My priorities are God first, family second, and then the work; and I want those priorities to pervade the organization."

Again, interviewing the CCS staff members, one finds they speak of how clearly and how often the president articulates these priorities in his work with the staff. And, again, the staff members talk about how the president sets an example by his own behavior. He is active in his own church and makes ample time to be with his own family; he is viewed as open and honest in all his dealings with others. He has been experienced as having high expectations of staff members in their work, but also as being very supportive to them in both their professional and personal lives. The president said, "It is crucial for the executive to model the behavior he wants to see in an organization." However, he also uses policy to reinforce these efforts. For instance, he has made using one's vacation time mandatory for all staff, and has established training efforts to teach all staff members with supervisory responsibilities how to delegate so that they do not end up carrying all the work of their department or program.

It is interesting to contrast these examples with the patterns of behavior in two other organizations. First, in Gospel Outreach International, the organization seen as effective but that has pronounced problems with its corporate culture and staff stress and burnout, one finds a history of executives whose personal lives and health have fallen apart as they let themselves be consumed by the job. Whatever the espoused values may be about "valuing people," the examples offered by the CEOs is one of being so task-oriented that families and friendships—and even one's own health—could be sacrificed to the work of the organization. It is significant that, at GOI, not one staff person mentioned the CEO's role in either articulating or modeling the values the organization's literature says it wishes the corporate culture to embody.

The behavior of the executive offering the most pronounced contrast to those of the organizations with strong Christian cultures is that of the executive of Love in Action. An organization that demonstrates no operative commitment to caring for its staff, that is highly unstable and seems to lack any enduring focus on mission, that is very opportunistic, LIA is led by an individual who was never spoken of by the staff as articulating a clear mission, whose own behavior was described by a number of staff members as "inconsistent" or "unpredictable," and whose primary focus seems to be on finding the next grant to keep the operation running. Given that LIA is in dire financial straits currently, this last concern makes sense, but several people said they did not see any significant difference in the CEO's basic approach to his role in those times when the organization had adequate resources for the immediate future. In short, the CEO's responsibility to give the organization clear direction and to articulate—by word and deed—its mission and values in a way that focuses the rest of the staff, has either never been grasped here or is something of which the current president is incapable.

Working actively with their boards—in Drucker's words, "taking responsibility for assuring that the governance function is properly organized and maintained" (1990, p. 7)—is also something the CEOs of the most effective Christian service organizations do. I found them taking a number of different approaches to this responsibility, depending on the type of organization and its context. The clearest examples of this in our sample were in Caring for the Children, Christian Community Services, and the Denominational Service Committee.

The president of CFC listed five key responsibilities in his work, and one of them was "board development." He noted CFC takes great care in selecting board members. Persons are chosen for wisdom and work more than wealth. The board includes ten members, a number with considerable business expertise—some with international business experience—which is very helpful to CFC. Those placed on the board obviously bring a high level of commitment; "the board meets three times a year and attendance is almost always 100 percent," according to the president. He says board members are expected to give, but he tells them "how much they give is between them and the Lord." And all are contributors in that all are sponsors of children.

The CEO also commented on the value of having people with many years of continuous experience; "they bring a sense of history and perspective to the board's deliberations that is extremely valuable. They help us avoid making unnecessary mistakes in trying things that were tried and didn't work before." The president was asked if there have been people on the board who have been there too long; was there a potential problem with resistance to change or a lack of fresh thinking? He responded that his experience has been that the board members are very concerned to have the organization continuing to improve and stay on the cutting edge of service and business practice. In addition, he noted, even though they have a number of board members with twenty-five years of experience, they also have brought in a new member "every couple years or so." One way CFC keeps its board members' perspective fresh, and keeps them in touch with the programs, is to send them overseas to see the projects every third year. Most go overseas on tours to meet their own children as well as on trips CFC arranges for sponsors of children.

In terms of working with the board, the CEO said that there is an executive committee for the board—consisting of himself, the chair, the treasurer, and one other member—which meets by conference call every month. He generally talks with the chair once a week, and has frequent contact with other members as well. There is a formal orientation for new board members, and a clear statement of what is expected of board members in CFC's "policy book." A copy of this statement is given to new board members. The organization is presently working to increase the board representation of women and minorities. All of this energy given to board development has led to a situation where, according to the president, "our strong board is one of our greatest assets."

Christian Community Services has what its president describes as a "strong and active policy-setting board." It meets every month; ten times a year for business, twice a year for purely social functions. The president meets regularly with the officers—usually one-on-one—to strengthen CCS's relationship with them and provide information and support to them in their work. These meetings usually involve a time of fellowship and prayer as well as business.

There are eighteen members on the CCS board. Attendance at meetings is generally between 80 percent and 90 percent. Twelve churches started the organization, and the original board was composed of one representative from each church. The only condition on the board's composition now is that no more than six members can come from the same denomination, a regulation intended to ensure the organization's continuing ecumenical character. The board is now self-selecting, with candidates usually being suggested by the CEO. They serve three-year terms, and can be reelected as often as desired. Two members have served fifty years. In the CEO's view, these people are a real asset, providing much-needed institutional memory, but being in no way reluctant to try new approaches.

Board members are oriented by the CEO through a formal interview process, an overview of the facilities and programs, and the provision of materials. Expectations about the board's functions and members' responsibilities are clearly laid out for them. Board-member involvement in planning and problem solving is through ad hoc committees rather than standing committees. The CEO says this seems "to give the board members a greater sense of satisfaction, and allows the board more flexibility in meeting particular problems and opportunities." The board spends most of its time on issues of: (1) program effectiveness—"they want to see if and how we are touching people's lives"; (2) policies, especially in relation to human resources and issues of equity; (3) ethics in fund-raising; and (4) finances. Board meetings are held at the different CCS facilities, to give board members the chance to see them and the programs being run out of them.

All CCS's board members are significant contributors to the organization. In fact, a number have worked closely with the director of development to spearhead particular fund-raising efforts. The president says he is generally very pleased with the board's performance. He puts considerable time and energy into supporting the board in its leadership and management role. The one place he thinks there could be improvement is to have more representation of women and minorities.

The chief executive of the Denominational Service Committee also puts a great deal of energy into working with his board, though he has far less influence over its composition. As is generally true of denominational organizations, most of the members of the board are appointed by different judicatories and related bodies; the DSC board is not self-selecting. It is also a very large board. Thirty of the thirty-eight board members are selected by the DSC's denominational or regional structures to represent the constituency. (Six more are members-at-large, appointed by the board, and two are ex officio.) The working body for the board is the executive committee, which must have twelve members, geographically representative for the denomination.

The full DSC board meets once a year. Attendance is "always excellent" (95 percent). It meets for a day-and-a-half. Its primary role, according to the CEO, "is to make policy, review our financial condition, and set a budget." An effort is made to have the board meet out in the areas—primarily small towns and farming communities—where most denominational members live, in order "to keep us in touch with those whom we represent, and give the DSC increased visibility for them." The executive committee meets an additional four times a year to conduct further business in oversight of DSC operations.

In this context, one of the most important functions of the board is to represent the DSC to the individual members, congregations, and judicatory structures of the denomination. The CEO gives considerable energy to helping board members in this role, by encouraging them and providing information and materials that can be useful in that function. In his opinion, which was echoed by a longtime board member, "the board has always been very strong, a great asset of the organization." Some of the most active board members have served the DSC in its fieldwork. Priority is given to seeking such people for the board for the perspective and understanding they bring. Board members are expected to bring wisdom more than wealth to the board. The CEO commented, "It is not expected that board members be major contributors, although certainly all do give. What is important is that they be active, committed church people."

The behavior of these CEOs in working with their boards stands in marked contrast to what appeared to be the case at Love in Action. Though the CEO was not available to be interviewed there, other staff members painted a picture of a weak board, one that is dominated by the CEO and another staff person who are both full members of this small—ten-member—body. (The board had been smaller yet, and was apparently enlarged only to meet requirements for certification by the Evangelical Council for Financial Accountability.) The CEO's administrative assistant observed that the CEO gives very little time or attention to work with the board. The LIA board generally only meets as a full board once a year, with an executive committee—two of whose four members are staff people—acting on its behalf in between meetings. Some of the board members are not contributors to the organization at all, and the supporting constituency is largely unrepresented on the board. In short, this board is a body that cannot provide leadership or management oversight to the organization, and the CEO is not choosing, equipping or empowering it to do so in any way.

In brief, our encounter with these organizations confirms the observations of the studies of Herman and Heimovics (1990, 1991). Effective executives in effective organizations build and support both the leadership and management capacities of strong boards of directors. They work closely with those boards to involve them in policy formulation and performance-assessment activities, and they involve them in representing the organizations to important constituencies to interpret their missions and programs and help them raise resources for these purposes.

We noted before that executives must be actively engaged in representing their organizations to their constituents and larger environments, and in garnering from those constituents and that environment the information and resources their organizations need. Much of the executives' work with their boards may fall into this category—especially if one sees the board as a potentially important "bridging mechanism" between an organization seeking resources and its environment (Middleton, 1987). Part of the difficulty many of these executives face, however, is finding a balance between devoting energy to those activities that are directed to external, environmental concerns and devoting the attention needed to managing and integrating the internal affairs of their own organizations. Even if they are delegating much of this administrative work, they cannot—as we observed earlier—delegate the *responsibility* to see that it is done well. Certain aspects of administration—such as the effort to focus individuals' efforts on an organization's mission and reinforce the key elements of organizational culture—require a chief executive's personal involvement and presence with some regularity. It is useful, then, to look at these external and internal elements of the executives' functions together.

All of the executives of effective organizations interviewed articulated a list of priorities for or key aspects in their own jobs. Every one of them put the responsibility to be a forceful spokesman to the public and key constituencies about his organization and its mission near the top of that list. The CEO of International Christian Relief said,

> It is my responsibility to help this organization maintain its clarity—for itself and its constituency—about its biblical mandate, while keeping its vision fresh for the changing realities of the world. . . . And I need to be the primary representative for the organization to the world.

Part of this description addresses internal needs, but I also asked more explicitly about how he is involved in actual administrative work. He said he has "tried to delegate that work to [his] 'leadership team,' and decentralize decision making." His role, he said, "is in helping define the [organization's] structure and the way it should function." The executive's role at ICR may be altered somewhat by the fact that ICR has no board of its own. Thus, the CEO has no one to help with the work of representing the organization to the world, and he down-plays his administrative role more than some other CEOs.

Even where board members are available to handle some of the work of representation, however, other CEOs still speak of this representation as a crucial part of their work. For the DSC, the concern is not so much representing the organization to the world as it is representing the DSC to the members of its denomination, and the CEO sees this as among the most important things he does. He said that, "by virtue of position, I am the most prominent representative of the DSC to its constituency. So I spend a fair amount of time at gatherings of members of the denomination—to listen and to be seen." How is this balanced against tending to administrative work? The DSC is, according to the CEO, "the kind of organization that places a great deal of trust in its staff, and has decentralized decision making to a large extent. . . . But I am the one person responsible to see that the whole system functions, and does so in a way that keeps our vision vital and clear." Accordingly, this CEO, while he delegates, has not removed himself from day-to-day administration; he follows up regularly with other staff to keep informed about and on top of issues of implementation and coordination of program and support activities.

Similarly, the president at Caring for the Children puts "cementing relationships [for the organization] with key groups: international partners, significant evangelical organizations, and our donors," near the top of his list of job priorities. He gives these tasks large amounts of time. To free up that time he has also created a "leadership team," and delegates major facets of administrative functions freely. He meets regularly with that team as a group and individually to ensure coordination of their efforts. The CEO is, as noted before, often available and present to lower levels of staff as well, a regular participant in the organization's worship activities, and in this way clearly the one who articulates and embodies the organization's mission and values in a way that focuses all the staff.

A similar picture emerges at Christian Community Services. The president of CCS puts "representing this organization to the public" and "overseeing and supporting the staff in its work" as two of his four primary responsibilities. As part of his representation effort, he does a great deal of speaking to local churches and groups and has a brief radio show three times a week to tell the community "the story of CCS's work." In his oversight and support effort, the CEO structures his own day (generally) so that he comes in early to have several hours to get his own paperwork done, and then has several hours to be at the sites of various CCS programs, while his afternoons are free to meet with people outside the organization. About his visitations to program activities, he said, "I do not mean to intrude on my staff [and programs], but I do mean to be available to them by being around our operations."

In all of these cases, then, we see the chief executives making a major effort to get out to the world and important constituencies with their organizations' stories and to learn about what is going on out there, scan the environment, find out what their organizations need to know, and help in securing the resources the organizations need. However, in each of these cases, the executives also balance this outside activity with a commitment to be present inside their organizations to provide solid oversight and leadership. They delegate, but for the most part do not distance themselves from, administrative and program work. They create "teams" of administrators to work with them to further enhance internal communication and coordination.

In these respects, my study did not generate good data for comparison with less effective organizations, in part because the executives of those organizations were not available for interviews. The only obvious contrast that emerged was with the behavior of the CEO of Love in Action, who appeared to have devoted himself so completely to representing the organization to others as to have no effective role in internal management. The result was an absence of internal coordination of activities between staff members and departments, which was creating serious problems in every aspect of the organization's work. The lesson is plain from the illustration of the most effective organizations—and perhaps it is confirmed by the one counterexample—that the CEOs will make the tasks of representing their organizations to and integrating them with their external environments one primary responsibility, and the task of integrating the various elements of internal operations another key concern; and they will strike a balance in the energy and attention they give to these two realms of leadership.

One last area in which effective executives appear to play significant roles, another way in which they can provide leadership to their organizations, is by initiating and engaging others in formal planning activities. I want to examine more fully the whole question of planning in these organizations. Before doing that, however, I want to turn our attention back to the roles and responsibilities of boards and their members in leadership and management.

### Board Members' Leadership Activities

Several of the areas in which boards and board members can contribute to the leadership and management of an organization overlap with the functions of the executives just described. This is but one more confirmation of the need for a genuine partnership between the board and the executive. Certainly, two areas in which this overlap exists are the representation of the organization and its mission to others and the work of raising resources. Indeed, in many cases, it is in efforts to raise funds that the board members are called on to speak for and about the organization.

In virtually any circumstances, the board members of an organization can help clarify and reinforce its basic mission and values by periodically re-examining, clarifying, and restating them. As we saw in Chapter 6, when we examined the broader concerns of management of Christian service organizations, it is important for a variety of reasons for the board to work at this task. In addition to the reasons cited before, a board's attention to these issues serves to remind all participants in an organization of the significance of these matters. In every instance, among the most effective organizations studied, there was evidence that the board regularly returns to examinations of the organization's basic mission, either as an exercise undertaken for the board members' own sake as part of a board retreat or some other occasion, or in relation to their efforts to resolve specific policy or program issues.

Most commonly, though, board members get involved in articulating the raison d'etre of their organization because they are trying to make a case for the organization to someone else, often in an effort to secure resources for the organization. This may occur as a board is trying to develop a "case statement" for a major fund drive, as an individual board member prepares for an invitation to speak to some group about the organization's work, or as an individual board member is involved in helping secure a gift or other support from some other individual in the community. Of course, how board members can be useful in this respect varies, depending on the nature of the organization and the nature of the communities it serves and the constituencies it represents.

So, for instance, it appears Christian Community Services makes substantial use of its board in these ways. This may be easier for CCS than for an international relief and development agency, however, because the community to which CCS provides services and the community in which it needs legitimacy and from which it requires support are one in the same. Its board members come from this same community, and to ask them to go out and talk to people about the organization's work is to ask them to talk with their own neighbors, members of their own congregations, leaders of their own community. The relationships on which CCS (or any other community-based organization) is building in asking its board members to fulfill this role of representing the organization are relationships that are natural and often preexistent for those board members, making it easier for the board to be helpful in this way.

A denominationally based organization is in somewhat similar circumstances. The community to which the DSC asks its board members to represent the organization is usually the community from which they come, their own denomination and churches. The DSC asks board members to help other members of the denomination see the ways in which the DSC is their organization, part of their church, and committed to being their instrument for reaching out to the world; and the DSC asks board members to help the organization understand how it can best live up to that commitment. When they can do both those things well, the board members greatly enhance the relationship from which resources should—and the DSC's experience suggests do—naturally flow. This is not to say that such a relationship is easily achieved and maintained, nor that it will always be easy for board members to fulfill this role in denominationally based organizations, however. The members of the board of the Sectarian Charitable Society, for example, have not traditionally been very effective in representing the organization to its own denominational base (except perhaps to a small segment of the denomination). This seems to be both a contributing factor in, and now a symptom of, the erosion of its relationship to that denominational base.

Where there is not a clearly defined "natural constituency" for an organization, as for the independent relief and development agencies, it is not so clear how the board members may best help in representing the organizations to the world and in resource development. For ICR, which has no independent board, whose "board" is rather a subcommittee of the board of its parent organization, one important role those subcommittee members play is in lobbying for support for ICR's operations in the board of the parent organization. This is a task like that of board members in other organizations in that it entails helping people on that larger board, who have little idea of how the work of international relief and development is to be understood as a ministry, comprehend ICR's mission in those terms. Organizations like Gospel Outreach International and Caring for the Children have some people on their boards with connections that can be helpful in raising resources, but they both seem to select board members more for the wisdom they bring. What these and other Christian service organizations are inclined to do is try to find prominent Christians—for the organizations in this study, often well-known evangelicals—who lend these organizations additional legitimacy and visibility when they act as spokespersons on their behalf.

Although I noted earlier my agreement with the idea that boards' responsibilities should not be limited to setting policy, and the distinctions between making and implementing policy are not as cut-and-dry as some would suggest, I would contend that formulating policy remains an important board function. It is no accident that the boards of all of the effective organizations in my study were described in the organizations' literature and by their executives as "policy setting boards." Moreover, there was ample evidence in every case that these boards took this role seriously.

At four of the five most effective organizations one of the things I was given to review was a "policy book." These books were compilations of the decisions, policies, and procedures by which the operations of these organizations were governed. In each case, there was a clear distinction made between "board policies," the areas in which decisions and policies needed to be made by the board; and "management policies" or "operating policies," the areas in which the executive or other staff members had authority to make decisions and formulate procedures that did not require a decision from the board. In general, the distinction is that "board policies deal with principles and fundamental areas of [the organization's] purpose, scope and functions" (GOI Policy Book); whereas management or operational policies deal with how particular practices are to be implemented to adhere to those principles and address those functions. So, for example, at CFC it is a board policy that all inquiries about the organization's financial operations will be answered as fully and quickly as possible, and it is a management policy that such inquiries will be referred to and answered by finance staff to ensure accurate information is provided.

What is striking about the policy books is how comprehensive and clear they are. The boards of these organizations have addressed directly a wide range of issues and questions—most of those that would bear directly on the operation of these organizations—in the formulation of policies to guide executive and staff behavior in the areas of decision making, resource development, financial practice and accountability, public relations, and human-resource management. Furthermore, the boards have addressed these issues at the level of principles and operative values, emphasizing crucial values and desired outcomes, rather than the particulars of programs and procedures that ought to be in the purview of management policies and the executives' discretion. While the mere presence of such a collection of policies is no guarantee that a board is doing its job or that good management prevails, it is not surprising that LIA does not have any such documents for review.

In the final analysis, though, the formulation of such policy is not enough. The other thing I found the boards of the effective organizations doing was actively engaging in evaluation of programs and procedures to see if the values they believed the organizations should embody were manifest, and the outcomes they sought were being attained. I cited before the involvement of Christian Community Services' board in visitations to programs and facilities and their engagement in program-evaluation efforts and policy reviews. Similarly, at Caring for the Children, the board spends roughly half of every meeting in committees focused on specific areas—finance, human resources, development, information services, and others—meeting with the staff from those areas and reviewing their goals, plans, and performance. Here we see evidence of a strong board actively seeking information and engaging in activities to assess organizational performance, not just waiting to hear what the staff has to say. Similar efforts by the DSC board could be described.

These efforts to clarify organizational goals, to determine the appropriate paths to take to attain those goals, and to evaluate how much progress is being made once decisions have been taken and action initiated suggest one more type of activity in which a board can be engaged to help lead and manage these organizations. It is the same activity I suggested executives might initiate as one more mechanism for leadership, and that is formal planning. I want to conclude this chapter by looking at what formal planning is, the use the organizations studied made of formal planning, and the role this might play in other Christian service organizations.

## Planning as Leading and Learning

One more way executives can lead their organizations is by engaging them, including as many participants as possible and helpful, in formal planning activities. Insofar as the executives can involve the board in planning processes—or perhaps the board might even be the initiator of such a process—this becomes another way the board can lead as well. We may not usually think about planning as leadership, but if there is merit in some of the concepts of planning mentioned before—planning as an activity that teaches people to think in certain ways, or planning as learning—then it might become a very important form of leadership.

Conventional management texts often put planning at the center of an executive's responsibilities (see, for example, Stoner and Wankel, 1986), and in "management by objective" (MBO) approaches to management—which have had a profound influence on management practices in many organizations over the last twenty-five years—planning is a primary activity of managers at all levels of an organization. However, there is evidence of a changing attitude toward, and perspective on, planning in much progressive management literature. This literature (for example, Peters, 1987; Vaill, 1989) raises important questions about the limits of the usefulness of planning in the conventional sense in all kinds of organizations—business and government as well as nonprofit. Vaill says the conventional view is that

> planning is the specification of a sequence of events or action steps that will move a system from where it is at present to some intended new state, usually called the planning objective. . . . But the logic of a sequence of events depends on the surrounding context . . . [and] if the context changes, the sequence may no longer make sense. (1989, p. 89)

Vaill's point, which is similar to Peters's, is that in a world where dramatic and continuing change is the norm, all forms of planning based on assumptions of linear logic will be of limited value. Indeed, Peters notes, "strategic planning, as we conventionally conceive of it, has become irrelevant, or worse, damaging" (1987, p. 615).

Still the newer, less-conventional conceptions of "strategic planning" and "long-range planning" (Bryson, 1990; De Gues, 1988) may be very useful. These focus on benefits that may accrue from formal planning processes, not in terms of the generation of foolproof plans for an organization's future, but rather in terms of the ways engaging in these processes can help an organization clarify what it wants to do and be, and help people in the organization learn to think and act in ways that will make it more likely this can come to pass (see also Ackoff, 1981; Senge, 1990).

Bryson distinguishes between long-range and strategic planning by saying, "strategic planning relies more on identifying and resolving *issues*, while long-range planning focuses more on specifying goals and objectives and translating them into current budgets and work programs" (1990, p. 7, emphasis in the original). In addition, he defines strategic planning as "a disciplined effort to produce fundamental decisions and actions that shape and guide what an organization (or other entity) is, what it does, and why it does it" (p. 5). Our study of Christian service organizations offers a mixed picture of their interest and participation in either sort of planning.

Three of the seven organizations examined do, for all practical purposes, no formal planning—long-range or strategic—and these include two of the most effective organizations and one of the less effective. Two others do some formal planning, but the activities are limited and do not involve their boards; and this group includes one of the most effective and one of the less effective. The remaining two, both among the most effective, do a great deal of formal planning, and these organizations involve their boards in planning. There is, interestingly, a correlation between the pattern here and a recent study on the involvement of nonprofit organizations more generally in planning (Stone, 1991). That study found that "having a board that concerned itself with higher-level policy issues, such as goal attainment, was a key characteristic" that marked organizations more likely to engage in planning (p. 208). This was true among the organizations in my study. Still, in this context, it is not possible to establish a clear correlation between participation in formal planning activities and effectiveness. We can, however, look at least briefly at the nature and effect of formal planning activities—or the lack thereof—on the individual organizations.

One of the most interesting cases is that of International Christian Relief, which has clearly benefited greatly from a previous planning effort, though it is doing little in this regard now. Faced with a major crisis of both finances and credibility a few years ago, ICR entered into a strategic planning process. This was an initiative that apparently involved everyone in the organization above the clerical level in a major effort to clarify the organization's mission and create guidelines "to produce fundamental decisions and actions that shape and guide what the organization is, what it does, and why it does it," as in Bryson's description (p. 5). The result was the system ICR developed and still uses to focus and screen all decisions about initiating, augmenting, or discontinuing programs. It is evident that the use of this system for decision making has led to ICR's staying focused on a distinctive mission, which is now a major factor in its fine reputation.

The irony in this case is that similar attention was never given to resolving and planning around strategic issues in the internal and administrative operations of the organization, which is where it now experiences some difficulties. The current CEO has made some effort to encourage such planning for internal matters, but given his somewhat hands-off stance toward administration, he has not succeeded in developing a staff commitment to this. Each department at ICR produces an annual plan on the SWOT model (which focuses on strengths, weaknesses, opportunities, and threats), but the director of administration said, "To tell you the truth, if you look at those plans for this year and last year, you will see, for the most part, people just copied last year's plans over with a few modifications." When it was suggested this process should lead to strategic thinking, he said, "You won't find very much of that around here. The current CEO is trying to get people to change that way, but he hasn't had much success yet." ICR's history certainly demonstrates the considerable value a Christian service organization can derive from engaging in formal planning processes that teach people new approaches to thinking and decision making; ICR could benefit even further if it would engage the organization in such processes again and more fully.

Another interesting example of an organization using planning successfully at some levels but not using it at all at others is the Sectarian Charitable Society. This agency, as was noted before, has been a leader among Christian service organizations in developing and using sophisticated fund-raising techniques. In relation to its fund-raising activities and some of its administrative functions, considerable energy has been invested in planning, and the efficiency and effectiveness of those functions appear to be related to that planning. The SCS, however, has never undertaken strategic planning of the sort Bryson describes, around "what the organization is [or should be], what it does, and why it does it"—a type of planning that would necessarily involve its board as well as senior staff. And it is disputes about these kinds of issues, issues centering on definition of the organization's basic mission and character, that are the cause of most of the SCS's difficulties now. The SCS appears to be another example of how planning might be useful, and of how planning could be more useful, helping an organization avoid what are now serious problems, if it were implemented more fully.

The most successful example of the application of formal planning among the organizations we studied is the case of Caring for the Children. Over the years, CFC has made a major investment of both staff and board time in planning activities, and this has been a significant advantage to the organization. CFC's executives attribute the organization's ability to serve ten times as many children as it served ten years ago, with only four times as many staff members, to planning efforts. They believe this attention to planning—along with other factors, obviously—has led to the steady, controlled growth that has allowed CFC to expand so dramatically while keeping its clear focus on its distinctive mission and retaining its strongly evangelical Christian organizational culture.

A commitment to and engagement in formal planning activities pervades CFC. The board has established policy committing the organization to both long-range and strategic planning as *regular* functions of the staff. CFC's policy book includes outlines for both types of planning processes. The board's role is to ensure this is happening, and to review and confirm (or challenge) plans as they are formulated. However, the board also has undertaken another role in this process by mandating that it must review the "statement of corporate philosophy" for CFC every year as part of its attention to strategic issues of the conformity of operations and policy to mission. As noted earlier, the board extends this role by meeting in committees with departmental staff to assess both plans and performance on a regular basis.

The managers and program staff at CFC are also fully involved in ongoing strategic planning processes. Each department must report once a year to the leadership team about its plans and objectives for the coming year, as well as to review how its plans for the previous year were implemented and goals met. The director of information systems spoke about the regular planning sessions he has with his own staff to identify and prepare to meet emerging needs in the organization, and to assess projects already undertaken. The leadership team also meets for planning purposes on a regular basis. I was given the paper that emerged from a recent staff planning retreat, and was struck by its discussion of both issues of mission and values and issues of implementation. It addressed the need, and offered a plan, to improve the "spiritual leadership" provided by managers to their departments and employees; it also talked in practical terms about what kind of organizational structure was going to be needed to ensure the continuing quality of CFC programs in the face of expected growth over the next decade.

Caring for the Children is a most impressive organization in every respect: in its clarity in and passion for its mission; in the effectiveness and efficiency with which it pursues that mission; and in the vitality of its Christian organizational culture. There can be little doubt that this is in part a function of the way in which it has used formal planning processes to focus people's attention on key issues and values; to help the staff and board think about tasks, problems and opportunities confronting them in terms of those issues and values; and to facilitate the integration of different functions and operations within the organization. CFC's experience offers a powerful example of how formal planning efforts can be immensely valuable to Christian service organizations.

One of the most effective organizations, however, the Denominational Service Committee, presents an anomaly. The DSC eschews formal planning activities altogether, and remains a very effective and efficient organization with a strong Christian corporate culture. Two factors appear to be significant in this context. First, the external environment with which DSC is most concerned is more stable than those of many other organizations in that the values, desires, and circumstances of the denomination to which it relates have remained fairly constant (or changed rather slowly) over the years; and, regardless of the changes in the world, the kinds of projects DSC wants to undertake and the way it wants to undertake them have also remained relatively constant. Second, the religious culture of that denomination, from which the DSC draws most of its workers, is so strong that much less has to be done than would be the case in other situations to help the staff and board see and think about the world in terms that will facilitate their participating successfully in and furthering the DSC's mission. Simply put, the need for some of the kinds of learning that should come from planning has been less pronounced in this context. It is interesting to note, however, that changes in the world seem to be having a more immediate effect on members of the denomination now, and those changes are producing more pressure on the DSC to undertake different kinds of projects as well as creating new challenges in securing resources. Whether the DSC can continue to thrive in the future without getting involved in more careful and formal planning activities remains to be seen.

Finally, we should recall that the DSC's reservations about planning, as the CEO described them, were that "there is a real aversion to MBO types of things." This seemed to reflect the idea that formalized planning is incompatible with a "spiritual" organization. While this does not have to be true, it does point up the need to adjust our view and use of planning to embrace the spiritual or theological insights that are central to many religious traditions. In religious organizations, managers need to focus their attention inward as well as outward—not just on the visible strengths, weaknesses, opportunities, and threats—in order to pick up signals about what is needed for their organization. An undeniable reality of the spiritual life and the nature of individuals' and groups' callings to mission and service is that they change. The managers of religious organizations may undertake planning, but they should do so with the recognition that the desirability of the intended new state they seek for their organization may have to be re-evaluated—even as they progress toward it—not only because of changes in their environment, but also because of changes in God's aspirations for and call to their organizations.

This is to say that approaches to planning—strategic or otherwise—based *solely* on logic will prove incompatible with organizations that aim to be "spiritually guided" in defining and fulfilling their mission. The religious organization that fails to employ prayer as well as analysis, that does not look at its spiritual resources as well as its technical capacities and environment in trying to determine its opportunities, goals, and strategies will not long be effective in offering the witness of service. One of the most impressive aspects of the most effective organizations in the study was the way they recalled the need to seek divine guidance in all their activities; planning and prayer were often integrated, frequently part of the same meetings or conversations (as people recounted them). In the realm of planning, these organizations seemed always mindful that it was *God's plans* to which they ultimately needed to give the most attention.

## Summary and Conclusions

Our society has high expectations of leaders, despite differing perspectives on leadership. Some researchers and theorists in the field of management tend to make hard-and-fast distinctions between the functions of leadership and those of management. These functions may be more interwoven than such distinctions would allow, however. It is important to look at the roles both executives and boards can and should play in both leading and managing nonprofit organizations. There is a range of possible relationships between executives and boards (and board members). Exploring this range in the Christian service organizations in our study leads us to an articulation of the key functions of boards and board members in leading (and managing) these organizations, and the key functions of executives in these same areas.

The effective executives in the effective organizations: (1) articulated and modeled their organizations' missions and key values; (2) worked actively with their boards to ensure that the boards fulfilled their responsibilities for governance; (3) represented their organizations to the world and important constituencies, and helped garner necessary information and resources from those constituencies; and (4) and involved themselves in making sure that the internal operations and activities of their organizations were well integrated and carried on smoothly, efficiently and in a manner consistent with organizational values. We noted and commented on some contrasts between the behavior of these executives and executives in the less effective organizations, and on the behavior of some executives in effective organizations that nevertheless were experiencing specific difficulties—difficulties that could be related to these executives' behaviors.

The functions and activities of the boards of these Christian service organizations in leadership and management seem to center on four roles: (1) representing the organizations to others, (2) helping secure needed resources, (3) formulating policy, and (4) reviewing organizational performance to assess the validity of policies and the effectiveness of their organizations more generally. Again, although the number and range of organizations studied does not allow for broad generalizations to be drawn about patterns in more effective organizations versus those in less effective ones, I did try to point out some noteworthy contrasts along these lines.

Some of these organizations engage in formal planning, and some do not. There are different perspectives on and approaches to planning, but our observations suggest that, when planning activities are designed and implemented with the intention of engaging staff (and board) members in helpful ways of thinking about an organization, the circumstances and issues it faces in its mission, and options for fulfilling that mission, these activities can become a potentially significant mechanism through which an executive and board may exercise leadership. There was no obvious correlation between the effectiveness of these organizations, at least as that was determined in the survey process, and the use of formal planning: some effective ones planned, some did not; one less effective one did not plan, one made limited use of planning. Still, the history and activities of some of the organizations in the study illustrate how engaging in formal planning can be useful to Christian service organizations. If these organizations are going to engage in formal planning, they need to remain mindful of their origins and value commitments in doing so. Such planning activities ought to be integrated with ongoing efforts to seek and remain faithful to divine guidance about their missions and attempts to provide Christian service. The most effective organizations seemed to reflect this understanding in their behavior.

In terms of leadership and planning, what finally stand out in the study of these Christian service organizations are the vitally important roles of executives and boards in providing sound leadership and management. Strong executives and effective boards help establish and maintain the Christian corporate cultures of these organizations; set policies, work with staff, and review performance to help the organizations increase their effectiveness; and take an active role in helping the organizations secure needed resources. The boards and executives of the effective organizations appeared to work in partnership toward these ends. One or more of these elements was absent in the less effective organizations; and even in the effective ones, the most obvious problems often seemed to relate to a deficiency of the executive or board in one of these areas.

One final point: in every one of the effective organizations, the senior executives and board members I spoke with were inclined to attribute some of their organization's success to "the grace of God." In this context this factor, however hard it may be to substantiate or measure, should be taken seriously. We obviously cannot know how the grace of God enters into the life and history of these organizations. It may be that one of the most obvious functions of that grace is to call the right people to these organizations, and to guide and sustain them in their work, to make possible the ministry these organizations provide in a hurting world. There can be no doubt that effective leadership from the people who become the executives and boards plays a key role in the success of effective Christian service organizations providing needed services and making a powerful witness to God's love to the world.

# 10

# Toward a Philosophy of Management for Christian Service Organizations

## Some Tentative Conclusions

THREE GOALS WERE articulated for this volume in the Introduction. One was to show how religious service organizations are an integral part of the American traditions of philanthropy, voluntary association, and nonprofit enterprise, as well as of the church. A second was to examine the place these organizations occupy and the functions they serve in the political economy and culture of the United States, representing those cultural traditions just mentioned as well as their own theological traditions. The third goal was to evaluate how this distinctive context for their existence and operation, and the unusual facets of their character, influence how Christian service organizations can and should be managed.

These three objectives have been met over the course of the last nine chapters. At the beginning I also noted, however, that one additional purpose for this effort was to make an initial, admittedly tentative attempt at developing a philosophy, or set of organizing principles, for managing Christian service organizations. That is the ultimate purpose of this last chapter. Here I also outline briefly some possible implications of the findings of this study for a broader range of organizations; first, other religious—not just Christian—service organizations, and second, philanthropic, values-expressive organizations. It seems best to begin, though, with a quick review of the bases for these principles and generalizations.

### A Brief Review and Summary

This volume began with a brief history of the evolution of American culture and the traditions of philanthropic practice in the United States, which revealed some striking parallels in their development and essential characteristics. This history supports Merle Curti's claim that "philanthropy has been both index and agent" of "the American national character" (1958, p. 424). In particular, this history demonstrates how a number of key elements and tensions in American culture—between the values of individualism and community, and the values of pragmatism and idealism—frame the context for the development and behavior of philanthropic organizations, including religious organizations, which it is crucial to understand in thinking about their management.

Taking this historical and sociological examination a step further, we next looked more specifically at the role of religion in shaping both the American national character and philanthropic ideals and practice. Religious ideals, images and values were shown to be central to this society's self-definition. Moreover, we saw the key role of religion in creating "the social space" in which the voluntary sector and values-expressive organizations could form, as well as religion's continuing role in motivating altruistic behavior and individual participation in endeavors to enhance the common good. In the close ties and interactions between religious values and institutions and philanthropic values and institutions, we found one basis for the public expectations that religious organizations should function as philanthropic organizations, and how they are thus likely to be subject to the same kinds of supports and constraints as philanthropic organizations. I highlighted some examples of how this has been the case in recent times.

All these external environmental factors create a situation in which philanthropic organizations, especially religious ones, are expected to fulfill a dual-faceted function in this culture—both providing services or somehow contributing concretely to the common good, and giving expression to moral, ethical, social, or spiritual values that enhance and support a more just, more humane, and healthier society. Fulfilling such a dual-faceted function creates a set of challenges in the management of these organizations which is distinctive, if not unique, to them.

Giving closer scrutiny to the circumstances of Christian service organizations, we then went on to explore how internal influences—theological factors—create reinforcing dynamics that also push them toward those dual-faceted missions, requiring the integration of works and faith, of service and witness. In this we saw that, in order to be faithful to their scriptural heritage and their historical roots, as well as to meet public expectations, it is crucial for Christian service organizations to be as concerned with the way they provide services (and raise resources) and the message that sends as with the practical effects of the services themselves.

In the final piece of this examination of the environments and circumstances of Christian service organizations salient to considerations about management, we explored some perspectives of organizational theory that are relevant to religious organizations. In particular, we looked at the ways in which having a dual-faceted mission, being committed to both service and witness, might affect these organizations. We observed that there were important implications in this regard for organizational goals and structures, and for questions about the "institutionalization"—as Selznick (1948, 1957) defines this—of these organizations. We saw that, viewed through the lenses of organizational theory, questions about how open or closed religious organizations are to their environment, about how they define their own boundaries and interact with that environment, become crucial.

Examining the character and functions of Christian service organizations in this way raised a number of questions that appear to have special significance for managers. Among these are: How are the goals of these organizations to be defined, and by whom? How can they or should they evolve over time? Are the structures of these organizations compatible with the values they profess and that they want their work to embody? How can they successfully adapt to their environments, garnering the resources they need to do their work, without assimilating to them? How can they manage the resource dependencies they experience in ways that do not undermine the organizations' integrity?

The questions pointed us to the data from my study of a number of Christian service organizations. The field data confirmed the centrality of these questions and raised some others.

Chapters 5 and 6 provided an overview of the field studies, describing the methodology and the organizations examined, and analyzing the major issues, questions, and insights that emerged from that process. In Chapter 6 in particular, we saw that these field studies indicated that questions about defining and articulating an organization's mission, and defining effectiveness in that mission; about establishing and maintaining an organization's integrity; and about preparing an organization for its future are fundamentally important for the managers of Christian service organizations.

Finally we saw how these questions highlighted the areas of (1) organizational culture and the management of human resources, (2) fund-raising and resource development, and (3) executive and board member roles in leadership and planning as especially significant in determining the effectiveness of Christian service organizations. Chapters 7, 8, and 9 were devoted to closer scrutiny of how the organizations studied functioned in these three areas.

From all of these historical, theoretical, and empirical studies, can any generalizations be drawn about how best to manage Christian service organizations? Do any general principles present themselves that might guide management practice, or at least help focus our questions about what management approaches will be most effective and most appropriate in these organizations? I believe these studies begin to suggest some possibilities along these lines.

## Principal Concerns in Managing Christian Service Organizations

What follow are ten principles or points of focus for the attention of those responsible for the leadership, management, and governance of Christian service organizations. The experiences of the organizations studied, as well as the insights of the literature and history we have examined, point to the areas and ideas these address as vital to the effectiveness of Christian service organizations. These are the concepts, issues, or functions which demand the attention of managers and board members of Christian service organizations. There may be more specific issues requiring management's attention subsumed within these larger principles, but these highlight what I believe are the most important concerns for making Christian service organizations effective in witness and service.

### 1. Focus on Vocation

To be effective in service and witness, Christian service organizations must focus on their own vocation. That is to say, when the board and executive of one of these organizations are trying to understand and articulate its mission they should be asking, What is God's call on this organization? What does God want us to be and do as a corporate entity? These are different questions than, What is its market niche? or What is its greatest opportunity for growth? or even What is the most pressing need or urgent problem it can address? The question these organizations need to ask in regard to their mission and vocation does not look outward first, but rather inward or upward first. To ask about one of these organization's calling is to ask, What is its part, its *particular* mission, within the range of compassionate ministries the church as a whole, as the body of Christ, should offer to the world?

Several corollaries derive from this principle. One is that choices to be made about a Christian service organization's mission and the programs undertaken to realize that mission, should grow out of a sense of *spiritual leading and giftedness*, as well as the more usual analysis of strengths and opportunities. By prayer and discernment as well as by analysis, boards and executives should be focusing on the special qualities of the individuals in their organization and the organization as a whole—spiritual as well as practical qualities—that might suggest how this organization is equipped (in some way others might not be) to undertake particular ministries.

Another corollary is that the determination of mission has to be the business of believers. If the purposes these organizations are to serve and the character they are to take on should finally be an outgrowth of their faith commitments, then the processes by which these determinations occur must involve the spiritual work of prayer and discernment, and those involved in these processes must be persons who share similar fundamental assumptions about how one comes to know God's will. This does not mean these organizations should ignore what the people they serve would tell them about what needs are greatest or what program priorities ought to be, even where those served are not Christians. It does mean that the ultimate and most basic decisions about what work these organizations should take on and how they should approach it should be decisions of believers acting in and under the guidance of a common faith and a shared commitment to discern God's will in these matters.

### 2. Focus on Witness as Well as Service

Following from the focus on vocation will be a focus on witness as well as service. We have discussed before, at length, how maintaining such a dual-faceted mission satisfies both theological imperatives and societal expectations for these organizations. To maintain such a mission requires that boards and executives—and all the other participants in these organizations—be consistently attentive to questions about *what statements are made and what messages are sent*, as well as what practical needs are met by the work these organizations do.

### 3. Focus on Means as Well as Ends

Immediately conjoined with the focus on witness is a focus on the means an organization employs to achieve its purposes as well as the character of those purposes. The manner in which services are provided, the relationships created between servers and served, and the relationships created among the servers and resource providers and those served are all critical factors in shaping the message or witness that emerges from acts of service.

The experiences of the most effective organizations as well as thoughtful consideration of these issues tell us that if Christian service organizations want to testify to the good news of God's love at work in the world, and give hope—and possibly faith—as well as aid to those in need, then they will find ways to involve those being served in the design and implementation of the programs that serve them, and create programs that empower as well as help these people. In so doing, they will also look for ways to structure these programs so that workers and donors may be given the opportunity to learn from clients and recipients. The examples of those in service programs who went to help and teach and ended up learning more about life and faith than they could ever teach are numerous.

This focus on means as well as ends must extend to questions about organizational structure. My study offered several striking examples of organizations that said they were committed to embodying—and so testifying to—certain principles of faith in their work, but whose structures and dynamics clearly undermined those intentions. Organizations that wish to emphasize the values of equality, the need for recognition of people's giftedness regardless of their status or background, and the need for genuine partnership in designing and engaging in ministry cannot achieve this through organizational structures that are essentially hierarchical, that separate personal qualities from the work to be performed, and that encourage competition rather than cooperation. There must be consistency between espoused and operative values.

### 4. Focus on Servanthood

Related to these questions of means and ends is an issue of attitude—organizational as well as individual attitude. One characteristic that was striking in all but one of the most effective organizations in the study was a pervasive sense of servanthood, of genuine humility. At an organizational level, this was manifest, for example, in the comments of one CEO who said,

> We don't have any illusions about what we can accomplish, but we know what we're called to. Jesus said we will always have the poor with us, but the Bible also tells us that with God all things are possible. So we try to serve as many children and families as we can within the commitments we've made to do that in certain ways and honor certain values; and we trust our Lord to make our efforts bear fruit in His time and in His wisdom.

At the individual level, an abiding sense of humility is related to the diminution of personal ambition, the absence of hierarchy—or, at least, any emotional and functional investment in hierarchy—and the presence of a strong cooperative spirit. This was evident in the statements of obviously effective executives who sincerely attribute their organizations' successes more to God's grace than to their own efforts, in the comments of program workers about how much they learn from those they help, and in the comments of managers who genuinely feel it is the contributions of those they supervise that make their departments successful. At a corporate level, this sense of humility prevents the onset of a destructive sense of urgency that leads to unmanageable organizational and personal stress.

In these settings, all participants need to see their roles as those of servants. Senior executives and board members should remember their authority to manage or govern relates to their responsibilities and the respect they have earned, not their rights; and every participant's efforts should be directed to ensuring that the organization serves those it was created and intended to serve. Ironically, this humility will also be reflected in a willingness to be served, where that is an act that empowers another or shows one's own willingness to learn.

## 5. Focus on Stewardship

One of the ways in which Christian service organizations serve others is as stewards of resources entrusted to them to carry on a ministry. One way of thinking about their function is to see them, as one development officer described it, "as a channel through which some Christians can put their wealth to work in supporting God's work of caring for those less fortunate." These organizations, like other philanthropies, hold their assets and resources "in trust," and they are responsible for exercising the utmost care in the ways they maintain and use them. We noted before, however, that stewardship cannot be simply equated with efficiency as an economist might define it.

Being good stewards does not mean buying the least expensive equipment if the difficulty of using that equipment may undermine the effectiveness of staff (or volunteers), or create great frustration for them, or erode essential qualities of the service to be provided. It does not mean refusing to invest in future organizational capacities—whether that takes the form of funding staff development, paying for planning activities, or investing in better equipment—because the needs the organization is addressing now are always urgent. It does mean that, within the context framed by the other principles articulated in this section, these organizations need to be prudent in their expenditure of funds. It means they should be analyzing the return on investment of program and other expenditures, and factoring that return into decisions, but insofar as possible doing so in social and spiritual terms as well as more easily quantifiable measures. And clearly, stewardship has implications for the way these organizations raise as well as use their resources.

### 6. Focus on Engagement in Ministry

Effective Christian service organizations can extend their witness of faith to others by engaging donors and volunteers in the substance of the ministry being performed. For example, CFC's use of the sponsorship mechanism involves the sponsors in the vital work of caring for the children; IRC's and GOI's fund-raising efforts attempt to educate donors in terms of their faith about issues and problems Christians need to address in the developing world; and CCS offers many ways for its supporters to become involved in the program work as well as provide resources for it.

Few people are changed simply by the act of writing a check, though the importance of giving—especially regular and sacrificial giving—for spiritual growth should not be underestimated. However, when people come to really know the stories of other people they are trying to help, and fully understand the circumstances that have led to their difficulties, those called on to help may begin to see the world differently and act accordingly. When it is possible to create vital relationships between the parties involved in the work of service and those providing support for that work, relationships based on mutual interest and respect, then possibilities for profound personal, intellectual, and spiritual growth open up for all.

Yet, it is not just donors that should be so engaged if a Christian service organization is to make its work a ministry; it is also its workers. The life and work of an organization can be organized so that only the program staff (and a few executives) have a sense of being involved in the *spiritual substance* of its ministry. Or it can be so organized that even those in clerical, purely administrative, and other support roles have a sense of being actively involved in ministry. In an interview a staff member of one of the most effective organizations commented, "What impresses me most is that there are guys in the warehouse who feel like they are serving God by stacking boxes. I could not feel that way about doing that kind of work, but I thank God for those people." This eloquently describes a situation all Christian service organizations should aim to attain.

Clearly, part of the explanation for people who can function in the way this staff member describes is the attitude they bring to their work. There are, however, a number of steps these organizations can take to facilitate this happening and sustain such conditions. One is to think about hiring and filling positions not just in terms of matching skills to job requirements, but also in terms of matching individuals' gifts and character to the type of work to be performed and the environment in which they will be working. Another is to offer every individual opportunities to be involved in the spiritual aspects of the organization's ministries—in worship, prayer, and efforts centered on discerning and guiding organizational character, direction, and mission. A third is to make sure that all organizational participants, regardless of position, are treated as being of equal worth in the eyes of God. When every staff member is treated as, and given the opportunity to be, a full contributor to the ministry of an organization, the power of the witness that organization makes will grow immensely.

## 7. Focus on Caring

One of the characteristics that will greatly enhance or detract from the witness of a Christian service organization is the way it cares for those who are involved in its work, along with those it serves. We saw several powerful illustrations of this—going in both directions—among the organizations examined in the study. There can be no question that a Christian service organization that does not care for and nurture those who work for and contribute to it becomes ineffective as a witness to Christian values, at least for those people who come to know the organization well. This commitment to nurture and care for its own must be balanced with accountability to donors and those to be served; but it is simply unacceptable on moral and spiritual grounds for, as GOI's literature put it, "the accomplishment of goals [to come] at the expense of people" in Christian service organizations.

## 8. Focus on Creating and Sustaining a Christian Organizational Culture

The previous seven principles can only be implemented, and certainly management's attention to these principles can only be sustained, within an organization that has a solidly Christian corporate culture. Chapter 7 discussed the development and maintenance of such a corporate culture. I stress again how crucial this appears to be to the effectiveness of Christian service organizations.

## 9. Focus on Integrity

One facet of a Christian organizational culture that was apparent in all the most effective organizations was a clear and pervasive emphasis on "integrity"—using the term in two senses here. First, each of these organizations made a special point of being open and honest, providing full disclosure in all financial matters, and emphasized these values in fund-raising and public-relations efforts as well. They all had policies mandating full disclosure of financial information in response to any and all inquiries; their audited financial statements were published annually and were, generally, clearly and helpfully presented for others to understand; and they had solid policies to prevent self-dealing and conflicts of interest by board or staff members. In the area of fund-raising, all had policies against the use of "representative" images or stories in fund-raising material, and each had a policy of going back to donors and getting permission to reallocate gifts if those gifts came in support of a project already funded. In this regard, each of these organizations met a standard against which every Christian organization should be measured: "to take pains to do what is right, not only in the eyes of the Lord but also of men" (2 Cor. 8:21), and to "abstain from all appearance of evil" (2 Thess. 5:22).

Second, Christian service organizations must concern themselves with their integrity in the sense of being what they claim to be. The Denominational Service Committee goes to great lengths to be representative of its denomination in every aspect of its operations, just as its name would suggest it should be. Caring for the Children says it is an evangelical organization, and everything about its work indicates it fulfills that commitment. This is not the case with all organizations. Yet, when there is a manifest disparity between what an organization claims to be and what it is, even when that disparity is not immediately evident to outsiders, a kind of dishonesty is present that will ultimately undermine the organization in many ways.

Just as it is with other philanthropic organizations, integrity in the sense of honesty about financial and legal matters is a sine qua non for Christian organizations. Without it, they eventually lose their ability to raise the resources they need to undertake the ministries to which they are committed, because they destroy the trust on which their resource-development efforts depend. Moreover, as we observed earlier, they may also subvert the trust donors should have for other religious or philanthropic organizations that are, in fact, more trustworthy. A similar argument can be made about the importance of integrity in the second sense as well. When donors and others come to have the sense these organizations are somehow not what they claim to be, trust in them and support for them erodes. For all these reasons, *and as a moral imperative*, the integrity of these organizations—in both senses—ought to be a fundamental concern of their boards and managers.

## 10. Focus on Leadership

We have cited before Schein's (1985) argument that the most significant function of leadership may be that of establishing and maintaining organizational culture. We saw in the field studies the potential importance of executives and board members in both representing Christian service organizations to the world—one key element of the organizations' witnessing function—and in directing their operations to ensure the effectiveness of their service functions. In addition we saw how the most effective executives seemed to strike a balance in their own roles so that, on the one hand, they gave careful and consistent attention to the function of representing their organizations to others and, on the other hand, took an active part in the oversight of internal affairs and in working with their boards.

To establish and adhere to any of the previous nine principles for good management of Christian service organizations, to give them regular attention and see to their implementation requires, above all, effective leadership. Excellent leadership and excellent management were a common denominator among all the most effective organizations in the field studies. All had strong boards and strong executives.

It might seem the call to focus on leadership should be directed primarily to boards. It is clearly important for these bodies to choose executives with great care—with an eye, perhaps, to whether those they would appoint can understand, focus on, and act upon the principles I have outlined here. It is still the case, however, that when these executives have been appointed, they may have significant roles in selecting new members for the board; and there is no doubt they can and should have vital roles in developing and working with the board. The executives need to help create boards that can understand, focus on, and act upon these principles, too. So the call to focus on leadership is addressed to executives as well. My studies indicate that strong, effective leadership from both boards and executives is vital to the effectiveness of Christian service organizations.

The pages preceding this chapter have offered many pieces of advice and many illustrations of how one might approach particular management functions in ways that incorporate the principles just cited. In this regard, I looked carefully at the management of human resources, fund-raising, executive and board leadership roles, and efforts at formal planning. The ten principles derive from the extensive examination of the place, functions, and operations of Christian service organizations detailed here, and serve, I hope, as points to focus attention on the most important aspects of managing these organizations and to generate useful questions about their management. Those who are more conversant with other specific areas of the operation of these organizations are invited to consider how these principles may or may not usefully be applied— or might need to be modified—to management responsibilities and tasks in those areas.

## Applications to Other Religious Organizations

The philosophy of management just outlined can be usefully applied, I believe, to some other kinds of religious organizations, beyond just Christian service organizations of the type scrutinized in my field studies. This way of thinking about the management needs of religious organizations may be valuable for Christian organizations that are similar in theological background and direction to those examined, but that are not specifically "service" organizations, such as judicatory structures or evangelistic ministries. It may also be useful for religious service organizations that are not rooted in a Protestant, free-church tradition, or even in the Christian tradition. In both cases, some cautions and adaptations are required, however.

### *Other Christian Organizations*

In the case of other Christian organizations, not narrowly defined as service organizations, the adjustments required in approaches to management stem from the fact that the clarity and concreteness of the organizations' goals may be considerably lessened. For example, many judicatory structures—district, diocesan, or presbytery offices and the like—have been created to provide specific types of support or administrative services to congregations and individual church members; but they serve also, more generally, to support the religious life and ministry of the denomination with goals that are hard to specify and desired outcomes—like strengthening the denomination's spiritual vitality—that are hard to measure. In addition to the lack of specificity (or measurability) of goals, the character of goals also changes in this context. Given the focus of most of these organizations on serving members, they tend to be more like member-benefit and less like philanthropic organizations than those we studied. Most of these structures also lack independent boards, leading to very different needs and dynamics in staff-board relationships and altering what expectations can and should be placed on board members.

Nevertheless, many of the principles suggested for good management might be usefully applied. For instance, denominational structures often are less effective than they might be because they operate without a sense of calling, without thoughtful and prayerful consideration of the particular part they may play in the ministry of the church at this point in time, instead merely doing whatever convention and tradition dictate they do. A clarity about mission that is regularly renewed; a focus on the means employed to fulfill that mission and the message this sends; and a focus on modeling servanthood and promoting stewardship (in the fullest sense of the term) are all attributes that judicatory and other ecclesiastical structures should strive to attain and maintain if they want to be effective agents for building up the church.

Similarly, these will all be characteristics that mark evangelistic ministries that are effective in building up the church. We have seen numerous counterexamples in recent years to make this point. In the Bakkers' organization, the PTL, we saw a lack of clarity about mission, a failure to understand the significance of the message sent by the means employed to reach organizational goals, and no evidence of a sense of humility or servanthood nor of any commitment to stewardship. The results were a "ministry" (to use the term loosely) that appeared to connect with individual Christians as consumers of religious goods and services, but almost certainly did more finally to tear down the church than build it up.

It is important to recognize that, if the purpose of an organization is to bring people into a life-changing relationship with Jesus Christ, then measuring organizational effectiveness is finally going to be very difficult, for no one can see into another person's soul. Still, it is possible to get a sense of whether an evangelistic organization is bringing people into the church and helping them build a strong and enduring faith, and building up the church by embodying the values that are most admirable in the Christian tradition. For evangelistic organizations, the points made in this volume about fund-raising practice, the management of human resources, and the character of executive leadership would seem to be especially important.

## Other Religious Service Organizations

I observed at the beginning of this work that, if I had focused on a different set of organizations—different in terms of their theological foundations—the principles for management developed might have a different cast to them. Clearly, some values that are embodied in these principles—for example, the idea that it is important for these organizations in their decision-making and planning processes to be open to the "leading of the Holy Spirit"—assume certain theological understandings that many non-Christians, and even some Christians, would not or could not affirm. Insofar as this is true, then organizations representing the religious traditions in which those people stand should (presumably) treat the principles regarding the focus on vocation and discernment of mission differently than has been suggested here.

Similarly, in much of the discussion that has gone before, claims have been made about the apparent incompatibility of hierarchy in Christian service organizations with the values and ideals in the New Testament. However, we know some elements of the Christian tradition read those texts differently and find hierarchical structures to be perfectly acceptable. The Catholic church is, after all, the original model of a bureaucracy in many of the senses Weber defined for that term. So for some, what constitutes a Christian organizational culture differs considerably from the description offered here, and their approach to creating and sustaining such a culture may differ as well. Still, if they want their organization to give expression to the religious tradition they represent, it seems safe to assume they will need to make the establishment of a Christian corporate culture, as they understand it, a primary concern.

Obviously, these kinds of differences become even more pronounced when we move outside the Christian tradition altogether. The Christian tradition, or at least elements of it, holds a commitment to giving public expression to the tenets and beliefs of the faith, and to proselytizing, which many other religious traditions do not. A Jewish organization is not likely to have the same concern for combining service and witness, for instance, as a Christian one. That is not to say, however, that a Jewish service organization will not see itself as having a responsibility to embody the highest ideals of Judaism in its work, or not see itself as having an important role to play in giving Jewish people a way to express those ideals in service, and in so doing strengthening the identity of the Jewish community. In fact, my conversations with people involved in Jewish service organizations indicate they see them very much as serving these purposes as well as providing needed services. As far as that is true, those responsible for the leadership and management of these and other—Islamic, Buddhist, whatever—religious service organizations may find the philosophy outlined here useful, although they may well have to adapt the principles suggested to reflect the basic beliefs and assumptions of their own traditions.

## Applications to Secular Philanthropic Organizations

The first chapter of this volume makes the case that secular philanthropic organizations in our society are generally expected to be values-expressive. Most people expect them to uphold, and even promote, a range of humanitarian values by the way they do their work as well as by the practical significance of that work. I have explored at greater length elsewhere (Jeavons, 1992) how the character of their management sends the message, or at least part of the message, that secular philanthropic organizations convey to the public. It is enough simply to say here that, with some modifications, all the principles for management articulated in this chapter, with the possible exception of the first one (with its explicit focus on seeking divine guidance), could usefully serve as a focus of attention—and as a basis for self-assessment of the performance and direction of secular philanthropic organizations—for those responsible for their leadership and management.

Sometimes the benefits to be accrued from following this philosophy may be different. For example, these organizations may not be seeking to engage their supporters in their work because it provides opportunities for the supporters' spiritual growth; but engagement will build a stronger sense of identification among donors with the organizations. And while secular organizations may not wish to develop a sense of stewardship in their donors as a spiritual virtue, it is clearly to the organizations' benefit (just as it is to the church's benefit) to have donors who understand the value of regular and thoughtful giving.

Right now it would appear that many secular philanthropic organizations may have much to learn from their religious counterparts about how to better attend to the values-expressive facets of their missions, if they want to be more effective in that way. No doubt, it is also true some religious service organizations may be able to learn valuable lessons from secular agencies about how to work with greater efficiency in some areas. The religious organizations, however, must always remember the ideals and values from which their missions spring, and make sure that management approaches pursued to improve efficiency never compromise those ideals and values.

## A Final Word

We saw in the first part of this study how vital religion, religious organizations, and especially religious service organizations have been in shaping and sustaining the more humane elements of American society. That is not to say the church has been without sin; nor that secular, philosophically rooted ideals and organizations have not also played important roles in the endeavor to create a better society. It is to say, however, that all those who work in, study, or just appreciate the voluntary sector would do well to remember its origins in the church. We would do well to remember that many of the philanthropic organizations in our society were created to uphold and promote specific moral and social ideals as well as to offer practical services, and that the impetus for both kinds of efforts to serve the common good often come from religious motivations.

For those of us who start in the religious realm, it is crucial to remember how important it is to put our faith into action as a way of testifying to its meaning, value, and power. One of the volunteers interviewed at the Denominational Service Committee, when asked what she thought was most special about the organization, said, "It is taking Christianity out of the church and into the community where it belongs." Robert Wuthnow's (1988) studies of the changes in the role of religion in the United States over the last fifty years suggest that those who are not part of the church believe its most important contribution to our society may be in promoting and nurturing the moral and social values of altruism, service, and community. Those studies go on to suggest that it is the para-church organizations—like service agencies—rather than congregations that people see most readily in trying to identify and understand religious values and commitments today. Both these perspectives, from inside and outside the church, indicate how important it is that Christian service organizations function in ways that give the best possible representation of the Christian tradition—or of whatever branch of that tradition they embody—to the world. When we consider what "effectiveness" means for these organizations, we need to see that for them the proverbial bottom line is "faithfulness."

For these organizations to be faithful, to represent the Christian tradition well, finally requires just two things of them. First, being mindful of Jesus' call to feed the hungry, to aid those in need, and to care for the sick, and of His call to be good stewards of the resources with which they are entrusted, these organizations have to provide needed practical services in accordance with their missions and vocations as effectively and efficiently as possible. Second, mindful of another call that echoes through the New Testament, the call to share the good news of God's love for the world, these organizations need to operate in ways that make the provision of the services they offer a living testimony to that love. These two requirements may seem to be at odds with each other in some instances, and where that is the case it is the responsibility of the managers of these organizations to reconcile them, making sure that the witness their organization is called to make is not compromised.

In this volume, I have attempted to provide a better understanding of the place and function of Christian service organizations in our society, insights about these organizations deriving from organizational theory, illustrations of effective and ineffective management practice, and suggestions of principles for management based on all this analysis. My hope is that this will help those responsible for the leadership and management of Christian service organizations think about how they can be better managed to be more faithful in both the practical and the spiritual aspects of their work, to fulfill effectively both their service and witness goals. If these organizations can be so managed, they can continue to make an essential contribution to both the creation of a better world and the nurture and growth of a vital Christian faith in that world.

# References

*The Holy Bible.* New International Version. Grand Rapids: Zondervan, 1979.
*The Greek New Testament.* Kurt Aland et al., eds. Stuttgart: United Bible Societies, 1968.

AAFRC Trust for Philanthropy. *Giving USA, 1990.* New York: American Association of Fund Raising Counsel Trust for Philanthropy, 1990.
Ackoff, Russell L. *Creating the Corporate Future.* New York: John Wiley, 1981.
Adams, David S. "The Imperative to Volunteer: Religious Themes in the Public Pronouncements of American Presidents—Hoover to Reagan." In *Working Papers for the Independent Sector Spring Research Forum.* Washington, DC: Independent Sector, 1989.
Adams, James Luther. "The Voluntary Principle in the Forming of American Religion." In J. Ronald Engel, ed., *Voluntary Associations: Socio-Cultural Analysis and Theological Interpretation.* Chicago: Exploration Press, 1986.
Aldrich, Howard E. *Organizations and Environments.* Englewood Cliffs, NJ: Prentice-Hall, 1979.
Anderson, John C., and Larry Moore. "The Motivation to Volunteer." *Journal of Voluntary Action Research,* 1978, 7, 120–29.
Aquinas, Thomas. *Summa Theologica.* O. P. Batten, trans. New York: Blackfriars (with McGraw-Hill), 1964. (Originally published in 1273.)
Argyris, Chris. *Personality and Organization.* New York: Harper & Row, 1957.
Banner, Lois W. "Religious Benevolence as Social Control: A Critique of an Interpretation." *Journal of American History,* 1973, 60 (June), 23–41.
Barnard, Chester. *The Functions of the Executive.* Cambridge: Harvard University Press, 1938.
Basil of Caesarea. *Longer Rules.* Sr. Monica Wagner, trans. In *The Fathers of the Church,* vol. 9. Washington, DC: Catholic University Press, 1952. (From an A.D. 370 manuscript.)
Bellah, Robert N. *The Broken Covenant.* New York: Seabury Press, 1975.
Bellah, Robert N., et al. *Habits of the Heart: Individualism and Commitment in American Life.* Berkeley: University of California Press, 1985.
Bellah, Robert N., et al. *The Good Society.* New York: Alfred A. Knopf, 1991.
Bendix, Reinhard. *Work and Authority in Industry.* New York: John Wiley, 1956.
Bennis, Warren G. *The Unconscious Conspiracy: Why Leaders Can't Lead.* New York: AMACOM, 1976.
Bennis, Warren G. *Why Leaders Can't Lead: The Unconscious Conspiracy Continues.* San Francisco: Jossey-Bass, 1989.
Benson, Kenneth J., and James Dorsett. "Toward a Theory of Religious Organizations." *Journal for the Scientific Study of Religion,* 1971, 10, 138–51.

Borst, Diane, and Patrick J. Montana. *Managing Nonprofit Organizations*. New York: AMACOM, 1977.

Boulding, Kenneth. *The Economy of Love and Fear*. Belmont, CA: Wadsworth Press, 1973.

Boyte, Harry, and Sara Evans. *Free Spaces: The Sources of Democratic Change in American Society*. New York: Harper & Row, 1986.

Bread for the World. "Hunger Pornography." *Bread for the World Newsletter*, 1991 (January–February), 6.

Bremner, Robert H. "'Scientific Philanthropy,' 1873–1893." *Social Service Review*, 1956, 30, 168–73.

Bremner, Robert H. *American Philanthropy*. 2nd ed. Chicago: University of Chicago Press, 1988.

Bryson, John M. *Strategic Planning for Public and Nonprofit Organizations*. San Francisco: Jossey-Bass, 1990.

Burns, James McGregor. *Leadership*. New York: Harper & Row, 1978.

Carnegie, Andrew. "The Gospel of Wealth." *North American Review*, 1889, 148, 653–64.

Clark, Burton R. "Interorganizational Patterns in Education." *Administrative Science Quarterly*, 1965, 10 (September), 224–37.

Clark, Peter M., and James Q. Wilson. "Incentive Systems: A Theory of Organizations." *Administrative Science Quarterly*, 1961, 6 (September), 129–66.

Clary, E. Gil, and Mark Snyder. "A Functional Analysis of Volunteerism." In Margaret S. Clark, ed., *Review of Personality and Social Psychology: Pro-Social Behavior*. Newbury Park, CA: Sage Publications, 1991.

Cohen, Michael D., James G. March, and Johan P. Olsen. "A Garbage Can Model of Organizational Choice." *Administrative Science Quarterly*, 1972, 17 (March), 1–25.

Curti, Merle. "American Philanthropy and the National Character." *American Quarterly*, 1958, 10, 420–37.

Curti, Merle. "Tradition and Innovation in American Philanthropy." *Proceedings of the American Philosophical Association*, 1961, 105, 146–56.

Deal, Terrence E., and Allen A. Kennedy. *Corporate Cultures: The Rites and Rituals of Corporate Life*. Reading, MA: Addison-Wesley, 1982.

De Gues, Arie P. "Planning as Learning." *Harvard Business Review*, 1988 (March–April), 70–74.

Denton, Patricia, and Mayer Zald. "From Evangelism to General Service: The Transformation of the YMCA." *Administrative Science Quarterly*, 1963 (September), 214–34.

De Tocqueville, Alexis. *Democracy in America*. Richard Heffner, ed. New York: NAL Penguin, 1984. (Originally published in 1835.)

DiMaggio, Paul J., and Walter Powell. "The Iron Cage Revisited: Institutional Isomorphism and Collective Rationality in Organizational Fields." *American Sociological Review*, 1983, 48 (April), 147–60.

Douglas, James. *Why Charity? The Case for the Third Sector*. Beverly Hills: Sage Publications, 1983.

Douglas, James. "Political Theories of Nonprofit Organization." In Walter Powell, ed., *The Nonprofit Sector: A Research Handbook*. New Haven: Yale University Press, 1987.

Drucker, Peter F. *The Practice of Management*. New York: Harper & Row, 1954.

Drucker, Peter F. "Lessons for Successful Nonprofit Governance." *Nonprofit Management and Leadership*, 1990 (a), 1, 1, 7–14.

Drucker, Peter F. *Managing the Nonprofit Organization*. New York: Harper Collins, 1990(b).

Ellis, Susan J., and Katherine Noyes. *By the People: A History of Americans as Volunteers*. San Francisco: Jossey-Bass, 1990.

Etzioni, Amitai. *A Comparative Analysis of Complex Organizations*. New York: Free Press, 1961.

Etzioni, Amitai. *Modern Organizations*. Englewood Cliffs, NJ: Prentice-Hall, 1964.

Etzioni, Amitai. *The Active Society*. New York: Basic Books, 1968.

Fayol, Henri. *General and Industrial Management*. London: Pitmann, 1949. (Originally published in 1919.)

Ferguson, Kathy E. *The Feminist Case against Bureaucracy*. Philadelphia: Temple University Press, 1984.

Fink, Justin. "Community Agency Entrepreneurs: Formalization and Change in Community Based Organizations during the Reagan Era." In *Working Papers for the Independent Sector Spring Research Forum*. Washington, DC: Independent Sector, 1990.

Franklin, Benjamin. *The Autobiography of Benjamin Franklin*. Leonard W. Larrabee, Ralph Ketcham, Helen Bonifield, and Helene Fineman, eds. New Haven: Yale University Press, 1964. (Originally published in 1791.)

Galbraith, Jay. *Organization Design*. Reading, MA: Addison-Wesley, 1977.

Gallup, George, and Jim Castelli. *The People's Religion*. New York: Macmillan, 1990.

Gardner, John. *On Leadership*. New York: Free Press, 1989.

Goldner, Fred H. "The Division of Labor: Process and Power." In Mayer N. Zald, ed., *Power in Organizations*. Nashville: Vanderbilt University Press, 1970.

Greenleaf, Robert K. *Servant Leadership*. Ramsey, NJ: Paulist Press, 1977.

Griffin, Clifford S. "Religious Benevolence as Social Control, 1815–1860." *Mississippi Historical Review*, 1957, 44, 3, 423–44.

Hall, Douglas John. *The Steward: A Biblical Symbol Come of Age*. 2nd ed. Grand Rapids: William B. Eerdmans, 1990.

Hall, Peter Dobkin. *The Organization of American Culture, 1700–1900: Private Institutions, Elites, and the Origins of American Nationality*. New York: New York University Press, 1984.

Hall, Peter Dobkin. "A Historical Overview of the Private Nonprofit Sector." In Walter W. Powell, ed., *The Nonprofit Sector: A Research Handbook*. New Haven: Yale University Press, 1987.

Hall, Peter Dobkin. "A Bridge Founded upon Justice and Built of Human Hearts: Reflections on Religion, Science, and the Development of American Philanthropy." In *Working Papers for the Independent Sector Spring Research Forum*. Washington, DC: Independent Sector, 1989.

Hall, Peter Dobkin. "The History of Religious Philanthropy in America." In Robert

Wuthnow and Virginia Hodgkinson, eds., *Faith and Philanthropy in America*. Washington, DC: Independent Sector, 1990(a).

Hall, Peter Dobkin. "Conflicting Managerial Cultures in Nonprofit Organizations." *Nonprofit Management and Leadership*, 1990(b), 1, 2, 153–66.

Hannan, Michael T., and John Freeman. "The Population Ecology of Organizations." *American Journal of Sociology*, 1977, 85, 5 (March), 929–66.

Hay, Robert D. *Strategic Management for Nonprofit Organizations*. New York: Quorum Books, 1990.

Heale, M. J. "From City Fathers to Social Critics: Humanitarianism and Government in New York City, 1790–1860." *Journal of American History*, 1976, 58 (June), 21–41.

Herman, Robert D., and Richard D. Heimovics. "The Effective Nonprofit Executive: Leader of the Board." *Nonprofit Management and Leadership*, 1990, 1, 2, 167–80.

Herman, Robert D., and Richard D. Heimovics. *Executive Leadership in Nonprofit Organizations*. San Francisco: Jossey-Bass, 1991.

Hershey, Paul, and Kenneth H. Blanchard. *Management of Organizational Behavior*. 5th ed. Englewood Cliffs, NJ: Prentice-Hall, 1988.

Hickson, David J., et al. "A Strategic Contingencies Theory of Intraorganizational Power." *Administrative Science Quarterly*, 1971, 19 (March), 22–44.

Hinings, C. Robin, and Bruce Foster. "The Organization Structure of Churches: A Preliminary Model." *Sociology*, 1973, 7, 93–106.

Hodgkinson, Virginia. *Research in Progress, 1986–87: A National Compendium of Research Projects on Philanthropy, Voluntary Action, and Nonprofit Activity*. Washington, DC: Independent Sector, 1988.

Hodgkinson, Virginia, and Murray Weitzman. *Giving and Volunteering in the United States; 1990*. Washington, DC: Independent Sector, 1990.

Hodgkinson, Virginia, Murray Weitzman, and Arthur Kirsch. *From Belief to Commitment: The Activities and Finances of Religious Congregations in the United States*. Washington, DC: Independent Sector, 1988.

Houle, Cyril O. *Governing Boards*. San Francisco: Jossey-Bass, 1989.

James, Estelle, and Susan Rose-Ackerman. *Nonprofit Enterprise in Market Economics*. London: Harwood Academic Publishers, 1986.

Jeavons, Thomas H. "Giving, Getting, Grace and Greed: An Historical and Moral Analysis of Religious Fund Raising." In D. Burlingame and L. Hulse, eds., *Taking Fund Raising Seriously*. San Francisco: Jossey-Bass, 1991.

Jeavons, Thomas H. "When Management Is the Message: Relating Values to Management Practice in Nonprofit Organizations." *Nonprofit Management and Leadership*, 1992, 2, 4.

Jeavons, Thomas H. "Identifying Characteristics of 'Religious' Organizations: An Exploratory Proposal," PONPO Working Paper #197. Yale University, 1993.

Johnson, Robert Matthew. *The First Charity*. Cabin John, MD: Seven Locks Press, 1988.

Joines, Jean. "An Organizational History of the Moorestown Female Charitable Society." Unpublished paper, 1990.

Karl, Barry. "The Secularization of Philanthropy: Benevolence and Taxes." In *Working Papers for the Independent Sector Spring Research Forum*. Washington, DC: Independent Sector, 1989.

Kimberly, John R., Robert H. Miles, et al. *The Organizational Life Cycle*. San Francisco: Jossey-Bass, 1980.

La Barbera, Priscilla Ann. "Commercial Ventures of Religious Organizations." *Nonprofit Management and Leadership*, 1991, 1, 3, 217–34.

Lawrence, Paul R., and Jay Lorsch. *Organization and Environment*. Homewood, IL: Richard D. Irwin, 1967.

Layton, Daphne N. *Philanthropy and Voluntarism: An Annotated Bibliography*. New York: Foundation Center, 1987.

Lodahl, Thomas M., and Stephen M. Mitchell. "Drift in the Development of Innovative Organizations." In John R. Kimberly, and Robert H. Miles, eds., *The Organizational Life Cycle*. San Francisco: Jossey-Bass, 1980.

Lofland, John, and James T. Richardson. "Religious Movement Organizations: Elemental Forms and Dynamics." *Research in Social Movements, Conflicts and Change*, 1984, 7, 29–51.

March, James G., and Herbert A. Simon. *Organizations*. New York: John Wiley, 1958.

Martin, Mike W. "The Study of Philanthropy as an Avenue into Values Education." Paper presented at the conference of the Association of American Colleges on "Collegiate Education and the Cultivation of Civic Consciousness," Chicago, April 1991.

Mather, Cotton. "Essays to Do Good." In Brian O'Connell, ed., *America's Voluntary Spirit*. New York: Foundation Center, 1983. (Originally published in 1710).

Mayo, Elton. *The Social Problems of an Industrial Civilization*. Boston: Harvard University Graduate School of Business Administration, 1945.

McGregor, Douglas. *The Human Side of Enterprise*. New York: McGraw-Hill, 1960.

Meyer, John W., and Brian Rowan. "Institutionalized Organizations: Formal Structure as Myth and Ceremony." *American Journal of Sociology*, 1977, 83 (September), 340–63.

Michels, Robert. *Political Parties*. Eden Paul and Cedar Paul, trans. Glencoe, IL: Free Press, 1949. (Originally published in 1915.)

Middleton, Melissa. "Nonprofit Boards of Directors: Beyond the Governance Function." In Walter Powell, ed., *The Nonprofit Sector: A Research Handbook*. New Haven, Conn.: Yale University Press, 1987.

Miller, Perry. *Errand into the Wilderness*. Cambridge: Belknap Press, 1956.

Moseley, James G. *A Cultural History of Religion in America*. Westport, CN: Greenwood Press, 1981.

Neilsen, Waldemar. *The Golden Donors: A New Anatomy of the Great Foundations*. New York: E. P. Dutton, 1985.

Neusner, Jacob. "Righteousness, Not Charity: Judaism's View of Philanthropy." *Liberal Education*, 1988, 74, 4 (September–October), 16–18.

Nevins, Allen. *John D. Rockefeller*. New York: Charles Scribner's Sons, 1959.

Niebuhr, Reinhold. *Moral Man and Immoral Society: A Study in Ethics and Politics*. New York: Charles Scribner's Sons, 1932.

Niebuhr, Reinhold. *The Nature and Destiny of Man: A Christian Interpretation*. Vol. 2, *Human Destiny*. New York: Charles Scribner's Sons, 1943.

Niv, Amatai. "Organizational Disintegration: Roots, Processes and Types." In John R. Kimberly and Robert H. Miles, eds., *The Organizational Life Cycle*. San Francisco: Jossey-Bass, 1980.

O'Connell, Brian. *America's Voluntary Spirit*. New York: Foundation Center, 1983.

O'Dea, Thomas F. "Five Dilemmas in the Institutionalization of Religion." *Journal for the Scientific Study of Religion*, 1961, 1, 30–41.

Odenhal, Teresa. *Charity Begins at Home: Generosity and Self-Interest among the Philanthropic Elite*. New York: Basic Books, 1990.

O'Neill, Michael. *The Third America*. San Francisco: Jossey-Bass, 1989.

Ostrander, Susan A. *Women of the Upper Class*. Philadelphia: Temple University Press, 1984.

Ostrander, Susan A., and Paul G. Schervish. "Giving and Getting: Philanthropy as a Social Relation." In Jon Van Til, ed., *Critical Issues in American Philanthropy*. San Francisco: Jossey-Bass, 1990.

Parsons, Talcott. *Structures and Process in Modern Societies*. Glencoe, IL: Free Press, 1960.

Payton, Robert. "Philanthropic Values." In Kenneth W. Thompson, ed., *Philanthropy: Private Means, Public Ends*. Lanham, MD: University Press of America, 1987.

Payton, Robert. *Philanthropy: Voluntary Action for the Public Good*. New York: Macmillan, 1988.

Perrow, Charles. *Complex Organizations: A Critical Essay*. 3rd ed. New York: Random House, 1986.

Peters, Thomas J. *Thriving on Chaos*. New York: Harper & Row, 1987.

Peters, Thomas J., and Robert Waterman. *In Search of Excellence*. New York: Warner Books, 1982.

Pfeffer, Jeffrey. *Organizations and Organization Theory*. Boston: Pittman, 1982.

Reichley, James A. *Religion in American Public Life*. Washington, DC: Brookings Institution, 1983.

Robbins, Stephen P. *Essentials of Organizational Behavior*. 2nd ed. Englewood Cliffs, NJ: Prentice-Hall, 1988.

Schein, Edgar. *Organizational Culture and Leadership*. San Francisco: Jossey-Bass, 1985.

Scherer, Ross P., ed. *American Denominational Organization: A Sociological View*. South Pasadena: William Carey Library, 1980.

Scherer, Ross P. "A New Typology for Organizations: Market, Bureaucracy, Clan and Mission, with Application to American Denominations." *Journal for the Scientific Study of Religion*, 1988, 27, 4, 475–98.

Scott, W. Richard. *Organizations: Rational, Natural, and Open Systems*. Englewood Cliffs, NJ: Prentice-Hall, 1987.

Selznick, Philip. "Foundations of the Theory of Organization." *American Sociological Review*, 1948, 13 (February), 25–35.

Selznick, Philip. *Leadership in Administration*. New York: Harper & Row, 1957.

Senge, Peter. *The Fifth Discipline: The Art and Practice of the Learning Organization*. New York: Doubleday, 1990.

Slater, Philip. *The Pursuit of Loneliness*. 2nd ed. Boston: Beacon Press, 1976.

Smith, Timothy L. "Biblical Ideals in American Christian and Jewish Philanthropy, 1880–1920." *American Jewish History*, 1984, 74, 3–26.

Stackhouse, Max L. "Religion and the Social Space for Voluntary Institutions." In

Robert Wuthnow and Virginia Hodgkinson, eds., *Faith and Philanthropy in America*. Washington, DC: Independent Sector, 1990.

Stone, Melissa Middleton. "The Propensity of Governing Boards to Plan." *Nonprofit Management and Leadership*, 1991, 1, 3, 203–15.

Stoner, James A. F., and Charles Wankel. *Management*. 3rd ed. Englewood Cliffs, NJ: Prentice-Hall, 1986.

Taylor, Frederick W. *The Principles of Scientific Management*. New York: Harper & Row, 1911.

Taylor, Frederick W. *Scientific Management*. New York: Harper & Row, 1947.

Thomas à Kempis. *The Imitation of Christ*. William C. Creasy, trans. Macon, GA: Mercer University Press, 1989. (From a 1441 manuscript.)

Thompson, James D. *Organizations in Action*. New York: McGraw-Hill, 1967.

Tosi, Henry L. *Theories of Organizations*. Chicago: St. Clair Press, 1975.

Vaill, Peter B. *Managing as a Performing Art*. San Francisco: Jossey-Bass, 1989.

Van Til, Jon. *Mapping the Third Sector*. New Brunswick, NJ: Transaction Press, 1988.

Weber, Max. *A Theory of Economic and Social Organization*. A. H. Henderson and Talcott Parsons, eds. Glencoe, IL: Free Press, 1947. (Originally published in 1924.)

Weick, Karl E. *The Social Psychology of Organizing*. 2nd ed. Reading, MA: Addison-Wesley, 1979.

Weisbrod, Burton. *The Nonprofit Economy*. Cambridge: Harvard University Press, 1988.

Whyte, William Foote. *Man and Organization*. Homewood, IL: Richard D. Irwin, 1959.

Williamson, Oliver E. "The Economics of Organization: A Transaction Cost Approach." *American Journal of Sociology*, 1981, 87 (November), 548–77.

Winthrop, John. "A Model of Christian Charity". In Brian O'Connell, ed., *America's Voluntary Spirit*. New York: The Foundation Center, 1983. (Originally published in 1630).

Workman, Herbert B. *The Evolution of the Monastic Ideal*. London: Epworth Press, 1913.

Wuthnow, Robert. *The Restructuring of American Religion*. Princeton, NJ: Princeton University Press, 1988.

# Index

THOMAS H. JEAVONS is the Director of the Center on Philanthropy and Nonprofit Leadership at Grand Valley State University. For ten years, he was a denominational executive for the Religious Society of Friends (Quakers) and has served in staff and board positions with a variety of nonprofit organizations in the arts, education, religion, and social services.